Calling the Shots

Calling the Shots

MY AUTOBIOGRAPHY

SUE BARKER

with Sarah Edworthy

EBURY
SPOTLIGHT

3 5 7 9 10 8 6 4

Ebury Spotlight, an imprint of Ebury Publishing
20 Vauxhall Bridge Road
London SW1V 2SA

Ebury Spotlight is part of the Penguin Random House
group of companies whose addresses can be found at
global.penguinrandomhouse.com

Penguin
Random House
UK

First published by Ebury Spotlight in 2022

www.penguin.co.uk

A CIP catalogue record for this book is available from the British Library

ISBN 9781529149036

Printed and bound in Great Britain by Clays Ltd, Elcograf S.p.A.
Imported into the EEA by Penguin Random House Ireland,
Morrison Chambers, 32 Nassau Street, Dublin D02 YH68.

MIX
Paper from
responsible sources
FSC® C018179

Penguin Random House is committed to a sustainable future for
our business, our readers and our planet. This book is made
from Forest Stewardship Council® certified paper.

CONTENTS

CHAPTER 1

MR ROBERTS

Not many 11-year-olds are lucky enough to know the day when their dream might start to become reality or to be able to identify the person who can shape their destiny. I recognised both with certainty. With every whack of the ball against our garage wall at home, every rally on the public courts where I played with my family in mixed-age groups on Saturdays, I visualised the moment when I would be talent-spotted by one man.

His name was Arthur Roberts and he was the resident tennis professional at the Palace Hotel in Torquay. Mr Roberts – as I would always call him – was a legend far beyond our stretch of the South Devon coast, with a reputation for coaching players to the top flight and a parallel notoriety for being formidably strict in his approach. In the early 1950s, before I was born, he had taken on Angela Mortimer – and she had gone on to achieve Grand Slam success, including winning the Wimbledon title in

1961. In that same Championships, another player from his small Torquay cohort reached the men's semi-final: Mike Sangster, famed for his 150mph cannonball serve. Arthur Roberts's success rate was phenomenal for an independent provincial coach – a one-man band, whose bread-and-butter job was to manage the courts at a popular seaside hotel.

I'd been introduced to tennis by my older sister Jane, who was a good player, and initially I was determined simply to emulate her. But tennis turned into a personal, all-consuming passion. By the age of 10 or 11, I was reading all I could about the game, largely to follow the progress of Corinne Molesworth, Mr Roberts's latest protégée, who came from Brixham, a fishing port on the other side of Torbay. She had just won the junior girls' singles title at the French Open on the clay at Roland-Garros. From his training set-up at the Palace Hotel, he had launched her as a tennis player, and now, at the age of 18, she was travelling from tournament to tournament in the United States, living the dream. To me, Corinne was a goddess. I studied pictures of her in the local paper. I admired her competitiveness, the way you could see she poured every ounce of effort into each shot. I desperately wanted to be like her.

So you can imagine the butterflies I felt on a cold October day in 1967 when word got around that Arthur Roberts was due to visit my school, the Marist Convent in Paignton, to assess PE teacher Mrs Embury's new intake. It was the first term of my first year in the senior department, a period when every aspect of life felt like a transition into a bigger, more thrilling adult world. Mrs Embury told us that Mr Roberts was coming to potentially pick two girls for private tuition – and I was determined to be one of them. I just had to be. I can see myself now, bouncing from foot to foot in my Aertex games shirt, racket in hand, shivering as a light sea breeze gusted across the courts. It wasn't the autumn chill that got to me, but the surge of nerves, the excitement and heady expectation as we started to hit balls, awaiting the arrival of this scary character. Every article I read about Corinne included a mention of how uncompromising Arthur Roberts was in his coaching methods, how he sought a high standard of dedication from his players, not just to tennis but to him personally, and how, in return, he would go to untold lengths to further their tennis careers.

This man with the gargantuan reputation had acquired mythical status in my imagination, but here he was, a small, wiry, slightly stooped figure in his early sixties, escorted by Mrs Embury to observe our afternoon PE session. Tweedily dressed, he stood at the back of the courts, pipe in hand, expression unreadable. The air was full of the sounds of rackets thwacking balls and shots skidding off the shale court surface and landing in the net, of girls screeching 'Sorry!' and 'Aaaargh!' After watching us closely for some time, Mr Roberts conferred with Mrs Embury. I noticed she nodded and then called out his first selection: 'Judy Reeve.'

I started to hit the ball harder, and move around the court with more intent, panicking that he wouldn't notice me. In my heart of hearts, I knew I wasn't the next-best player on court that day: there was a girl called Jane Burnell who presented a more accomplished all-round package. It seemed inevitable that hers would be the next name to be called out. I scurried after every ball, putting everything into the rallies, trying my best to get him to take note. Agonising minutes ticked by before Mr Roberts leaned towards Mrs Embury again ... 'Susan Barker' ... and I was beckoned over.

Mr Roberts was gruff and to the point, but I lapped up his comments. He said I wasn't the second-best player in the group, but he had observed how I was able to play shots even with the wrong foot forward and get myself out of trouble. He admired my balance on the court and said there was a rawness to me that he could work with, as opposed to someone who'd been overcoached. Later I would hear him say over and over again, 'A coach cannot put in what is not there. My only job is to bring out what is there.'

Potential was all, and I have always realised how fortunate I was to be born in this tennis hotspot in Devon at a time when this absolute guru of a coach actively sought out local talent. Mr Roberts said he had also picked up on my determination to impress him with every shot – a quality he rated because he knew that sort of resolve would develop into long-term commitment. Once I was under his guidance, he would refer to me as his 'alley cat', saying he was confident I would scratch, claw and bite my way to victory.

That autumn day 55 years ago set me on my incredible journey in life. When Mr Roberts said he saw in me a determination that he hadn't seen in any other kid, I took his words to heart. If determination was a quality that opened that first door, I soon learned that it would also carry me through the ups and downs of pursuing my professional tennis dreams and lead to opportunities that I would never have imagined possible. But first I had to listen and learn.

At the end of my first coaching session on the Palace courts, I handed Mr Roberts the £1 note my parents had given me. He took it slowly, eyes locking with mine. 'If you give me this money, it means you are employing me and you can tell me what to do,' he said. 'If you come back on Thursday and don't pay me, can I tell you what to do?'

And so began a 19-year relationship that shapes my life to this day. Mr Roberts was a tough taskmaster, a brilliant but formidable tennis coach, a source of wisdom and inspiration, yet also something of an enigma. With a huge emphasis on work ethic, he coached me in every aspect of the game, honing my shots and schooling me in positioning and tactical awareness; he taught me how to approach competition, how to handle defeat, how to continually self-analyse in order to improve. He had exacting standards and there were plenty of tears along the way – but he was always there for me, a constant in the spinning whirl of junior, national and professional tennis competition. Behind that dour, uncompromising manner was a remarkably generous man, always ready to guide, or chide, me (even if I won, he might not have liked the manner in which I won). He understood me better than I did myself. Throughout my entire career in tennis, Mr Roberts refused to take any money from me apart from that initial £1, even when I started earning good prize money. I used to beg him to let me give him a fair percentage, but he was adamant. It was my money; I'd earned it. It was me out there on the court, not him. A shared passion for tennis was all he wanted; his pleasure came from seeing me chase my dreams and do well.

Mr Roberts was so much more than my tennis coach and mentor, he was my confidant ... my hero. And I hear his voice ringing in my ears to this day.

CHAPTER 2

WIMBLEDON HIGHLIGHTS

Clearing out a cupboard in my mother's home, I found some storage boxes that hadn't seen the light of day for years. Among these was a large plastic container with a clip-top lid, and I could see through the transparent sides that it was full of the old scrapbooks my father began to collate when I started competing in local junior tennis events back in the late 1960s. My daily sessions with Mr Roberts quickly led to a busy schedule of junior tournament play. Dad took great pleasure in sticking in news cuttings, photos and programmes, labelling each new addition with the occasion and date to create what is now an Aladdin's Cave of memorabilia. He'd found 'Susan' in large letters in a random headline and cut it out and glued it on the inside cover of the first album, 1969–70. And he went to the trouble of adding extra details in neat black pen under the entries. Beneath a picture snipped from the local paper of an array of trophies won by our tennis-mad Marist Convent team, he itemised 'Susan's Contributions'. My haul, as per Dad's list, was three shields, one trophy, one cup, five medals, one spoon and the Aberdare Cup, the trophy awarded to the top national girls' school tennis team. At the time, I had no idea he put so much effort into these albums – I was just playing tennis.

Thinking about the early scrapbooks makes me chuckle. I was always 'Susan' at home; it wasn't until I was picked out for individual coaching by Mr Roberts that I became 'Sue'. We were all a bit scared of Mr Roberts's brusque manner. Early on, he made no bones about the fact that he didn't like my name. Susan was too soft, he said. 'Sue' had more bite. A view you might say was underlined many years later when I was presenting the BBC's *Sports Personality of the Year* show in 2012. On stage at ExCeL London, I addressed Bradley Wiggins, the Tour de France and Olympic time trial champion, as Bradley, instead of Brad – not having had the chance to ask him what he would prefer to be called. Throughout our live exchange on stage, he persisted in calling me 'Susan' with pantomime formality, much to everyone's amusement. *Touché!*

I didn't dare open these boxes and their cache of nostalgia when I found them at Mum's. I knew that no sooner had I spotted a photograph of Arthur's stable of kids on the Palace Hotel courts, or read a report of 12-year-old me playing for the Devon Under-14 team at Bristol, or seen a headline from the *Paignton News* anticipating a victory for the Marist Convent in the national schools' competition at Wimbledon, or a picture of me jumping the net alongside the world's best player Rod Laver at a junior international tennis clinic, than I'd be wandering down a long and winding memory lane of happy reminiscences for hours.

But something caught my eye: a cream envelope, wedged between two turquoise albums. I recognised it straight away as a talisman I'd squirrelled away more than 50 years ago, and my heart leapt. I plunged into the box and drew out this long, thin paper packet that had been sealed and folded in half again to doubly protect its treasure. Dad's looping handwriting was as clear as the day he wrote it: 'Grass from the Centre Court (Aberdare Cup. July 1969)'. The Centre Court. No need to say where.

Summer 1969! I didn't want to risk opening the envelope in case those carefully preserved clippings evaporated into dust. Wrapped up in crumpled black tissue paper inside was a precious harvest of grass from Centre Court, nicked on my first visit to the home of tennis to play in the national schools' event. Just to hold the packet in my hand again was such a magical feeling. From the moment I first picked up a racket, Wimbledon signified the ultimate goal. These matted blades of grass were the symbol of my passion for tennis.

And what did they mean to me today?

I recalled the fun of that first visit to the All England Club, home of the Championships known universally as Wimbledon. Our squad of ten, drawn from various year groups, travelled up from Devon in the old school bus, driven by our patient PE teacher, Mrs Embury. There were only 198 girls at the Marist but, thanks to Mr Roberts, who coached several of us outside of school, we were the best tennis team in Britain for four consecutive years.

We stayed at our sister school, the Marist in Sunninghill, Berkshire, which we dreaded because the older girls said the convent food was unpleasant. Sister Evaristus, Sister Placidus and Sister Moira accompanied us for the trip and on the short journey from Sunninghill to our destination in south-west London they would whip out their rosary beads, poised to channel all the powers they could muster to give us an extra competitive edge. They used to say that they would be praying hard if our matches got tight – and I'd wonder if nuns should be taking sides like that! The sisters from Sunninghill used to pack into the old bus, too, to boost our support. We were so embarrassed by our holy barmy army, cheering us on in their black habits and headdresses. They were the noisiest spectators. You can imagine our street cred.

We filed off the school bus and crossed the road excitedly. I've never forgotten the first time I walked through the grand wrought-iron gates on Somerset Road: it was an incredible moment seeing the sun glittering on the golden 'AELTC' lettering on the gates and the picture-perfect vista through the railings – the purple and green club crest spelling out 'The All England Lawn Tennis & Croquet Club' and the formidable Virginia creeper-clad clubhouse. We played on the shale courts in the south of the grounds – roughly on the site where the new No.2 Court is today – and once the competition was over we were offered a tour of the landmark clubhouse as part of our prize for winning. We took photographs of each other under the famous clock, right in front of the doors where just a week or so earlier that year's Wimbledon finalists – the Australians Rod Laver and John Newcombe, American Billie Jean King and the British champion Ann Jones – had gone in and out, and we were then led down through the inner sanctum to walk out on to *the* Centre Court. I already had plenty of reverence for the place Billie Jean calls 'the cathedral' of tennis. I loved Billie Jean's feistiness; her competitive spirit had become my benchmark ever since I'd watched her on the black-and-white TV that we'd sat around as a family, our eyes glued to her epic battles with her great rivals – the Australian Margaret Court, Maria Bueno from Brazil and Ann Jones – in Wimbledon finals. My awe for the whole scene intensified when we filed on to the hallowed turf below the Royal Box. Standing there, drinking in the atmosphere and thinking of all the epic matches played in this grand yet intimate stadium was just surreal. The empty, undressed court was alluring, inviting: *Come play on me one day,* it seemed to say. I knelt down to pick some blades of grass, wrapping them up in a bit of tissue and shoving them in my pocket to take home. My own piece of Wimbledon.

That first visit cemented it for me. I collected the grass much as you pick up a souvenir from a foreign city you may never visit again, but I knew Wimbledon would always be a special place for me. Who knows, maybe I manifested my life here through my dreams and determination? For in my imagination, I had played on Centre Court many times before I crossed the threshold of the famous gates on that early Aberdare Cup adventure. Centre Court was the garage wall at home in Paignton, where I pummelled Billie Jean on a daily basis, always beating her in a close final set, 7–5 or 6–4. It was the swingball in our sloping back garden where I whacked the ball with my older sister Jane, with the sea across the Torbay skyline sparkling in the background. It was also the public courts at Oldway Mansion – a park situated between our house in Barcombe Heights and Paignton Beach – where I played on weekends with my family and locals of all ages. A bit later, of course, it was the indoor courts and the hitting wall at the Palace Hotel, where I was drilled by Mr Roberts to emulate the feats of his former protégés, Angela Mortimer and Mike Sangster. Not that he'd let me dream about Centre Court: Mr Roberts was all about a steady work ethic and small steps to build confidence in my technique and competitive ability – he would have had me dreaming about winning an Under-12 event in Exeter! Privately, every single swing of the racket edged me one ball closer to my ambition of actually competing on Centre Court at Wimbledon; every winner I struck was a crucial point in a fantasy match on my way to glory there.

I didn't foresee when I sealed that first envelope of Centre Court grass that every year for the next half-century, I would be back in some capacity – as a junior aged 15, as a Grand Slam winner ranked No.3 in the world and as a broadcaster sharing all the action as it unfolded to an audience of millions with the likes of Chris Evert, Martina Navratilova, John McEnroe (Mac), Boris Becker, Tracy Austin, Tim Henman and Pat Cash as my studio guests.

Wimbledon and me, we go back a long way, and the magic of the place is still entwined with the pride I felt walking in as that 13-year-old kid who had earned the right to play there. Each of the four Aberdare Cup schools' finals I competed in and won from 1969–72 – and the junior national championships, which were also held on the club's shale courts – gave me a sense of belonging, and a longing for more. For the short duration of those events, I was a bona fide insider at the home of tennis. Centre

Court, and the history of all who had played there, loomed large in my peripheral vision as I mortared the lines with sledgehammer forehands to smash the junior opposition.

Holding these clippings in my palm again, I had to pinch myself to think about what happened subsequently in my career, and the way my passion for tennis has shaped my life. The grass-clippings collection became a ritual for me and Dad; I would pluck some grass every year over the next four summer trips to and from Wimbledon on the old school bus, and hand it to him as soon as I got home. Was I keeping it as a memento? Or to nurture continuity in my association with this special place? The more I claimed a tiny piece of Wimbledon, the more it became a part of me. If someone had told me then that I would actually play on Centre Court, that I would twice be just a match or two away from reaching the Wimbledon ladies' singles final, and that I would go on to present the BBC coverage alongside such TV legends as Des Lynam and Harry Carpenter, I would have laughed in their face.

But I did, and I have Mr Roberts to thank. Had he not picked me out for special individual coaching when he came along to the Marist Convent courts to watch the first-year seniors play, my life would have gone in a different direction. Had our little school not had tennis courts and a proud tennis history, or a PE teacher like the wonderful Mrs Embury, who forged the connection with Arthur Roberts, I would never have developed my love of the game. One thing led to another, and it all stems from travelling to school competitions with a busful of nuns and being coached by a maverick hotel tennis pro in the seaside town made famous by *Fawlty Towers*.

• • •

Wimbledon is the constant that runs through my tennis and broadcasting years, like the letters that spell out 'Paignton' in the traditional sugary sticks of rock sold in the sweet shops along the seafront of my hometown. I've never missed a year. For me, that green patchwork of grass courts down the hill from Wimbledon village has been a place of eternal sporting drama and a place of work. It's both a professional touchstone and my home from home. Courtesy of my indispensable floor manager Liz Thorburn, I have my own coat hook in the BBC studio within the Club's Broadcast Centre marked 'H.R.W.H.' (Her Royal Wimbledon Highness) and my own nickname among our close-knit crew (DOC, short for Demanding Old Cow – far too complicated to go into here).

Every July, I'm still down there on the edge of Centre Court, no longer worshipping the grass myself but with a camera and sound crew and the likes of Boris and Tim or Chrissie and Tracy. I might be previewing matches as players knock up before I rush back to my studio chair as a match gets under way – I consider myself the official Wimbledon warm-up correspondent, as I never see a ball hit live throughout the fortnight of a Championship. Or I'm tucked away behind a curtain just off Centre Court, watching the last minutes on a small monitor, primed to walk on to interview the champion and the runner-up. It's quite something to think how often I've now walked across that same patch of court I knelt down on as a kid, and watched a roll-call of great champions honour the court in their own way: kissing the grass, eating it, falling backwards on it in jubilant exhaustion, shedding tears of joy or disappointment. The ground staff today would be bemused to know I once showed such respect for their carefully manicured grass: after years of trotting down in heels with the camera crew, the wary groundsman's team eventually found a bit of green carpet to protect it from my spikes!

These days I come traipsing in through the media entrance with my day's notes spilling out of a rucksack, which isn't half as fun as being with my mates on the old school bus or as glamorous as a player being delivered to the clubhouse door in a courtesy car. From 1993, Wimbledon became just one of the prestigious sports events I've presented each year for the BBC, alongside five Olympic Games (Atlanta in 1996 through to London 2012), five Winter Olympics, as well as Commonwealth Games from Canada, Malaysia, Manchester, Melbourne and Delhi; numerous World and European Athletics Championships, racing festivals, figure skating, 19 *Sports Personality of the Year* shows ... I've travelled the world and worked from the heart of the premier events of global sport to share the stories as they unfold. I'm immensely proud of being one of very few former athletes who have gone on to present multi-sports programmes on such a high-profile channel – but I still get chills when I walk through the gates of the All England Club. And I still have a ritual.

On the eve of a Championship I make a point of coming in early and going up to the roof above the Broadcast Centre to look out over the grounds and feel the transformative power of the place. I love that private moment. You hear the courts being mown, smell the freshly cut grass, the flowers; there's something special about seeing everyone scurrying around the walkways preparing for a glorious fortnight of action. It gives me goosebumps every year. What am I now, 66? And I first walked in when

I was just 13. Everywhere I glance from the rooftop prompts a host of memories and also a sense of wonder about what history will be made over the next 14 days while I'm in the presenter's chair. Once the tournament is under way I certainly don't have time for contemplation, but I enjoy seizing that moment for myself to just take stock and feel the timeless spirit of the place.

I always say I am a player first, a broadcaster second, but I mean that in spirit. I never dwell on the standout matches I played here myself. Frankly, there are a few I'd like to forget. But it's bizarre to glance towards the ivy-covered walls of Centre Court and think it's where I played the great Maria Bueno on my singles debut on the show court in 1976 – the year Björn Borg won his first title, beating Ilie Năstase on that same swathe of sun-scorched grass. After all my dreams of that longed-for occasion, I didn't have a sleepless night anticipating this head-to-head with one of the greats of the game. I only learned I was due to play in the second match on Centre Court that very morning when I was staying with my friend from junior days, Linda Mottram, in her family home in a Wimbledon cul-de-sac. I was tucking into bacon and eggs at the kitchen table when Linda's mum looked up from the newspaper and said, 'Oh, Sue, how exciting! Have you ever played on Centre Court before?' In those days we didn't get the Order of Play the night before; you had to look in the morning papers or ring up the referee's office. That was the first I knew of it.

From the rooftop, looking over to the left, there's Henman Hill, which didn't exist when I first came to Wimbledon. The land was leased to a New Zealand sports club and was used as a car park during the tournament. As I survey its sweep of lawn and picnic tables and the giant TV screen, I smile to think that this landmark is named after a skinny ten-year-old who I coached at the David Lloyd Tennis Centre in Heston shortly after retiring in 1985. (I was shocked to hear Tim recently describe me as a 'borderline scary coach', but yes, I did expect 100 per cent effort in my drills!) Sometimes when I dropped the boys back at Reed's, their boarding school in Cobham, I would ask if they fancied a burger and take them to McDonald's, or pick up some Coke and chocolate at the service station. I felt sorry for these little lads dutifully eating their strict nutritionist-controlled diet. They loved me! To this day, Tim calls me Auntie Sue, and blames me for never winning Wimbledon, saying I compromised his athlete's diet from a young age. I think he's joking.

On the other side of Centre Court lie the club's original grass courts, separated by narrow walkways. If I close my eyes, I can almost hear the hysteria in the air when Borg, my one-time doubles partner, would be mobbed by hysterical fans. He was a superstar, to his contemporaries as well as his fans. I recall Chris Evert and me marvelling at the scene from the upstairs window of the women's dressing room; after hearing the screams, we looked down and saw a dot of blond hair in a sweatband and those broad shoulders in an orange Fila tracksuit top, Björn surrounded by policemen trying to ensure his safety. Today, there are underground tunnels to help players get from the locker rooms to the show courts without having to navigate crowded walkways, but he never had the benefit of that. Even when he was finishing matches, fans would run on court to grab his sweatbands. Those on-court invasions still seem extraordinary when everything else about Wimbledon was, and is, so formal, with the all-white clothing regulation and tea lawns, the band playing jaunty tunes and the army of service stewards helping the public find their seats. Borgmania was a sign that tennis suddenly had blockbuster glamour, and I was so lucky to be competing during those heady days when our sport became box office.

Of course, my dream was to win the ladies' singles title. I certainly had my chances, but I never converted them. My greatest successes were not on the grass courts of Wimbledon; it wasn't my favourite surface. Two matches that I should have won haunt me – a quarter-final against Martina Navratilova in 1976, the year I won the French Open at Roland-Garros, and a semi-final against Betty Stöve in the following year (I'll go into the gory details of both later). To have not capitalised on two chances at Wimbledon when your dream is to win it … well, you never quite get over it. I was never the same player again. Those painful losses broke something inside of me. But I blame myself, not the place. It hasn't affected my love for Wimbledon at all. And here's the great thing about working on television: I have all these great players on the programme as studio guests, and we've all had our nightmares as well as our triumphs. Thanks to our dear old British weather, and numerous rain breaks before the introduction of the covered courts, we've shown clips from bygone years of each other's milestone dramas just to keep the banter going. It's not just great fun, the comments amount to group therapy! Mac was in the studio once when I had the misfortune to sit through the end of my horrible match against Martina in 1976. I had two break points to go, two breaks up in the third set and then I just threw it away. I could hardly look as the footage played … I had a face like thunder as my 20-year-old self swept up her rackets, towel and handbag and stomped off the court. But all Mac could do was take the mickey.

'Your *handbag*!' he laughed.

And it did look ridiculous. Players today tote around their huge athlete's kit bags and there I was slinging on my little shoulder bag with my accreditation pass dangling from the strap.

'Your face may have got you through the gates,' I said to Mac, 'but I needed my competitor's badge and it was tied to my handbag!'

I've fronted the BBC Wimbledon coverage alongside many of my friends and former rivals for three times as many years as I was a competitor, and the former-player-turned-broadcaster is a fun club to be in. That's something I muse on every year when I'm having my private moment of reverie on the roof. It's a small world and the players who loved their tennis careers tend to stick around. During the Championship, you might see former Grand Slam champion Jim Courier interviewing Novak Djokovic for Tennis Channel on the raised terrace next to the Broadcast Centre or Mac coming down the steps in his Converse sneakers en route to taking up position in the BBC commentary box. There's the bench opposite the referees' office, close to the entrance of the Media Centre, where for years Venus and Serena's father Richard Williams used to sit, almost inviting anyone to come and talk to him. How the years whizz by. When Venus arrived at Wimbledon in 1998, already the previous year's US Open finalist aged 17,

I sat down to interview her. She had asked if she could bring her younger sister along and I said fine. On camera, Venus introduced Serena and told the world to look out because Serena was going to be better than her. I remember laughing out loud, thinking, *Oh yeah?* Venus herself had just burst on to the scene. She was so athletic, so powerful, so tactically aware, it seemed impossible that her baby sister could be even more formidable. That's the beauty of sport. You just never know what will happen next.

I wake up each morning during Wimbledon looking forward to the day. Nerves don't bother me any more, but I have the same feeling I did every day as a player. I'm either going to do a good programme or a bad one. It's like winning and losing in tennis – there's nothing in between. I leave the studio each day asking myself the same questions I did when I left a tournament, the questions Mr Roberts urged me to ask of myself. What worked and what didn't? And why? What could I have done better?

As a presenter, I've had my highs and lows too. Live television can be a white-knuckle ride as it is, but add in the emotion of watching a British player, and I'm a wreck. I make sure I am scrupulously impartial on air but I always want the home players to succeed because I know how special it is to play well at Wimbledon for an appreciative crowd. In 2013, Andy Murray was two sets and a break down in his quarter-final against Fernando Verdasco and I was living every point with him in the studio, so nervous as he looked like he was down and out. Jo, the sound lady, filmed me screaming and fist-pumping and sent the clip to Judy Murray, who later passed it on to Andy and his wife Kim. So embarrassing. I got an email from Judy after his eventual victory, saying I was getting more wound up than she ever would. I don't know how she sits so composed in the players' box with the cameras on her as Andy plays with his heart on his sleeve. Jane Henman, Tim's mother, always used to say she lost 5lb through tension every Wimbledon.

That year, of course, Andy went on to win – the first British men's Wimbledon champion since Fred Perry in 1936 – and that ranks as my absolute career highlight. Earlier that year we had persuaded him to take part in a BBC documentary. The British public had started to warm to him after his desperately emotional speech on Centre Court the previous year, when he lost to Roger Federer. I knew that if the public saw the 'real Andy' then they would take him to their hearts, as privately he is funny and personable. Andy agreed, and I travelled to Florida to film with him. We also filmed him walking his dogs and I interviewed him at his home in Surrey where he opened up about his memories of the Dunblane massacre, breaking down in tears as he relived the horrific shootings that took place at his primary school in Perthshire when he was an eight-year-old pupil.

Incredibly, from those two sets down through the Verdasco challenge, he went on to win Wimbledon. Without doubt, walking on to Centre Court to announce him as winner was the best day of my television career. The journey to that final was immense, and for him to beat Novak Djokovic and emerge victorious after such a seemingly endless last game really put us all through the wringer. That last game was the most terrifying ... I thought if Andy didn't win that service game he might lose the match.

The 1999 highlights programme produced my most morti-fying gaffe. Steffi Graf had announced at the beginning of the

It was about this time that Mr Roberts started sending me off to junior competitions in Europe by myself. Typically, his tactic was psychological. On one early trip to an Under-21 tournament in the South of France, he gave me a one-way ticket and told me to win enough prize money to buy my way home. There were times when I slept inside the host tennis club because I was worried about paying for a hotel. My tactic was to hide under a hedge and wait until the club was locked up for the night, then sleep in a *cabana* in the grounds. I knew I had to get through to the quarter-finals, at least, to make enough money for the fare home.

All of these things were so exciting and I needed time off school because a lot of the Under-21 competitions took place during school times. Even Sister Placidus – bless her – agreed to let me take my O-level exams with the retakers in November. That summer of 1971, I wanted to play in the Junior World Cup, I wanted to enter the Beckenham tournament and I wanted to compete at Wimbledon, and they agreed to allow me that. My parents paid for me to have private tutoring because they wanted me to have the back-up of education in case the tennis didn't work out.

By now there was a regular group of us representing GB: Glynis Coles, Linda Mottram and myself. Shirley Brasher was our captain. In Europe, we had the Princess Sofia Cup for Under-16s, which was mainly played in Spain, and the Annie Soisbault Cup, an Under-18 international team competition named after a French player and racing driver who juggled appearances on the tennis circuit with tearing around hairpin bends on the Monte Carlo Rally. We always seemed to be up against Czechoslovakia in year that she would be playing her last Roland-Garros and Wimbledon. Having lost the final to the hard-hitting US Open champion Lindsay Davenport, Steffi had taken her leave of Centre Court and I was asked to close the show by linking to a montage of her greatest moments. At the end of every show I hear a hard count through my earpiece to the moment when I should stop talking. It's not professional to underrun or overrun; I need to be saying goodbye as the count goes from one to zero. In those ten seconds, I decided I would close with the line, 'After a magnificent career, Steffi waves a final farewell to Wimbledon and her beloved Centre Court, but at least she walks away with some great memories.' In my ear, I could hear the producer ask where the closing montage was … this was ten seconds to go before I would deliver my line.

Adrenaline is running high. Where was the montage? Would my words work if we didn't have the clips? Needless to say, with seconds to go, the video compilation was ready – everyone had played a blinder to put it together on time – and I ploughed on and delivered my line: 'After a magnificent career, Steffi waves a final farewell to Wimbledon and her beloved Centre Court, but at least she walks away with some great mammaries.'

I lay my head on the desk as there were huge gasps from the gallery. Martin Hopkins, the daytime producer, burst through the doors in hysterics. 'At least you were factually correct,' he roared. We all burst out laughing. The next day I got a message from the men's locker room thanking me for 'stating the bleeding obvious'. My embarrassment was complete.

CHAPTER 3

COMING OUT FIGHTING

It was my sister Jane, six years my senior, who got me into tennis. I won't say 'introduced', because it was under duress. She'd started playing tennis at our junior school and she was very good. The Marist Convent, juniors and seniors, shared tennis courts. Some doubled as a netball court and a rounders field, but there'd always be at least one net up. I used to beg Jane to let me go and play with her after school. Mostly she'd let me tag along to act as a ball girl: 'Well, you run around quite well,' she'd say. 'At least you can pick up balls for me.' I was always the last resort. If she couldn't find anyone else to play, she'd let me have a go with a racket. I used to try so hard to hit balls back for her, but I was all over the place.

We had a fabulous PE teacher called Mrs Chadwick who saw how much I loved the game and the challenge to improve enough to give Jane a game. She used to stay back after school sometimes and give me a bit of coaching. At the time, there was a government or community initiative that set tennis challenges for junior school pupils. Can you hit 20 balls over the net inside the court? Can you get ten serves in a row in the box? Your teacher would sign the form to verify you'd met the goal and a few weeks later a certificate would arrive in the post. From the age of six or seven, I'd started sticking mine on my bedroom wall as incentives to improve. And then Mrs Chadwick would announce the next challenge. It would sometimes take me weeks to get there but eventually I would and she'd send off another form. I loved those days at school when she'd seek me out to say, 'Susan! Your certificate's arrived!'

After school, I'd trail after Jane into Oldway Mansion, which was halfway between home and the beach. Sadly it's semi-derelict now, but the grand nineteenth-century house had a formal garden modelled on the Petit Trianon in Versailles, with ponds and acres of informal 'pleasure grounds', including a dozen or so public tennis courts that backed on to our primary school. There was a lovely café and we used to pay half a crown or something to hire a court for an hour.

Oldway was heaven for kids. We liked to play hide and seek, ride our bikes there or muck around on the putting green, but what I loved most was going to the club to play tennis at weekends. Mrs Easterbrook, who I thought was about 100 years old, ruled the roost and welcomed all ages. Sometimes I'd play doubles with her against her fellow club regular Joyce MacDonell and another middle-aged lady. Their enthusiasm made a lasting impression on me. One of them served underarm – but trust me they were very competitive. It was a lot of fun. If you'd asked me my life's ambition when I was ten years old, I would have said I wanted to grow up to be Mrs Easterbrook. I used to think I would be that lady who is still playing tennis when she's 100.

My parents first met at the local golf club. My mum, Betty – who I sadly lost this year at the amazing age of 100 – had been engaged during the Second World War to a fighter pilot who was killed in action. Mum spent much of the war years in Sussex, looking after children who had been evacuated from London; her voluntary work included working alongside nurses, helping out however she could. After the war she returned to Devon and, as she said, there weren't that many men her age around. Her mother, my grandmother, was playing a lot of golf with a chap called Bob Barker – full name Robert Charles Barker – who had moved to Paignton from Leicester. Mum met him at the golf club and got to know him, and they married in 1948. Dad was born in 1905 and there was a 16-year age gap between them, but I never noticed that as a child. By the time I was born, Dad was 51, but he was always slim, fit and active, and very hands-on in terms of conjuring fun for us. After Jane was born in 1950, my parents bought a lovely house for £4,000 at 20 Barcombe Heights, which remained our home for 35 years. It had three bedrooms, one family bathroom and a sun lounge that ran along the back of the house, overlooking a steep garden with beautiful views over Paignton to Brixham and out over the sea. Barcombe Heights was a really happy street and I'm still in touch with our neighbours – two of whom play tennis and one is even a member at Wimbledon.

After Jane, Mum had a miscarriage and a stillborn child, and then my brother Neil arrived safely in December 1954.

Mum never had a salaried job in her life; she was happy to be a stay-at-home mum. Dad was an area representative for Bass Charrington, the brewery company; he was based in Plymouth, and his job was to oversee a group of pubs mostly in Devon with a few across the border in Cornwall. Mum and Dad decided that two children were enough on his salary, but less than six months after Neil was born, Mum found herself pregnant again. Jokingly, she used to tell me that she went to the doctor to say she didn't want another baby. She thought Dad really wouldn't want another mouth to feed. One night she drank too much gin and bounced herself down the stairs, thinking, because of her previous miscarriages, this might do the trick. It didn't, and I was born on 19 April 1956. It's part of our family lore that I came out fighting, determined to make my presence felt, as if I knew I had to.

My ability to battle through adversity was tested almost immediately. I caught whooping cough as a very young baby. Mum remembered me turning blue and at night she would have to walk backwards and forwards along the landing in our upstairs hallway for hours on end, holding me up against her shoulder, because I struggled to breathe any time she tried to put me down. Several times I just stopped breathing, and it was touch-and-go for three days. She had taken me to the hospital but they said there was nothing they could do. It was what it was. My parents would have to ride it out and hope for the best. It wasn't until I was a professional player on the women's tour that Mum told me I'd been so ill for so long I was never christened. I arranged that for myself when I was 21.

The Barker household was a very happy place, though my sister thought Neil and me annoying younger siblings. I can't blame her. Jane had been the apple of everyone's eye for five years and she didn't want a newborn to arrive. Suddenly, she had a brother, and then a sister who had to share her bedroom. On one occasion, she'd had enough of me and that was it. She threw me out of the car. There were no baby seats back then and she had been holding me on her lap in the back seat. Dad slowed the car to go around a corner and she just opened the door and out I went. Dad slammed on the brakes and I was scooped up from the side of the road. Jane wanted me to go and I very nearly did. I still have a dent in my head.

With just 15 months between us, Neil and I were close partners in crime. We were horrible to Jane and she was always telling us off. Being very much a girly girl, Jane liked her dolls and she had a Spanish one that she absolutely idolised. On one occasion when we'd had a row with her, my brother planned our revenge. He stuffed the doll in a branch of a tall conifer in our garden and pulled the branch back as far as he could. Ping! The catapult action sheared off the doll's glossy raven-black hair. And we just left the doll dangling there for Jane to find. I don't think she spoke to either of us for weeks after the scalping episode.

Sometimes I was too much even for Neil. I was always that child in a school photo with a wonky scarf, unbrushed hair and buttons askew. I never looked in a mirror. There's a family story about the time my brother and I were late walking home from school one day. Mum came out to meet us and caught sight of my brother, with me dawdling miles behind.

'Neil, why aren't you walking with your sister?' she asked.

He turned to point at me: 'Well, *look* at her!' My hat was off to the side, my school bag dragging along the ground. He refused to walk alongside me. I was that embarrassing sibling.

My father was in his late thirties when he arrived in Paignton from Leicester after the war. His early life had been tough and he would never talk about it, not even to my mum. On one occasion, his brother turned up on our doorstep and was sent packing. We don't know what happened. We didn't even know he had a brother. All Mum knew is that my father's father was sent over to France during the First World War and fought in the trenches. He survived, but only just. He returned home with syphilis (as did roughly 5 per cent of British soldiers during the war), and the disease sent him mad and ultimately killed him. He was admitted to an asylum and died when my father was no more than 18 or 19.

Dad was bright, especially good with numbers, and he wanted to become a bank manager. He had his future planned: to study more and go into banking. When his father died leaving no money, his mother told him he had to go out and bring home a wage. He had to be the breadwinner. So he shelved his ambitions and worked in a shoe factory to provide for his mother and younger brother. He didn't leave Leicester until his mother died, then he came to Devon and made a new life there. It's really sad. He had been married before, but Mum told me I mustn't let on to Dad that I knew because divorce was a major issue in those days. I don't know what happened, and I don't want to find out, because I'm not going to hear both sides of the story now and

Dad certainly never wanted to discuss it. I'm sure it's why he was such a lovely father. His fresh start in Devon was a second chance and he was intent on creating a happy family.

My parents always wanted us to be outdoors, playing in the fresh air. We were always being kicked out of the house to play pirates or other games to tire us out among the apple trees at the bottom of the back garden. We persuaded them to get us one of those giant swingball contraptions. It was a big pole with a ball on a piece of elastic and we used to be able to stand there and hit it between us, hoping that it didn't fly off the elastic and go into someone else's garden. We also used to hit balls – much to our neighbours' annoyance – against the garage door. There were lots of fun days out to the beach or to play tennis, cricket and golf. My mother was the ladies' captain at Churston Golf Club in Brixham. Jane and I used to go riding every Sunday and I loved hanging out at the stables. I can still remember every pony's name, from Spotty, a tiny bay with a white blaze that everyone started on, to Tessa, the big mare my sister fell off. We used to ride on the beach. We even did jumping. I just loved it, and I built little jumps in our garden for my own imaginary stable of horses. But I had to give up when I was 12 and tennis took over my weekends.

In the summer, we used to venture up to Dartmoor for picnics beside a stream. Dad bought this inflatable rubber paddle-boat and he would sit on a rock with a rope attached to the boat on the end of his foot. More often than not, Neil and I would be in it, paddling like mad, thinking we were setting off downstream, but not actually going anywhere. And Jane would be laughing her head off watching us. Even in my teenage years, when Dad was in his mid-sixties, he, Neil and I often went climbing on Dartmoor. Jane was at university by this stage, shot of us at last. We'd clamber up to the top of Haytor Rocks and wave at Mum, sitting in her deck chair below. Dad was pretty fearless and she used to hate it: 'He's taken them up there again!' But she could talk. Diving off Paignton Pier was strictly prohibited, but that didn't stop her. She loved swimming and preferred to dive in rather than wade out. She got into awful trouble for doing that, but that was her. She was such a character.

Once a year we took the car over to De Panne in Belgium or to France on the ferry and rented a holiday flat above a beach, often with uncles and aunts and cousins. The flat opened out on to a promenade and, beyond that, a beach. The boys used to visit war sites and German bunkers. We had fabulous family holidays on the seafront. But we never flew anywhere.

There wasn't a lot of spare cash. For years, we didn't have a fridge at home; we used to keep milk in buckets of cold water and Mum had an outhouse with marble shelves for butter and cheese. We had a coal-fired boiler. Almost every day, I had to fill the coal bucket and bring it into the kitchen to get the boiler going for heat and hot water. Meals were good but basic – meat from the butcher with vegetables from the greengrocer and always lots of gravy. Every plate used to swim in gravy. Mum used to spend a lot of time cooking and every night she produced a big dessert. She did all the steamed jam and syrup puddings and my favourites, Queen of Puddings and Apple Charlotte. I do remember the excitement of the day we got our first fridge, but it seemed quite a utilitarian thing. I was more fascinated by our first telephone.

I'd look at this big heavy contraption with its rotary dial and wonder if it would ring, and what it would sound like.

Our television was encased in a wooden box on four legs and stood in our lounge. Initially, I don't remember watching anything on it except for Wimbledon. Later, in my early teens, I watched a lot of different sports with Dad. He'd let me stay up and watch *Match of the Day* with him, and our favourite, *A Question of Sport*, hosted by David Vine. We absolutely loved that. Dad loved his football, but racing was his main interest. Every weekend, we'd choose our horses from the paper and then watch how they'd do. Sometimes he'd take me to Newton Abbot, which was only about ten miles away; he would allow himself one quid to bet (the equivalent of about £20 today). That was it, no more. He wasn't a gambler. We were all sports mad and spent many happy hours around the family TV. I look at photos of that room now and remember how much I loved roasting chestnuts on the open fire, or toasting little teacakes and crumpets when the nights had drawn in. But I don't know what my mum was thinking when she decorated it: she had one wall papered with a green and yellow psychedelic swirl and a heavily patterned sofa. You know those classic looks from the 1950s and 1960s? Well, we were living that dream.

Dad was the rock of our family and always provided for us, but times could be tough. That hit home when I was about six or seven and Mum gave my sister her purse and asked her to go and get some apples because she was going to make a pie. I tagged along too. On our way home from the greengrocer, we became distracted by some boys on bicycles. We went with them down to the courts at Oldway, where we used to hang out. Jane left the bag with the apples and the purse in a courtside shelter. The boys were just bothering us, actually. When we came back, the purse and the bag of shopping had gone, and the boys were riding their bikes around munching on our apples. So we knew they had the purse, too, but they just cycled off and that was it. Gone! When we got home, Mum just burst into tears and said, 'That's all the money I've got in the world!'

That stuck with me, her look of despair. I thought, *Oh my God, we're poor.* I quickly learned that we weren't so much poor as living on a tight budget, and Dad used to give Mum a weekly allowance for housekeeping, so it wasn't like she had lost thousands of pounds. It was just the week's shopping quota. But at the time, it terrified me to think we were that short of money. And, of course, Jane got in a lot of trouble.

Usually it was me being sent up to my room with Mum's voice ringing in my ears: 'Just wait till your father gets home!' I was always very close to my mum but I was mischievous and I pushed her buttons. She would be in our sitting room while I was out playing 'nicely' in the garden and then she'd see that I was up at the top of one of the 25-foot-tall conifer trees that flanked the sun lounge, trying to make it violently sway. Mum used to get so angry because she thought I'd fall and kill myself, so she got Dad to cut the bottom five feet of branches from each tree so I couldn't climb them. But I just got on my brother's shoulders and climbed up again. I definitely tested her patience. Mum would have said that Dad was a lot stricter than her, but when he arrived home from work and came into the bedroom I shared with Jane to follow up on Mum's reprimand, he was gentle. He had this ruse. He never used to tell me off. He'd shut the door and ask me what I'd done. Then he'd say, 'I'm going to shout so your mother can hear, but just give it five or ten minutes and come down and apologise to her and everything will be all right.' And it always was, and then he'd give me a fireman's lift over his shoulder to take me upstairs at bedtime.

He'd often fall asleep in an armchair when he came home from work. Being a rep for the brewery, he must have had a few half-pints in the pubs he visited each day. He used to let me comb his hair, though that stopped when I decided to give him a crew cut at the front of his head while he was dozing.

He'd let me sit on his knee when he was driving the car. He'd be doing the gears and I'd be steering. When I was a bit older, he let me sit in the passenger seat. 'I've got the clutch in,' he'd say. 'You change the gear.' Courtesy of his job, he received a new car every couple of years, and its delivery was just so exciting for everyone in the street. It was always a Ford Cortina, and we never had a choice of colour. He'd let us know in the morning that he would be coming down in the afternoon to pick us up from school in the new car. I would be fired up all day wondering what colour it would be – and so disappointed when it turned out to be another yucky green. His workday started early and finished when pubs closed after lunchtime, about 3pm. He planned his route so that his last calls were the most local pubs and he could then come and pick us up from school. There must have been a few occasions when he'd had way too much to drink because he rolled his Cortinas at least three times that I can recall. Once, he arrived home having had one too many of his company's samples – he came down our steep driveway and smashed straight through the garage door. Mum was furious.

In terms of sporting genes, Dad obviously loved his golf – it's where he met Mum, after all. And he once let slip he had a cousin who played rugby for Leicester Tigers. My mother, like her own mother, was mad about golf. Churston Golf Club was a big part of family life, but I never caught the bug. Most of my parents' friends came from the club; my godmother, Judy, was one. She was the funniest lady I'd ever met. She swore like a trooper. She'd be effing and blinding and Mum would keep saying, 'Hush, Susan's in the car.' I used to caddy for them sometimes, but Mum banned me because I used to laugh whenever she messed up a shot. One side of Mum's family was from New Zealand and she has always said her grandfather played for the All Blacks, but my brother – who did a lot of family research before he passed away six years ago – couldn't find anything to confirm it. I think it was in her dreams. He probably played rugby for Auckland.

Mum's family was very different to Dad's. Her paternal grandparents, the Wilsons, owned the *New Zealand Herald* newspaper in Auckland, which was how they made their money. Their son, my mother's father, came to London and fell in love with a girl from Balham called Ethel. She wasn't welcomed by his family because she was deemed not to come from a suitable background. But my grandfather apparently said to his family, 'You can choose my career, but you will not choose my wife.' Before long, my grandmother became pregnant with my mum. We didn't know this until July 2006, when the *Daily Telegraph* wrote an article based on my family tree without my knowledge. It was really irresponsible journalism because it was through this piece that my mother learned that she was conceived out of wedlock. She was in her mid-eighties, and it left her extremely upset – especially the fact that it said it was a real scandal and that my grandfather had been forced to marry my grandmother, when she'd always been told they were so in love. They were very happy and went on to have three children: Mum (Betty Valerie), Uncle John and Auntie Barbara.

My grandfather was a dentist and when Mum was five, he moved his practice to Torquay. Literally months after they moved, he died of blood poisoning – something which could be cured easily today with a simple course of antibiotics. Poor Gran was left with three young kids and not the greatest support from her in-laws in New Zealand. A few years later, there was a change of heart in that her father-in-law wanted to look after his son's children by paying for their education. So Mum was sent to Malvern Girls' College. I've driven Mum back to see it and she regaled me with the old stories of her grandfather coming over to visit and driving around in a Rolls-Royce. The long-distance family support remained. Later, Mum, to her surprise, was left some money by the New Zealand relations – which proved to be a game changer for me.

The big stroke of luck in my life came when Jane failed her 11-plus. Although she's incredibly bright and became a head teacher herself, she failed the entrance exam for the grammar school. Thanks to that small sum of money Mum had been left by her father's family, my parents were able to send her to the fee-paying senior Marist Convent school instead, where she thrived and became head girl and tennis captain. Six years later, I was at the Marist Convent junior and did manage to pass my 11-plus. I was all set to go to Churston Grammar School, which had massive sports facilities ... and boys. I had my bus pass ready and was just hopping with excitement. But I came home from school one day and it was clear from the atmosphere that there was to be a change of plan. Mum had heard, out of the blue, that she was to inherit more money, this time a substantial windfall – and my parents made the decision that I would join Jane at the Marist Convent.

They explained it was for the ease of logistics. At the time I was devastated, but it proves some things are meant to be. If I hadn't gone to the tennis-mad convent, I would never have come to the attention of Mr Roberts and gone on to forge a career in professional sport or television.

CHAPTER 4

IT'S JUST YOU AND ME, KID

On my first day at the Marist, I met Giovanna Ficorilli, who is still my best friend today. Jane was friends with her sister Tonia. Their parents owned Mario's Ice Cream Parlour in Paignton and they lived in the flat above; both girls often had to work in the shop after school and on weekends. Giovanna and I sat next to each other in class and giggled our way through lessons. There's a classic picture of us struggling to keep straight faces during one of the nuns' sponsored silences. We were always paired up to do projects: our best effort was Travel in Tudor Times, complete with drawings of a dray and the Spanish Armada.

Sport was a serious part of the curriculum and we loved netball (Giovanna was wing attack and I was goal attack), but in other lessons we got up to all sorts of pranks. Once we took the staffroom door off its hinges and hid it in the science block. Our friend Melanie (known as Mel) remembers the three of us putting up 'Don't feed the penguins' posters around the convent. We always seemed to be in detention. Sometimes, Jane, as head girl, would have to give us our punishment: 100 lines of 'I must wear my hat' or 'I must not run in the corridor.'

I was destined to be the naughty girl all through my school years, but sport saved me. I got over my disappointment about not going to the grammar school with all its incredible facilities as soon as I heard about the planned visit of Arthur Roberts to eye up potential talent to join his stable of youngsters at the Palace Hotel, down the road in Torquay. My collection of junior-school certificates had continued to grow; I loved working at my game. My next challenge was to impress this famous coach enough to be taken on for private individual coaching out of school hours. The autumn of 1967 is notable for historic milestones such as the formation of BBC Radio stations 1, 2, 3 and 4; the unveiling of the Concorde supersonic aircraft in Toulouse and the launch of the *QE2*; for Britain being vetoed by French president Charles de Gaulle for membership of the EEC; and Henry Cooper winning the first of his two BBC *Sports Personality of the Year* titles. I can pinpoint a seismic shift in my life's direction from the moment when Mr Roberts named me the second of his two selections for free tuition. I was to be taken on by him! I would benefit from the same coach/guru as the local superstar Corinne Molesworth! I was over the moon and my parents were as proud as punch.

And so it began, a routine of playing every day after school, and all day on Saturdays and Sundays. On my first visit to one of his training sessions, Mr Roberts introduced me to Nuala Dwyer, one of his pupils, who was a little older than me and who lived in Plymouth so only came at the weekend. She seemed as calm and collected off the court as – I would soon learn – she was on it. He said quietly to her, 'If you keep it on her forehand, she'll give you a reasonable game.' Nuala did just that and remembers thinking, *Wow, you're good!* Soon I was doing 20 hours' training a week at the Palace. Dad would collect me from school at four and we used to stop at a bakery so I could pick up a bread roll or another snack for energy. At 6.30pm, I'd lug my bag to the bus stop to make the journey home; sometimes Mr Roberts would give me a lift. In the first few years, when I was being drilled in the basics, he personally would hit with me during these after-school sessions, or ask Bob, his assistant coach, to direct balls at me while he stood at the end of the court, coaching me shot by shot. He always encouraged me to keep moving forward. He'd hit the ball a little bit short – or ask Bob to do the same – drawing me on to the front foot to strike the ball with more aggression.

At weekends, the group dynamic was magical, with Mr Roberts and Bob overseeing up to 14 players, all of us nationally ranked for our age, all of us challenging ourselves and each other to improve. We had mini-tournaments in which we were hand-icapped individually to make sure it was competitive. If I played the older boys, I'd start each game at love–30 (on their serve) or 30–love up. It made for sharp competition; I'd win quite a lot of games against the guys, and then someone would end up with the silly little trophy that we'd come back and play for again the following weekend.

In those early days, it seemed glamorous just to be dropped off at the entrance of the Palace Hotel to make my way to the tennis court complex. The hotel was vast, a grand country-house establishment freshly painted mint green, trimmed with white, and surrounded by beautiful, landscaped grounds. Not at all like *Fawlty Towers*. Set back from the seafront, it was a sheltered sporting oasis with a manicured golf course, squash courts and well-maintained indoor and outdoor swimming pools.

You'd see people having afternoon tea on the garden terrace, strolling along to tee off at the next hole, arriving in their evening finery for silver service dinner in one of the Palace's opulent dining rooms. We weren't allowed inside the hotel very often and I don't remember the tennis courts being used that frequently by hotel guests – Mr Roberts probably scared them off. He used to fix the hotel booking system so that the courts were unavailable to guests between 4.30pm and 6.30pm on weekdays – just so that his kids didn't have to pay for court hire. He'd scrutinise the hotel guest list and look for names with initials that matched his players, then enter them in the system to pretend the courts were booked for guests and their friends. For me, he'd enter a name that began with a 'B' and ended with 'er' (Baxter, Baker and so on); for Nuala Dwyer, it might be Danver or Darmer, and Nicky Salter, another regular player, something like Sadler or Saunder. He was endlessly inventive. The hotel manager knew what was going on, but turned a blind eye because he loved the prestige Arthur brought to the hotel.

Every November, the Palace hosted a major international tennis event, the Dewar Cup, which was televised because it attracted the best players in the world, men and women – Ilie Năstase, Ken Rosewall, Evonne Goolagong and Virginia Wade, among others. Arthur Roberts organised the tournament, employing his young players as ball kids. It was at the first of these that I realised how respected Mr Roberts was in the tennis world: I was working as a ball girl in the final and in his commentary, Dan Maskell, Arthur's childhood mate from the back streets of Fulham, pointed me out, saying he'd been told on good authority that young Susan Barker was a player of the future. My dad nearly fell off his chair. Apparently, Arthur had told his old friend to look out for the blonde girl and remember her name. Dan asked how he would recognise me. 'Oh, you'll spot her,' Arthur said. 'She'll be everywhere!'

Without making a thing of it at all, Mr Roberts gave me special attention. He referred to his group of players as his 'stable', explaining that every stable has different sorts of horses – a couple of racehorses, a few plodders, some reliable hacks and the odd carthorse. He'd say, 'Everyone's different, everyone's important.' But no one else got a daily call from him to discuss their performance in training. He used to phone me after my allotted homework time and spend a good 15 minutes, often half an hour, talking about what I'd done well that day and what I hadn't done well, setting me up to improve incrementally, session by session. He was more of a psychologist than a technical coach because it was always about getting me in the right frame of mind.

He would give me goals that were attainable. He never let me look too far ahead. If I started doing that – dreaming of becoming the British No.1, for instance – he would quickly slap me down.

He used money as an incentive. I'd get a few pence a point, a shilling a game or a pound a set. It was all about tuning me as a fighter, using each goal achieved as motivation to fly higher.

Mr Roberts's tennis realm at the Palace comprised four outdoor shale courts and two indoor courts, which he managed from his cramped, stove-heated tennis professional's room overlooking the walkway next to the outdoor courts. His abrasive manner was evident from my first day when he straight up renamed me 'Sue', practically spitting 'Sue' out. He preferred short, monosyllabic names that sounded as emphatic as a winning shot whistling off his shale courts: 'Mike' Sangster, or 'Mort', as Angela Mortimer had been known. Most often, he just used to call me 'Kid'. He really didn't like my name.

He was tough on us and I was frightened of him. At the start I couldn't speak in his presence. He was quick to tell me that he wouldn't tolerate a single loose shot. Every ball had to be struck with a purpose in mind. From the very first ball we warmed up with, we had to have a rally of at least 15 to 20 strokes to show we were concentrating from the off. On one occasion, I missed a shot after about nine strokes.

'Go home!' he barked. 'Just go home.'

Really? It had taken me an hour and 15 minutes on three different buses to get there that Saturday, but he was adamant. And furious. He made me pack my bags and I scarpered with harsh words ringing in my ears.

'Come back when you can concentrate from the first ball!'

'Well, I'm not coming back, ever!' I shouted back through tears.

'Fine,' he said.

For several days I was too frightened to go back. And he never phoned to suggest I return. Of course, I was itching to return. As I tentatively sloped along the walkway next to the courts a week later, I could see him watching me from the window of his office, his eyes tracking me as I approached with my kit bag. Weak at the knees, I meekly went in and he just said, 'Help yourself to the basket.' I picked up the balls and headed down to the courts. It was never mentioned again.

There were so many occasions when I'd arrive home in tears. The rest of the family would have eaten supper at six o'clock and I didn't get home until 7.30pm, when I'd sit at the kitchen table, eat, do my homework and go to bed exhausted. Often, I would be sobbing over a plate of crusty mashed potato surrounded by a pool of gelatinous gravy that had been kept warm in the oven and my poor dad would say, 'That's it! You're never going back there.' It was difficult for him to see me so upset.

He thought Arthur's authoritarian behaviour was unfair on someone so young – but Arthur was like that with everyone. All his players had stories to tell. Everyone was terrified of him. My parents wanted to support my love of tennis; they could see how much I adored playing. But they weren't allowed to watch me practise and he would brook no interference whatsoever. When I came home in tears, Mum would calmly suggest I take some time to cool down. And of course I always went back. It was my choice. That was the way with Mr Roberts, and we all accepted it because he was universally known to be a tough taskmaster. There was no doubting that he was brilliant, a master tactician, and we all knew we could improve under his vigilance.

He expected a lot from me, but I learned that he would also always be there for me when I lost a match. I could cry my eyes out in front of him in the frustration of defeat and he would sit there and listen. He was generous with both his time and his lack of interest in taking fees.

Our payback was to help maintain the courts. At least twice a week, we had to sweep the green wooden indoor courts and walk up and down across the outdoor courts, dragging a wide sheet of netting behind us to comb the dusty shale surface; then pick up a stiff bristle brush and clear the lines so that the white markings were visible. Mr Roberts used the annual Dewar Cup as motivation. It was such a special event, with the world's best players descending on Torquay, and we all looked forward to it so much.

He actually entered me for the tournament when I was just 13. Crazy! Nicky Salter, another girl from the Marist Convent, was also one of Arthur's players. She was a couple of years older than me. He entered us both that year and said he'd give money for points to whoever won the most in our respective matches. I won three games against the Scottish player Winnie Shaw, and 31 points, which won me this particular battle. Arthur gave me the money and with it I went straight to the tennis shop run by Mike Sangster in Torwood Street and bought my first tracksuit. It was navy blue, and my prized possession, largely because there was no heating at the Palace Hotel's indoor courts and it was always absolutely freezing.

There was no hot water in the showers either. The courts were inside a brick building with a corrugated iron roof, lit partially by glass panels along the top. Some of the glass in these windows was smashed, allowing icy draughts to funnel down. Snow would drift through and there'd be leaks from the roof in between points. We had to get the squeegee out and get the water off the courts, because painted boards are like an ice rink when wet. We had to be really careful on the court surface. No money was ever spent on the facilities. I asked how the windows had broken. Mr Roberts said it happened when Mike Sangster had been learning how to serve. Until Mike had mastered the timing of his rocket serve, the ball would hit the top of the racket frame and fly upwards, smashing pane after pane of glass. That was in the 1950s and the windows still hadn't been replaced when I was playing in the 1970s.

Mr Roberts had a lot of strict rules. He didn't want his girls in tennis skirts and dresses, he insisted we wore shorts. Not just for training, for competitions too, when players tended to put on their best tennis outfit. There was one junior tournament where they wanted to take a photograph of the winners and I wasn't allowed to be included in the line-up because I wasn't in a nice skirt. I was always in shorts. Nuala thinks it was all about us not attracting male attention, even though we were kids.

Certainly if we were ever spotted chatting to one of the teenage boys, we'd be reprimanded or at risk of being closed out of the squad. Mr Roberts said we had to be focused, businesslike, and get on with it. The shorts were symbolic of it all.

Out of the blue, he would reward me if I'd done well. On one occasion, he was pleased with how impressively I'd played in a junior tournament and said that as a prize I could pick out a new racket from his silver-steel lock-up kit cupboard. He had a stock of about a dozen brand-new rackets on pegs – perhaps for hotel guests to purchase – and he let me try them out and help myself to a new one. This was a huge thrill; I had never played with anything other than my trusty wooden Slazenger, which Dad had bought for next-to-nothing and was now a rickety old thing. I picked out the nicest-looking racket in the cupboard and went to try it out on the hitting wall. Mr Roberts questioned my choice, saying the grip was way too big for me.

'No, it feels great,' I said. 'I've been hitting with it and I really want to work with this one.' He thought I'd give up on it, but I didn't. It was the racket I used all through my career and, believe it or not, it was exactly the same $4\frac{5}{8}$-inch tapered grip that Rod Laver favoured. I said, 'If it's good enough for the great Rod Laver, it is certainly good enough for me!' I discovered that was true a few months later, when I was invited by BP sponsors to a junior international tennis clinic in Maida Vale with Rod and Ken Rosewall. I was so proud to be able to bounce up to Rod and tell him I had the same grip even though my hands were half the size of his. Everyone now says, 'Who even uses a $4\frac{5}{8}$?' But we didn't have so much choice back then; it was very amateur compared to today's abundance of customised rackets. Mr Roberts used to add weights to the end to give me more power on the racket head, and it felt just right.

Dedication for him was a two-way dynamic, though I didn't realise at the time how much he was prepared to sacrifice for me. In one of the cuttings I recently discovered in my father's scrapbooks – from the *London Evening News* in 1970 – Mr Roberts let it be known that he had found in me another exceptional talent to launch. 'Sue hits the ball hard and comes racing into the net. Most girls of 13 are only too happy to plod safely along the baseline but not this one. She has no tendency to play safe. She is the most fluent hitter of the ball for her age that anyone has seen in this country for a long, long time,' he said, comparing me to the standard set by Angela Mortimer. He certainly didn't tell me this!

Trawling through the scrapbooks full of carefully cut-out press reports, I can see now my junior career was exceptional. Mr Roberts, however, was not lavish with his praise to me; he was all about setting the next goal. Today, though, I feel great pride in reading his early appraisal of me. 'Sue is very different from Angela in style,' he continued. 'She is more like Virginia Wade. She has an ideal temperament too and the only real problem is that she has no opposition in her age group in this part of the country. She's always playing against girls of 16 or 17.'

At this stage, Arthur received funding from the Lawn Tennis Association (LTA) for coaching his nationally ranked players, and with that came opportunities for us to attend clinics with great champions like Laver and Rosewall, and even to go on a trip to Texas to play in minor-league tennis. Each year, the LTA-funded juniors were invited to a weekend of assessment where national coach Tony Mottram (father of my fellow GB juniors Buster and Linda) and his assistant Dan Maskell would scrutinise our technical game and monitor our overall progress. I have a picture of my last one of these review weekends at Crystal Palace – with Mr Roberts standing behind me on the court and Tony Mottram looking on. I thought I'd put on a good showing: I'd won my matches, played well, I was buzzing.

A few weeks later, however, Mr Roberts called me in and told me the report he had received from the LTA was not positive. Tony and Dan had concluded that my forehand was unacceptable: 'She plays it with a bent elbow too close to her body.' They insisted that, if I were to remain a funded player in the junior programme, Arthur must dismantle my forehand so that I hit with a straight, freer arm. This was a devastating blow. I was 13, and my forehand was my primary weapon (and my pride and joy), a stroke I could rely on to end any rally at any time from any part of the court. Mr Roberts was incredulous, and angry. He just ripped up the LTA report in front of me and said, 'Right, it's just you and me. I have resigned from the Lawn Tennis Association and I am going to fund your career myself.'

And he did. He knew my parents couldn't afford to support me financially – I was the youngest of three, and Mum and Dad believed in being fair to all of us. As it was, my siblings had to put up with two-week summer holidays based around the Eastbourne junior tournament when they would much rather have been on a beach in Belgium or France as of old. It was such a defiant gesture from Mr Roberts, such a statement of confidence in my ability – which I didn't fully appreciate at the time. It was just onwards and upwards, working every day to continue to improve.

CHAPTER 5

CINDERELLA HAS A BALL

M r Roberts's manner was daunting and his approach was intense, but I realised I had earned his respect when I brought my own ideas to him. I had read a lot of details about Margaret Court's training routine. The Australians were ahead of the game in terms of physical fitness.

'I'm not doing any fitness work,' I remarked. 'We have to start training like this.'

'Good idea,' he said. 'It's important to be fit and strong.' I didn't have a killer serve – at that time in the women's game, the serve was more an initiator of a point, rather than a potential winner in itself – and I wasn't a natural volleyer. Arthur knew that I would always need to work hard on court. Rallies would be long and I would have to do a lot of running around. I roped in Dad to help me.

He and I went to a local gym and I tried to lift the weights that Margaret was working with, and it was frightening. I couldn't begin to hoist them. She was superhuman.

I had my goal of getting to Wimbledon – kept secret from Mr Roberts, who just wanted me to focus on the next junior event in Budleigh Salterton – and I embarked wholeheartedly on a new morning routine. Dad used to wake me up at 6am and we'd put together a different challenge each day. One morning it would be sprints and another day it would be a three-and-a-half-mile run along roads that looped round our house so I couldn't cheat. Dad used to send me off, timer in his hand, and my aim was to better my record at each attempt. I'd finish off with a session of squats and burpees and a lot of skipping. And then I'd have my breakfast at 7.15am and set off to school. That was every weekday.

Mr Roberts approved of learning by example. He would encourage me to observe players I admired and copy them, even if they were my rivals. 'Just watch and mimic the good things,' he'd say. First, he pointed me towards Nuala, who was tactically astute, so clever with the different shots that she used while I was just bish, bash, bosh. He said I'd learn a lot from seeing which shot she chose and when. She had so much variety, little drop shots, little dinks. Nuala had a lovely game, but she didn't have the power. You have to go to your strengths.

And I wouldn't have had the power without my weird grip. I was five or six when I first picked up a racket, and I literally picked it up off the floor and that was it. That was the grip I used when I played with my family and at school, because I was never formally taught how to hold a racket. (The basic, traditional grip would have the V formed by your thumb and forefinger at 11 o'clock; my V was somewhere close to three o'clock, which allowed me to generate a lot of speed and weight on each shot.) Arthur saw that it enabled me to have this humdinger of a forehand and didn't want to change it.

Nuala was British junior champion when she was 15, which was a remarkable feat, but in the following year I beat her for the first time at a tournament in Torquay. She thought she'd never beat me again (though funnily enough she beat me the very next day ... and *then* never again) and decided that if she couldn't beat 'another girl from Devon', she was just going to have to give up. She went off to study medicine at Cambridge and rose to become an obstetrics and gynaecology consultant. We spent many happy years playing together in Arthur's stable and travelling all over the country to play in junior tournaments, and I'd seek her out for comfort after my most bitter loss at Wimbledon in years to come. But I get ahead of myself ...

Mr Roberts also suggested I study how Chris Evert constructed points. Chrissie, two years older than me, was a prodigy who had burst on to the scene at the US Open in 1971 at the age of 16. Arthur instructed me to analyse her shot selection. Why didn't she go for that winner when it would have been my instinct to go for it? We had no videos to obsess over in those days – it was literally looking at photos and being glued to Wimbledon on TV each year to pick up tips on how you can hit a backhand. I used to race out to get the *Daily Telegraph*, which carried tennis reports and detailed results from events all over the world, places with exotic names like Delray Beach. I'd commit the names of the players to heart, and then suddenly they'd be on television at Wimbledon, and I'd be able to put a face to the name.

From television, too, we'd subconsciously pick up the mannerisms of established players such as Billie Jean and Virginia. In Dad's scrapbooks, there is a report in *The Times* from when I was 13 or 14, which sums up that wannabe-itis:

> Even little Miss Barker shakes her head, dimples and all, as though it is an infinitely serious matter when she misses a volley or hits out of court. But if, indirectly, the television camera makes the young more histrionic than they might be, it must also be an instrument in the development of their game.

Arthur believed in letting his players build on their natural game. It used to be a running joke on the tour that you could spot a British player from the practice courts because they had the same game; they all came off the LTA conveyor belts with the same swing, the same grip, the same stance, you know, left foot forward for this, right foot forward for that. He picked me out at the age of 11 because he saw raw potential. He didn't dismantle my game.

He didn't even change my extreme grip. By the time I went to Mr Roberts he was just so excited by what I could do with that grip that he was never going to change it. He used to teach me maybe one new thing a month, and the rest of the month was spent working to incorporate it into my game, making it instinctive. 'I want to see it when you're playing in a match,' he'd bark. In the early 1980s, just before I retired, I remember visiting the Florida academy of Nick Bollettieri, the American coach who pioneered the concept of residential tennis schools, and seeing this little kid with long hair and funny shorts. It was a young Andre Agassi and he was whopping the ball unbelievably with beautiful timing, but none of his shots were going inside the court. Nick was laughing his head off.

'Crikey,' I said. 'What are you going to do with him?'

'Nothing,' he replied. 'He's going to learn how to hit them in. I don't want to change what he's got. He will find the way.'

I found that so refreshing, and it reminded me so much of Arthur and his determination to bring out natural talent in promising individuals – and Bollettieri, of course, had tremendous success with Agassi, Jim Courier, Venus and Serena Williams, and Maria Sharapova, to name just a handful of his Grand Slam-winning protégés. Kids will learn; kids adapt. I think sometimes that naturalness is taken away from young players because they're overcoached. I don't envy coaches right now, because parents are paying a lot of money and expecting their children to be learning three new things a week, but that's not the way it works. Sometimes it's just a little thing that often takes a long time to develop within your game, and that's why I was just so lucky with Arthur. And his biggest piece of advice was, watch someone you admire, and copy them.

That report in *The Times* was right: I wore my heart on my sleeve. Of course I did, I looked up to Billie Jean and she used to get so angry when she missed a shot. I was copying her style, her intense desire to win. Margaret Court always looked serene. Her expression didn't change whatever the outcome of a crucial point. But Billie Jean was a firebrand. There was one occasion at Eastbourne when I got incandescently angry with myself. I won my match, but not easily, and not in the manner I'd planned.

At the end, I hit a ball out of the court and threw my racket down. And this behaviour was unheard of. I was only 13 or 14 and not a massive favourite to win the event. The tournament referee was Captain Gibson, who was exactly as the name sounds, a blazer-clad disciplinarian with a meticulously trimmed moustache. He marched over to me, shouting, 'Get off the court! Get off the court!'

Mr Roberts rushed to me and said, 'What the hell were you doing?' before hot-footing it to the referee's office to beg Captain Gibson not to default me. He managed to persuade him to give me another chance. Afterwards Mr Roberts read me the riot act, but worse was to come.

My mother was visibly upset. 'I've never been so embarrassed to call you my daughter,' she said.

That was it for me. That hurt more than Arthur's anger. It taught me a heck of a lesson and it was a watershed moment in that it affected everyone's view of my tennis. Winning, and winning well, had become so important to me. Tennis was the only thing that mattered. I'd played badly and I knew Mr Roberts wouldn't be happy with the way I'd laboured to finish the match ... and I thought, *Dammit*, and just whacked the ball out of the stands. Nowadays, young players do it all the time and just get a point penalty or a warning. It was a wake-up call: it made me realise just how fragile my status was ... you know, I'd won my match, but I could still get defaulted. And that one instance drastically changed the way I reacted emotionally on court, *forever*. I would smack a ball down in frustration but I would never get to the point where I couldn't keep a lid on my emotions. If only I'd had a sports psychologist to teach me how to use emotion, how to channel it and make it work for my game.

If only I had a pound for every time I've thought that ...

* * *

John Barrett – a former player turned commentator and author who, a few years earlier, had married Angela Mortimer – arranged the BP Cup and he recommended that I attend a junior international clinic with Rod Laver and Ken Rosewall. I was 13 and this was the year that Rod achieved his calendar-year Grand Slam. The brilliant, nimble Australian was the god of tennis and, much to the other clinic attendees' annoyance, I was singled out by him as a future star. To mark the moment, a photograph was taken of Rod and me jumping the net in his trademark celebration.

The smile on my face could not have been broader. After our time on court, we had lunch with the Australian champions as well. We kids were given a school-dinner-type meal such as shepherd's pie, but Ken asked for fillet steaks for himself and Rod. I thought, *That's what I've got to eat to make me a champion.* I went home and said, 'Mum, I have to eat fillet steak.'

Rod Laver was my hero. I never felt prouder of the Rod Laver racket that I had selected from Arthur's cupboard than on that day. The same size and with the same grip as the top men's player in the world, it seemed ridiculously huge for a girl to use, but because I used it from the age of 12 it became a habit, and if I tried to use anything smaller I felt like I had a toothpick in my hand. I just kept with it right the way through. The bigger grip helped my forehand and, when I turned professional and signed a deal with Dunlop, they asked what I wanted and I said, 'A replica of this, please.' And that was it forever.

When I look at Dad's scrapbooks, I am amazed at the coverage of my junior career. Until I delved into the cuttings, I didn't realise how successful I'd been as a junior; I suppose I was always ahead of my age group. I was so lucky to go to the Marist Convent and to be coached by Mr Roberts. Both at the Palace and at school, we all pushed and brought out the best in each other. But Dad faithfully preserved evidence that I competed in all the tournaments on the junior circuit. At the British Junior Championships (Under-18s), I won every singles title at least once, on hard, grass and indoor courts. I won each age group's doubles championships at least twice and the mixed doubles as well. I do remember that Mr Roberts didn't just want me to win these titles once; I had to go back the following year and defend them. I wanted to move up a level, but he wouldn't let me. He insisted I learn how to handle the pressure of defending my titles.

Junior tennis was very different in the early 1970s. The tournaments ran from Monday to Saturday and if you lost, you played cards. Today, kids are taken home by their parents when they get knocked out – a quick call on their mobile phones – but in my day everyone's family mucked in for the week and we all got to know each other well on the circuit. In late December or early January, we met up for the Covered Court Championships at Queen's; August was the Grass Court Championships at Eastbourne (and the Under-18 in Manchester, on grass) and September was the big one, the Junior Championships of Great Britain at Wimbledon, which we all called 'Junior Wimbledon' (though that's not to be muddled with the junior girls' singles at the Championships).

There were a lot of keen rivalries, heightened by enthusiastic press coverage, but we made friends for life, with our paths often crossing through the years, certainly at Wimbledon. Nuala Dwyer says her husband has always found it amusing that she can recognise someone at Wimbledon today who she once beat 6–4 in the final set in an Under-14 event at Budleigh Salterton. Happy days. There were established tennis families like the Mottrams (Buster and Linda), the Lloyds (David, John and Tony), the Dwyers (Nuala) and the Pantons (Cherry). Mum and Dad were golfers and new to the tennis circuit, which was a bit of a whirlwind for them. When the tournament came to Torbay, they did the catering, providing soups and sandwiches. One of my diary entries notes that Nuala and I went to Torquay for a Wimpy because I didn't want to eat Mum's cooking. The great thing for me was that their lack of tennis experience meant they were not pushy parents – they never questioned me about my matches, or asked why I'd lost or why I hadn't employed a particular tactic. They wanted to let me develop naturally. They wanted me to do what I loved doing, and to do it to the best of my ability.

I found it terrific fun, but I have to apologise profusely to my brother and sister because every summer they got dragged to Eastbourne for our family holiday. Neil used to go fishing with Buster Mottram and that was about the highlight of his trip. My sister used to be bored stiff. In Eastbourne we started off staying in a hotel, but that didn't work out as we needed room to make breakfast and sandwiches for lunch, so then my parents rented a self-catering flat. The bad news for my siblings was that it was two weeks, not just one, because the first week was Under-14 and Under-16 and the second week the Under-18 event. These were the last events at which my parents came to watch me in person. They used to drive me to the local tournaments – the three main Devon events in Torquay, Exeter and Budleigh Salterton – and as time went on, they came to Bristol and to the national championship at Wimbledon.

They'd watch from a distance because they got nervous. After one Junior Wimbledon, I banned Dad. He had this horrible way of going 'oooh, hooh, tut'. I'd hear these sighs of disappointment in the stand and I just knew it was him.

'I could hear you! I'm trying my best, but I can hear you,' I'd say when I came off court.

He agreed to not watch my semi-final, but I heard the tutting sounds coming from behind a bush. He was watching from a hidden position but I could still hear him. He knew how much winning meant to me and he wanted me to win. Mum, on the other hand, was paralysed by the tension. 'I couldn't tut, because I was like ice,' she said. 'I couldn't move.'

I had lots of battles for titles on all surfaces with Linda Mottram, her glamorous cousin Cherry Panton, who had a solid back-court game, and Glynis Coles, but two milestones stick with me to this day. The first was winning the Under-12 West of England Championships in Bristol when I was just 11. I can't recall anything about the competition except that it resulted in my picture being published in the local paper. There was a photo and quotes from Mr Roberts tipping me for the top. My gran –

who was still alive, though she died quite young – was so proud of that. It was a huge deal in our family that I should have my picture in the *Torquay Herald Express* and the *Western Morning News*. It was a breakthrough moment, setting the foundation of confidence in my tennis – and so special to me because my gran, who I loved so much, was just beyond excited by it.

The turning point, though, was being thrashed by Glynis 6–0, 6–0 in the 1971 Under-18 Eastbourne final when I was 15. That was humiliating. Glynis had a strong all-court game and never showed much emotion on court, unlike me. I remember her being very tall, but that was probably because she was two years older than me, and wearing her long blonde hair in bunches or occasionally a ponytail.

She had burst on to the scene out of nowhere, it seemed. Shirley Brasher, who as Shirley Bloomer had won the French Open in 1957 and who'd become a respected coach, had spotted her playing in August 1970 and taken her under her wing. She'd collect Glynis from school and coach her; she even found her a sponsor. Just four months later, she won the Junior Covered Court Championships Under-18 title, and went on to win all the junior titles in 1971. She was the bee's knees. And I *hated* losing to her. I was chastened beyond belief by that defeat. I served first, was 40–15 up in the first game, had break points in the second, at least two or three game points in the third, and then it was downhill faster than Franz Klammer. I wasn't getting break points or game points. My brain just imploded with negative emotions. I couldn't understand it. How could I lose like this? I was very tearful and angry. Mr Roberts took me off to the beach afterwards for a pep talk.

'Remember how much this hurts,' he urged, as I stared down at the sand. 'Remember this feeling and don't let this happen again. You are good enough to beat her. And that's going to be your goal. You didn't stick with the game plan. You didn't do what you were supposed to do.'

The game-plan comment was true. Glynis used to come into the net a lot, and I was hitting the ball way too short. I wasn't giving her difficult volleys. The nature of that clobbering made me dig deeper. I played her only three months later and beat her – indoors at Queen's – and that made me realise what I could do.

Glynis and I have a laugh about it now. She takes tremendous pride in beating me so resoundingly, and I take pride in how I turned my mortification around. She never beat me again.

The lyrical press coverage of my bounce-back in *Lawn Tennis* magazine makes amusing reading. First up was the Green Shield Junior South West Championship, held at the Palace Hotel:

> At 11.05am on Thursday morning, 23rd December, 1971, it all came true for Arthur Roberts's golden-haired princess from Paignton Susan Barker as she flashed a forehand volley well out of reach of Britain's 1971 best girl junior Glynis Coles to win her first big championship at the age of 15 and on her home court.

The report ends with several thanks, including a mention of 'the caterers Bob and Betty Barker (washing up while their daughter was winning the title)'.

A few weeks later it was the British Junior Covered Court Championships at Queen's, where again I faced Glynis in the final, and won. The same reporter nominated me as his 'competitor of the month':

> It was a superb win … and I am not forgetting Virginia Wade's outstanding performance in the Australian championships when she beat Evonne Goolagong, the favourite, in straight sets. But I still think I am right to name Miss Barker for this first tribute. 'Competitor' is an apt name for her – she really is a cool customer in a crisis – and a bonny fighter – as she demonstrated when she knocked over the defending champion Glynis Coles in an outstanding fashion.

It was just amazing for a 15-year-old to be talked about in the same sentence as Virginia, who had won the US Open a few years earlier, and Evonne, who had won the French Open and Wimbledon. In tennis, age never matters; it's about how good you are. It is interesting for me, today, to read Mr Roberts's quote at the time, quashing comparisons between Angela Mortimer and me. 'Far better to look ahead, perhaps say another five years, when you will be hearing much more of Sue,' he commented. 'We don't intend to rush things.'

Ever since the bust-up with the LTA, Mr Roberts had an Us and Them mentality – Us being his players based at the Palace Hotel, Them being the players who trained at Queen's Club in London. I didn't realise until many years later that this rivalry was rooted in an incident in about 1921, when Arthur was a ball boy at Queen's Club alongside Dan Maskell. They had grown up together in Fulham, sharing the same ambitions to go into coaching. He always told me that a spin of a coin changed his life, and the spin was held to see who – Arthur or Dan – would be taken on as a junior coach at Queen's Club. Arthur lost, and was so upset he ran away to sea, working on a merchant ship that transported mutton from South America. He hated that experience, and returned to work as an assistant tennis professional at the Hurlingham Club, which was more of a genteel country club than a hothouse for tennis stars in the making.

In 1936 he moved to Torquay, to take up his role at the Palace Hotel, and I wonder if some resentment lingered. Certainly, his relationship with the LTA was conducted at arm's length. He was unmoved by the powers that be. He was a renegade, but Arthur had indisputably become the most successful coach in the country. He revelled in any success his players achieved, but the emphasis on the rivalry with the London players became even more intense after his falling out over my forehand. He wanted to prove them wrong. He had not just me, but Nicky Salter and Nuala Dwyer, really good players who were winning the Junior Championships, so among our group there was a wonderful camaraderie and a sense of being in Arthur Roberts's gilded circle. Everyone wanted him as their coach. When I was 13 and hoping to compete in my first Junior Championships, I was considered too young to be entered in singles, but I was allowed to enter the doubles. Mr Roberts must have kicked up a fuss, because my omission from the draw was a talking point among the journalists. My partner Nicky Salter and I went on to win the doubles, prompting a wonderful report from John Parsons in the *Daily Mail* under the headline CINDERELLA HAS A BALL, describing me as Cinderella, the girl who was not allowed to go to the party, but ended up bagging the doubles prize.

CHAPTER 6

THIS IS TEXAS, AFTER ALL!

From that point onwards, the sessions with Mr Roberts became even more focused, more about learning how to play and win matches. He used to invite adult players from the local Torquay Tennis Club to come and play with me. I used to compete against the headmaster of Torquay Technical College, and players in their thirties and forties. He would say, 'This is a match, not a social game. You come along, you play the best of three sets.' And Arthur would watch, beady-eyed.

Each of these fixtures was set up like a proper tournament match, with a change of ends and no chit-chat. He was teaching me to be a match player, with a robust competitive temperament; he would stand and observe every point from his office window, as inscrutable as ever. And sometimes, when he walked down the stairs, I'd think, *Oh no, I'm in trouble.* If he was courtside and turned on his heels, I knew I'd done something wrong, and I was in for a b******ing later. On those occasions, he would ask me to explain myself: why did I play that shot, why didn't I move my opponent around more, why did I keep going cross-court? We'd analyse every aspect of the match.

The emphasis was on defending titles I had won in the national junior tournaments. Winning the first one is easy in a way because you're not expecting it, and it's thrilling. Going back to defend it is not as exciting but it is far more rewarding. At least, that was Mr Roberts's line. I felt my success at national level just added immense pressure. And that was why he made me play them, because, he said, 'You've got to be able to deal with being the biggest fish. If you don't deal with it now, you'll never deal with it.'

He was right, of course, but I found it frustrating. I now expected to win the British events. Mentally, I'd moved on from them because I'd had a tantalising taste of international competition with the Junior Wightman Cup in the United States, and the Princess Sofia and Annie Soisbault Cups in Europe, where I could pit myself against the best in the business – fellow teenagers like Martina Navratilova, Renáta Tomanová and Mima Jaušovec, who I grew up playing at Under-16, Under-18 and Under-20 tournaments and who would be my rivals down the road in professional tennis. The national junior events didn't excite me any more; they were simply something I had to do to maintain my form.

My first trip abroad when I was 14 whetted my appetite. I was sent by the LTA along with Linda Mottram and Lindsay

Blatchford, another promising GB talent, to play in an international junior league event in Dallas, Texas. I had never even been on a hop-over flight to Europe let alone a long-haul across the Atlantic and six time zones. It was a big adventure, earned by working hard at tennis. We were put up by a lovely couple, Carole and Bill Hoffman. Carole had volunteered to look after an English-speaking player and luckily had a large, spacious house, as we three shy British girls wanted to stick together. Carole had worked for American Airlines before she married Bill, who was in the fashion business, representing a smart brand called JH Collectibles across the south-west United States. As Carole tells it, Bill wanted his 'American princess wife', so she 'retired' and took up tennis at the local country club that was hosting the event.

They were warm and welcoming, and seemed to relish driving us to and from the club to train and play our matches, feeding us and making us feel their beautiful sprawling residence was our home from home. Everything seemed huge, from the portions of food to the sophisticated bathrooms with power showers (something that was alien to 1970s England). We had so much fun. Lindsay loved her curly hairstyle ... and Linda and I left the taps on 'shower' mode so that when she came to have her bath, her hair got soaked. We giggled for days about that trick. When I look back to that first visit now, I imagine us on the set of *Dallas* or something. Every aspect of life here was eye-opening. Carole showed us the gun she kept in her bedside table – a little pearl-handled .25 pistol. Our eyes were on stalks. We were scared. She just laughed and said, 'This is Texas, after all!'

After our first day, Bill came home after watching us warm up and said to Carole, 'If that little blonde girl can learn to hit it in the court, she's going to be phenomenal!'

Well, that trip was my incentive to nail my accuracy. I can't recall anything about the tennis we played on that visit, but I was taken with the notion that tennis brought travel opportunities, and sold on American culture from this brief immersion. It was my 15th birthday during our stay and as a treat Bill opened his remote-controlled garage and took us in his baby-blue convertible Rolls-Royce to a drive-in McDonald's. Two years later I reconnected with Carole and Bill, and they became my American family, my second parents. They moved around Dallas a few times, but always kept a bedroom for me with a plaque indicating 'Sue's Room' on the door.

We also played the Junior Wightman Cup in America. The first one of these was staged in La Jolla, California. It wasn't until we arrived there that we realised it was pronounced 'la–hoy–a'. The event was held at the beachfront Kellogg Park and a member of the famous Kellogg family was there, and I just thought, *Wow, I eat Kellogg's breakfast cereal every morning.* It was such a revelation for a little girl from Devon. It was like I'd gone to Hollywood.

We got absolutely hammered by the American team. I'm not sure we won games, let alone matches. They were so much better. That also was a real wake-up call. It was the first time I'd been shown how far behind I was and how much more work I had to do to compete on the same level. And, of course, all the young American players looked like models.

the semi-final or final of the BP Cup and the Annie Soisbault Cup, pitting ourselves against Martina Navratilova, Renatá Tomanová and, much later, Helena Suková. We had fabulous times playing against the Czech girls. Martina was too talented for us but we were too good for Renatá, so it always came down to the doubles, and it was always close. Glynis and I had a very good record against them; Linda and I less so. Věra Suková, mother of Helena, was their captain and she was an unsmiling, menacing presence. She frightened me to death when she sat courtside. This was the Cold War era and our imaginations ran riot. We thought she was a super coach because she was from Eastern Europe; we always thought they had secrets.

In 1972 we finished runners-up to the USSR in the Annie Soisbault competition, but in Le Touquet the following year, we triumphed spectacularly over the same team of Marina Kroschina and Elena Granaturova – both juniors of pedigree, having won the Wimbledon and French Open girls' singles titles respectively. Again we faced the Czechs in the semis and, as usual, it boiled down to the doubles, which Glynis and I won eventually, taking the second set 11–9 and the final set 6–4. The September 1973 issue of *Lawn Tennis* magazine ran a fulsome report:

> Glynis had a three-set win over Miss Kroschina and then the little Devonian took the court against the second Russian. 'She was given the reception accorded Borg at Wimbledon,' said Shirley Brasher. 'The crowd adored her and screamed after each point she won.'

The report continues:

> It could have been her downfall as she got somewhat
> excited and after being 3–0 up in the first set, hit every-
> thing in the bottom of the net and was soon 3 all.
> However she eased out 6–4 but was 5–1 down in the
> second set and had three set points against her at 5–2.
> These she saved with a great surge of adrenalin and the
> help of the crowd before racing home a 6–4 7–5 winner.
> And so the Annie Soisbault Cup came to Great Britain.

All the while, on my doorstep, in the tennis mecca of Torquay, I had
the BP Cup to look forward to each year. Initially an international
Under-18 event, which changed to Under-21, the tournament was
held at the Palace Hotel, organised by John Barrett with Arthur
Roberts. Very forward-thinking, John had launched an international junior development programme in association with the petrol
company at the start of the Open Era in 1968. If you'd won a singles
title in your age group at one of the designated junior tournaments
on the LTA's list, you were eligible to enter. The draw included teams
from the United States, France, Czechoslovakia, Italy, Spain and so
on. Each country had two singles players and a doubles team, and
we played a round-robin tournament. It had a buzz about it: my
BBC colleague and former GB No.1 Andrew Castle and his brother
used to drive down to Devon to watch the world's best juniors and
he says the play he witnessed inspired his tennis career.

The Americans were a major presence. It's where I first met
Peter Fleming, who went on to win four Wimbledon doubles

titles partnering John McEnroe, and also became a BBC colleague. His fellow American Billy Martin was talked about as a future great player. On the girls' side, I remember meeting Kathy May, who went on to reach three Grand Slam quarter-finals, and Betsy Nagelsen, who was a top junior and doubles specialist and, post-retirement, married Mark McCormack, the founder of IMG, the first sports management agency.

It's also where I first met Martina Navratilova when she was 13 or 14. She knew no English but we acknowledged each other with a nod. We were the best girls there, so we guessed we'd be seeing a lot more of each other in the future. Martina had a deadpan demeanour; she didn't give a lot away. Later, of course, she became very emotional on court. Yet as a kid, she looked quite stern and serious. But when she smiled – just as now – her face lit up. I thought, *She's really tough*, but then you'd see a softer side with her beaming smile. Following Arthur's advice, I studied her because she had a very different game from me. At that age, Martina wasn't the superwoman she became. She was quite skinny but an incredibly athletic player.

What impressed me was her natural ability. She had this impressive, fluid lefty serve that was in place when she was 13. She was already a fabulous volleyer. Mr Roberts would say my volleys were manufactured; hers were natural. She just made it look so easy. And the only way I could play her was to try and keep her away from the net. If I hit the ball short, that was it, point over, because she could jump like a gazelle and hit blistering smashes. A smash is a shot that is rarely seen today. Few players like to come in and hit a smash. They always wait for the ball to bounce, or drive volley, but Martina had this whistling smash. Once she was at the net, she was almost impossible to pass. It was always a battle to try and keep her at the back of the court.

Renatá Tomanová – who I would beat to win the French Open at Roland-Garros in 1976 – was very pretty and feminine. She always had her hair in braids and wore lovely dresses, whereas I was in my workmanlike Arthur-issue shorts and a shirt. Martina was also in shorts. Renatá was much slower, more deliberate, more graceful than either of us. She went on to be in the world Top 25.

This was all when I was 14, 15, 16; competition against our international age group normalised the different challenges we posed to each other at a professional level. I'd grown up with Martina and seen her evolve so I had respect for her, but no fear of her. When Martina did bounce over to the States, it was like, *Wow, where did she come from?* Because there was no television, no internet, no form of media where you could follow someone's progress. You just read results in very small print at the bottom of the sports pages and that was it. And Martina did have a real aura about her, even as a kid. You knew she was special. The way she played, the way she carried herself; there was a champion's aura about her. As there was with Chris Evert, who famously never played juniors. She went straight into senior tennis and she was just awesome. In 1971, while I was still battling with Glynis for best GB junior-girl status, Chrissie had reached the semi-final of the US Open. The following year, she made her debut at Wimbledon and made the semis, playing – I remember so well – in a dress with little red stripes. (My dress envy continued!)

All the while, Mr Roberts had gradually introduced me to the buzz of top-level senior competition through the Dewar Cup. Sponsored by the whisky company, the series of indoor competitions moved around the UK and, as I've mentioned, attracted some top players. The Palace Hotel event was televised and played in front of a crowd of 500. I thought it was really bad luck that I always drew the top seed in the first round, but of course Mr Roberts was responsible for the draw and he fixed it to give me experience. He gave me incredible opportunities from the age of 13 onwards; to get to be first-round fodder for some of the greats of the game on my home courts was a confidence builder. It reduced their mystique.

One year I was drawn against the Scottish player Winnie Shaw, who represented Britain in the Wightman Cup, and won enough points to win the wager with Arthur and get my prized first tracksuit. The next year, I was up against Evonne Goolagong, the Wimbledon champion, and was overawed; I won just one game. In the following year, I played Virginia Wade and took a set off her.

That was a turning point. I started to believe in myself. I could see the incremental improvement, year on year. That was Arthur's aim all along. 'You can teach any old Charlie how to hit a ball,' he'd say. 'But a world-beater is one who has confidence in their technique and a strong competitive spirit.' It was just so much fun to be part of these glittering proceedings on the courts I knew so well. After playing the top seed in the first round, I was the ball girl in the final. I could watch these stars of the game in action and that was how I measured myself, more so than by my national junior achievements.

Evonne Goolagong turned up in Torquay in a glamorous fur coat. A Wimbledon champion in my hometown, playing on the very courts I trained on every day! That was special. When Evonne came on the scene, she was such a breath of fresh air, and when she won Wimbledon at 19, it was a huge story – the fairy-tale emergence of an indigenous Australian girl. Talent will out, as they say, and will travel. And here she was in the flesh. I waited for the right moment and asked if I could have a picture of us together. I still have it today – my hair looks awful, of course. Whether it was after a match and I hadn't washed it I don't know, but my hair was stuck to my head and the contrast between us is immense. She looks fabulous with her beaming smile and winter furs. I am holding a racket, looking like I'd been dragged backwards through a hedge.

CHAPTER 7

ARNOLD PALMER, BJÖRN BORG AND SUE BARKER

Meanwhile, on the other side of the Atlantic, Billie Jean King had led a group of the best female players to form a breakaway professional tour, independent from the men. This was the Virginia Slims Circuit, which later evolved into the modern WTA Tour. The aim was threefold: to give any girl in the world who was good enough a place to compete; to allow female players to be appreciated for their accomplishments and not their looks; and to enable them to make a living from playing the sport they loved. She had faith that the women's game represented by the Original Nine – herself plus Nancy Richey, Julie Heldman, Rosie Casals, Valerie Ziegenfuss, Judy Dalton, Kerry Melville Reid, Peaches Bartkowicz and Kristy Pigeon – had the talent and charisma to deliver great sporting entertainment that should command its fair share of financial reward. It was unfair, Billie Jean thought, that she should take home £750 in prize money when she won the first Open Era Wimbledon Championships compared to Rod Laver's £2,000.

Mr Roberts and I would chat about how things were beginning to kick off in women's tennis. We had started discussing my tennis future less as a hobby and more as a career. Our relationship had initially been one with me as little Sue sitting there going, 'Yes, Mr Roberts, no, Mr Roberts,' but it had evolved into a partnership. We butted heads. He wanted me to challenge him in the same way that he challenged me. That dynamic was important to him, and it was part of him preparing me for what he could foresee as a professional career. He said, 'You know, this is a game changer.'

And the formation of the Virginia Slims Circuit is when it got serious. I found an entry in my diary the other day, and the phrasing is a bit unfortunate but it reads: 'I've promised Mr Roberts I'm going to go all the way with him.' And that was when I said to him, 'Right, this year I'm dedicating myself to tennis. This is not my hobby any more. This is it. I'm going for it.'

In September 1973, Billie Jean King beat the 55-year-old retired American veteran player Bobby Riggs over three sets in the Battle of the Sexes match. Riggs, a colourful personality, had been one of the world's best amateurs and was known to be a bit of a hustler who loved the spotlight. With his face emblazoned on magazine covers, he was intent on proving the women's game was inferior. I read about it excitedly in the *Telegraph*, and then discussed it further with Mr Roberts, who said this was the breakthrough for the women's game that Billie Jean had long been talking about. Four months earlier, Riggs had taken on Margaret Court under the same challenge and thrashed her 6–2, 6–1, teasing her with drop shots and lobs. The result, and the manner of her loss – which was described as the 'Mother's Day Massacre' – set women's tennis back by years, not least because Riggs, basking in the limelight, continued to taunt the status of women's tennis.

Determined to put the record straight, Billie Jean, always the fighter, always a performer for the big stage, accepted an offer to take on Riggs herself. I knew she would win. I idolised this woman. She couldn't lose in my eyes, there was no chance, and this was my future on the line. It's lovely to hear Billie Jean talk now about fathers who, over the years, told her how important an achievement her victory was for their daughters. They were watching it as a televised spectacle, not as a serious stand against chauvinism, and yet it changed the way women's tennis was perceived. It was the first example of equality in sport (the prize money issue would be slower to resolve), but fans of tennis saw Billie Jean, Margaret and Evonne on a par with John Newcombe and Stan Smith. People were becoming fascinated with the women's game; they wanted to watch its stars. What it lacked in power, it made up for in finesse and intriguing rallies. The style of play was different but it was equally mesmerising to me as a kid and to my family too, my brother and my father. The Battle of the Sexes was a game changer for everyone.

By the age of 17, I had outgrown domestic junior competition and there was no one to stretch me at the Palace Hotel set-up – even the headmaster of Torquay Tech, who was an excellent player, couldn't get a set off me. It was time to move on, but there was no way Mr Roberts was going to let me go to Queen's to join the national regime. That's where I should have gone, of course. I should have joined Glynis and Linda, John and David Lloyd, John Feaver and Richard Lewis.

Mr Roberts just refused. 'I'm not sending you to London,' he said. 'I think you should go to America and get on the WTA tour.' When I dared to query this, he reminded me of Dan Maskell and Tony Mottram's critical assessment of my forehand, and the fact that they wanted to dismantle my major weapon. 'That's why you're not going to London,' he said.

He had set himself up against London, gone against the LTA, he was out on his own. He certainly didn't want his protégée to go and become part of a set-up he'd turned his back on. He preferred to send me 5,386 miles away to Newport Beach, California, than see me head up the A303 to London.

As the youngest of a close family, I was amazed that my father allowed me to go to America. I was on the cusp of leaving school, and had only just passed my driving test, and literally within a year I had left the childhood room I shared with my sister and set up base in Orange County, California, driving on the wrong side of the road and living the dream among palm trees and beaches and eating out in classic American diners. The way my life changed so dramatically was such a bizarre turn of events, and it was Mr Roberts who came to my father with the proposition. I wasn't allowed in on the conversation; he didn't want me to get excited about a plan my parents might not sanction. I'd had numerous discussions with Mum and Dad about possible careers and I went through the motions of giving them three options: I would follow my brother to catering college because that was in Torquay; I could go to secretarial college, which was also in Torbay; or I could sign up to be an air stewardess because I loved to travel. I didn't want to do any one of them.

Mr Roberts felt the time was right for me to join the fledgling women's tour in America, because I was already in the Top 20. Even at 17, I'd had some success. He had been approached by Mark McCormack's International Management Group (IMG), who wanted to represent me, and privately shared the idea with my parents. My mother was upset. I think my father was probably ready to get rid of me – I was the only one left at home! But he was worried about the financial implications. I had started to earn prize money but, because there was a 75 per cent tax bracket in 1974, I ended up with about ten grand from all the money I had already earned. And the top rate was due to increase to 83 per cent for the tax year 1974/75. Domiciled in the UK, I couldn't earn a living travelling to pursue the sport I loved, so I had to go somewhere. It was either catering/secretarial college or the United States.

The move was carefully planned. Billie Jean King's victory over Bobby Riggs had created a huge momentum for the women's game, and made a career in professional tennis possible. Just a few years earlier, I thought I'd play for as long as I could as a hobby. I'd be Mrs Easterbrook on the Oldway courts in Paignton. Even though players turned pro in 1968, it wasn't really a career option. Even in 1971, when I was 15, all the money was thrown into the men's game. Billie Jean fought to stop the women just being a sideshow at occasional men's tournaments.

Men's tennis boomed, with multiple circuits governing their own round of tournaments, including World Championship Tennis and its so-called 'Handsome Eight' – Dennis Ralston, John Newcombe, Tony Roche, Cliff Drysdale, Earl Buchholz, Nikola Pilić, Roger Taylor and Pierre Barthès. Fewer tournaments wanted the women because the men's draws were getting bigger, and the court space wasn't there. But the women's tour was now in its fourth year, and comprised the Grand Slams, the Virginia Slims Championship, the Virginia Slims Circuit and further-flung international events in Australia, Europe and South Africa. The WTA, formed in 1973, gave the players a voice. Women's tennis was getting more prize money, more attention. The biggest growth in the history of the sport was seen in the 1970s, and I was joining it, bang in 1974.

In a sure sign that it had traction with the public, the women's tour had just signed its first television broadcast deal with CBS. I couldn't have picked a better time to show up. Mr Roberts was excited for me because women's tennis was so much bigger than it had been, so much more global and high-profile. There was money to be had – not a fortune, but more than any other job I could possibly do. He wanted me to see my career to wherever it would take me; he wanted me to live the dream. I felt I was still improving. I always wanted to be the best I could be and with Mr Roberts that couldn't ever be 99 per cent.

He explained the nuts and bolts of the contract to my parents. IMG would take care of all the financial aspects: they would start me off with a sum of money in advance of prize money and set me up in a rental place in Newport Beach. IMG would manage my direct debits, my bills and schedule. I would have to book my own flights, hotels and hire cars as I travelled from tournament to tournament, but basically all I had to do was play tennis. It was a dream come true. I was so excited that Mark McCormack's agency, which had a roster of famous sportsmen and -women, wanted to represent me before I was even winning that many matches on the tour. I thought, *Wow, they must believe in me.* Years later, I found out that IMG used to sign at least 30 juniors every year, just on the off chance that one of them might make it, so it wasn't that I was so special. I was thinking, *Mark McCormack wants me. Arnold Palmer, Björn Borg and Sue Barker!*

Reluctantly, my parents agreed. I said to Mum: 'If you don't let me go, I'll never speak to you again!' I probably made that threat every week and she was never taken in by it. Mr Roberts had persuaded them to let me give it a go for one year. So I made a deal with my parents that if I didn't enjoy it after a year, I'd be back, but also that if I didn't establish myself inside the women's Top 20 within the year, I'd come home, because I wouldn't be earning enough to afford to pay IMG and stay on the tour. Yet again, Mr Roberts, who had instigated this opportunity, had given me a goal to fight for.

He knew Rod Laver was based in Newport Beach, and made the introduction. Rod turned out to be my new neighbour and we'd have the odd hit together. Surreal! Arthur's friends Teddy Tinling, the dress designer, and Shirley Brasher, the former British Grand Slam champion who coached at Queen's Club and led our Princess Sofia and Annie Soisbault Cup adventures, were often at tennis events in America and promised to keep an eye on me for him. And I had the wonderful Carole and Bill Hoffman, my American family, who kindly pledged to travel to tournaments to support me.

I had a lot to hold me in Devon – a close family, my Palace Hotel routine, and Mr Roberts, who was my absolute mentor in life. But I was off to join Billie Jean, Chrissie, Evonne, Martina, Rosie Casals, Olga Morozova … In a flurry of excitement, I packed up my things from the bedroom I had always shared with Jane and flew to Los Angeles. Talk about living the dream! At LAX, I upgraded my rental car to a convertible and drove to my new two-bedroom furnished townhouse in Newport Beach, California, not far from the John Wayne Tennis Club. I was 18. Mum had been in tears as I was waved off at Paignton station, but I hadn't been able to keep the smile off my face.

• • •

I had a year to make it work. Mr Roberts remained a daily point of contact, even when I was thousands of miles away across different time zones. He would send me a detailed letter once a week. We would plan my matches over the phone; I relied on him to help me walk out on to the court with a clear mission in mind. Maintaining our dialogue gave me confidence to put my game plan into action. He used to quip, 'I don't know how she's making any money because she must be spending it all on phone calls.'

The reality was that he insisted I make the reverse-charge phone calls to him. 'Reverse the charges, any time, any place, anywhere,' he said regularly. As I heard the phone ringing down the line at his home in Devon, I realised I couldn't picture him picking up the receiver, because I didn't even know where he lived or in what sort of circumstances. He was such an enigmatic, private man. He never gave anything away. We'd had the most incredibly strong bond since I was 11 and he totally understood me, but I knew absolutely nothing about him.

I only met his wife a few times. This must have been his second marriage and he did once let slip that his wife was a wealthy woman. That's all he said. I don't know whether he said that to make me feel more at ease about him wanting to fund my career. He never wanted me to worry about money. He used to say, 'I've got more money than I know what to do with. I don't want any more. I'm quite happy.' He lived a simple life. He never took a day off, never went on holiday. His whole existence revolved around being at that tennis club at the Palace. He lived for the excitement of seeing his players develop and flourish. He used to tell Mum that he got so much pleasure from working with me and seeing me do well.

That didn't mean he got any softer in his post-match debriefs. I couldn't hide anything. Even over a crackling phone line, he'd say, 'Why did you lose?' I would explain. 'Why didn't you try this? Why did you do that?' He always reminded me that when things started going wrong I had a tendency to panic. And when you panic, you can't think clearly.

'When you get into that state, just simplify it,' he'd say. 'Just say to yourself, every wide ball that comes my way I'm going to hit cross-court, I'm not going to overcomplicate things. Keep it simple to calm yourself down.' And he liked to hear about my matches from me, not from the radio.

Following my move to America, I could only spend 63 days per year in the UK, due to tax status, which limited the time when I could see Mr Roberts in person. By the time I'd played Eastbourne, Wimbledon and Wightman Cup matches each year, I was a fair way through my allowance – and I think that did affect my game. I'd go back to Devon when I could and he'd tweak my game, ironing out any bad habits I'd fallen into without his daily scrutiny. He'd get me back to where I was and send me off again.

I was playing 35 tournaments a season and earning well over $100,000 a year with endorsements and exhibition match fees and still he wouldn't take any money from me. I felt so bad about that. Most of my peers were paying their coaches 20 or 25 per cent of their earnings, possibly more, but he just wouldn't have it. 'You're the one who's earned it,' he'd say. 'Just put it aside for your future.' Eventually I forced him to accept four payments, but again, he stuck to his principles and, in cahoots with my dad, secretly invested the money in annuities in my name. He was an incredible individual. As I've got older, I realise just how special he was, how generous-spirited despite not suffering fools, and how he totally transformed my life and gave me such a magical time, just to be able to play and do something that I love so much.

CHAPTER 8

CALIFORNIA DREAMING

I remember my first few weeks in California as if they were yester-day. I thought I'd died and gone to heaven. My townhouse was in a resort-style set-up close to the beach with two private courts in the middle. I'd see one famous person after another playing there. The first time Rod Laver asked me to hit with him, I rang my mum as soon as we finished playing even though it was 3am in Paignton. I had to tell someone. IMG clients could also play at the John Wayne Tennis Club, where various American and Aussie pros would train, as well as Hollywood stars. It was a ridiculously glamorous scene.

After years of my entrenched routine with Mr Roberts based around the Palace Hotel, life on the Virginia Slims tour was a novelty – as it was for all of us who were the first generation of women vying for prize money and able to earn a living with our rackets. And that was exciting. I was lucky that Billie Jean and the

Original Nine had taken the women's game professional when I was 13, and not when I was 20, when it would have been too late. The timing couldn't have been better.

Sponsored by a cigarette manufacturer, the Slims tour had settled into an established circuit, running for three months from January to the end of March each year. It was a well-thought-out, points-based indoor championship in venues such as basketball arenas and country clubs. There were two parallel levels: the Championship level, with the stars to draw in the audiences, and the Future tour. If you got to the semi-final of the Future event, you'd earn two weeks of main-draw play at Championship level. It was a wonderful way of feeding in young talent. You earned points from matches, which graded you in a ranking system. I played in the Championship level, but the players I'd be up against were different at almost every event. Tournament organisers in each host city would demand one Top 5 player, perhaps two ranked 5 to 10, and at least six players ranked 10 to 20. We gave the WTA bosses our preferences for tournaments and they'd distribute as fairly as they could according to our ranking and the organisers' requests.

I learned as I went along that the top choices were Boston, New York, Miami, Dallas, Houston, LA, San Francisco, San Diego, Seattle and Atlanta. I loved New York and the experience of going to a diner for breakfast just like in the movies. Dallas drew a high-end crowd; the joke was that the men applaud and the women shake their jewellery. The tennis circuit was part of a glitzy life. I remember Glynis Coles telling me that she and our Wightman Cup teammate Lesley Charles were sitting in a hotel somewhere in the States and got chatting to a nice man in the foyer who said he played in a band. Glynis asked if it was a hotel band, and he said no, no, he was playing down the road. She carried on chatting, and later Lesley laughed and said, 'You hadn't a clue, did you?!' It was Eric Clapton.

The more industrial cities like Detroit and Akron, Ohio, were less popular. I always seemed to end up with Detroit and Akron, but I loved them because every city in America was fascinating to me after Torbay – though, even a few years down the line, I hadn't developed antennae for judging the safety of a neighbourhood. In Detroit once, I went out alone to see a 7.30pm screening of *Lipstick*, a psychological thriller with Margaux and Mariel Hemingway. When I emerged at 10pm, I thought I'd walk back to the hotel to get some fresh air, much as I would have done at home. It was about an hour's walk. As I entered the hotel, the concierge said, 'Hey, Miss Barker, where you been?' I told him I'd seen a movie and he asked where the taxi had dropped me. I told him I'd walked back. He was horrified and made me promise solemnly that I would never, ever do that again. Apparently I'd walked through some of the most dangerous neighbourhoods in the city. But that didn't stop me. I always used to try and walk back from the courts just to be outdoors. Naive to the end, I thought the edgy side of life was just on television.

I was excited to be around players that I'd watched on TV and followed in newspaper reports, though it was pretty intimidating to walk into the locker room. I was quite shy. They soon got that out of me, because I had to get on with it. There was no one there to help me. Billie Jean sat down with a group of us and explained the importance of giving our time to the press and presenting ourselves well to help build the profile of women's tennis. She told us to be full with our answers and always try to sell the tour.

Our figurehead and firebrand, she was so generous with her time. If I was sitting on my own, she'd come over and chat to me about my family, and ask how I was doing. She was intrigued by my forehand and thrilled me by asking if she could watch me practise to figure out how I struck the ball with such power. 'I could watch you hit your forehand all day long,' she said. It turned out she also associated my forehand with May Sutton, the first American to win the singles title at Wimbledon in 1905, who had learned to play on a clay court in Southern California. Ever the history buff, Billie Jean …

Sometimes I'd be quite homesick and she'd boost my morale by reminding me that every single one of us was important, that we all brought something to the tour. She liked the way I played my heart out. 'As an athlete you have to leave your guts on the floor' was her line. Physically, I wasn't big; I worked hard on court and I was quick. My style was not typical of either Americans or the British – which again she said was good for the show. 'We don't want everyone looking the same.' In the upswing of my career, everything about my new life was so exciting. I didn't even mind the losses because I was learning from the defeats.

Each week I was in another strange city; every day was an adventure. My fellow players were the only source of friendship. Most were American, with homes they could easily retreat to. Americans hopped on planes as if they were buses. I remember it all as a very happy time, but re-reading my letters home triggered

What were our parents thinking, or was it fancy dress?

When I think of how much I pay for a haircut now.

Arthur Roberts. The man who changed my life.

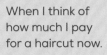

Off to school.

So excited about Dad's new company car, even in that colour.

My first tennis racket. What a proud day.

We won so many, I have no idea where we are or what trophy this is.

My dear old dad. Looks like we were off to a wedding.

Aged 12, getting tips from the great Rod Laver.

Queen's Club – in the snow, still hitting against a wall.

This is how I will always remember him. Pipe in hand, with plenty to say.

Not a bad junior career.

Playing for Great Britain with Virginia Wade. These were my proudest moments, playing for my country.

One of my first radio commentaries, sitting in the stands with the legendary Gerry Williams.

A hug for Dad on a rare visit to Devon in the early eighties, as I delivered my parents a new car.

One of my favourite photos. Rod Laver and Ken Rosewall. Two of the all-time greats. I showed this photo to Rod at his home in California a few years ago and we got quite teary.

The moment I became a Grand Slam champion, winning the French Open in 1976, having just turned 20.

French Open presentation. I found out over 40 years later that my nationality on the trophy is engraved as Australian. Well done, Roland Garros.

A school visit back to Marist Convent to encourage the next generation.

With my boyfriend Greg Norman. I'm so proud of the career he went on to have in golf. The sporting calendar worked against our relationship.

Beating the Americans in the Wightman Cup at the Royal Albert Hall. Always a major highlight.

My forehand. My biggest weapon and the reason I got to No.3 in the world. Voted by my peers as the best forehand in the game, five years in a row.

Tennis coaching vacation where I first met my husband.

Modelling my good friend Karen Scott Happer's clothing line One Love at 30,000 feet.

One of the first photos of me and Lance, my husband-to-be.

The only photo of our wedding. Hang your head in shame, Hugh. Our great friend and official photographer, who got his shutter speed wrong. Hilarious.

a lot of memories. It was a lonely existence because initially I didn't have many friends. Self-doubt stalked me when there were few distractions from my tendency to over-analyse my performances. We often only had one court for our women's tour event – for practice and competition – so matches were played one after another from 1pm to midnight, and there was a lot of hanging around. I didn't have much of a routine beyond practice, match, stretching, showering and talking to the press after a match. One day a match could be at 1pm; the next day, it could be 10pm. I had to drum up someone to practise with, someone to go out to dinner with, and that was dictated by who had played at about the same time as me, because other people were either on court or preparing for matches.

Sometimes I used to hang around the locker room. We might play backgammon or, years later, Trivial Pursuit or sit around and listen to music and chat. At one stage Virginia Wade taught me how to tackle cryptic crosswords. Sometimes I joined the Christian girls' meetings for the coffee and chat. Mostly I was bored out of my mind. I spent hours and hours in hotels. On one fleeting trip back home, I bumped into Mel in Paignton, and we went for coffee. It was so good to see her. I didn't feel like I was missing out on life in Devon, because I was obsessed with getting to the top in tennis – I really wanted to be the best I could be and win top tournaments – but I did tell her I often felt isolated and lonely. Giovanna remembers Mel passing this news on to her: 'Oh bless, it's not as glamorous as we think.'

I phoned my parents maybe once every two weeks, because it was expensive, but I used to write home every day, or every other day, using fold-over-and-lick pre-stamped Par Avion enve-lopes that were easy to post. My writing got smaller and smaller towards the end as I tried to squeeze in as much detail as I could. That was the only way we communicated and I found that hard, being separated from my warm and chatty family. I'd send post-cards from every new city I visited to Giovanna and Mel. 'I'm in Philadelphia!', 'Chicago!' It must be so different now with the internet, email and social media, but in the early 1970s, to go and live on another continent was like being cut adrift, trapped in a different time zone. You felt every mile of separation.

Our season started with the Virginia Slims tour, then moved to Europe for the clay-court season. Next up was the grass-court season, with Eastbourne and Wimbledon, then it was back to the States for the US Open and the hard-court tournaments. When the tour finished in America in the middle of October, we sometimes had the Wightman Cup in October or November and then it was on to Australia. As I mentioned earlier, to avoid the high UK taxation on my hard-won earnings, I could only spend 63 days every year on British soil. My passport was stamped 'Alien'. After allowances for days spent at Queen's, Eastbourne and Wimbledon, for the Wightman Cup and later the Federation Cup, that left precious few days to come home for a re-tuning session with Mr Roberts, let alone seeing my family and friends.

I might have a few weeks free in the late autumn, so I'd either try to arrange a holiday with my family in Europe or in America, or with my long-standing doubles partner Ann Kiyomura, who was from California. I got to know Ann in 1973, when she'd just joined the tour and was playing in the Wimbledon warm-up tournaments in Surbiton and Beckenham. A rising star, she beat Martina to win the Wimbledon junior title that year. We began our doubles partnership around 1976 – and went on to win the world doubles title in Tokyo in 1981 – and we played Team Tennis together in 1977. Ann was composed, measured and very much the leader on the doubles court. Lethal at the net, she was nick-named 'The Sword'. She calmed me down. She used to have a power nap before we went on court – how did she do that? I was always too wired. She was immensely loyal and fun to be with, and we roomed together on many occasions.

But often I went somewhere on my own. I flew to Antigua and played against tourists in the Antigua Open and collected a nice shell trophy three years in a row. I explored Sri Lanka; I visited Hawaii, Tahiti and Fiji. Jane, my sister, had trained as a schoolteacher and I enjoyed putting together projects for her classroom about each country. I'd take some photos and make little books and send them to her.

I missed my family and friends. I was fully committed to making a go of my tennis career, but I would be guilty of looking back through rose-tinted spectacles if I didn't admit to finding the flipside of life on the tour difficult. I wish Virginia and I had been closer at that stage, but there was a bit of an age difference between us, and also some tension as we both so desperately wanted to be British No.1. Billie Jean was always there for me. And Gerry Williams, the journalist and BBC radio commentator, joined the tour often.

But with both of us in the world Top 5 or Top 10, a larger-than-life posse of British writers would turn up, invited by tournament organisers keen to promote the Virginia Slims brand. Lance Tingay, known as 'the Dean' among his writing colleagues, and the flamboyant Laurie Pignon were both great characters and heroes of the Second World War who loved the game and who became friends of mine. As did Lance's successor at the *Daily Telegraph*, John Parsons. Collectively, they brought a nuanced sense of perspective to their roles as newspaper correspondents and an enthusiasm that was infectious. Laurie, having survived five years as a prisoner of war, was said to have vowed to relish every single day of the rest of his life – and he certainly lived up to that on the tennis circuit.

Gerry, as a one-man band on the radio, used to seek me out if I'd lost and ask if I'd come and do the commentary with him. The alternative was sitting alone in my hotel room in a strange place, so I loved it from the start. I have a picture at home of Gerry and me sitting in a stand in the sun, headphones on, mikes at the ready. I also had an early introduction to the world of TV broadcasting through Bill Macatee, the local sportscaster in Dallas, who ended up working for CBS and Tennis Channel. I met him through the Hoffmans, and I did some broadcasting with him during an event at the Moody Coliseum.

Carole Hoffman was a godsend. Just before I moved to America, I had been in Dallas for the Maureen Connolly Brinker International, run by the trailblazing tennis promoter Nancy Jeffett on the indoor courts at the Brookhaven Country Club, staying at the Fairmont Hotel. Nancy was such an influential figure: not only did she fund international junior tournaments in Dallas such as the one I'd been invited to play in with Linda and

Lindsay three years earlier, but the Maureen Connolly Brinker International evolved into the Virginia Slims of Dallas – the first televised professional women's tournament. (In 2015 I stood aside from a nomination for the International Tennis Hall of Fame so that Nancy had a clear run. I was grateful to her for all the chances she'd given me and so many of my peers. It was a proud day for her and her family when she was inducted into the Hall of Fame.)

Unbeknown to me, the Hoffmans were sponsors of the event, and had a courtside box for entertaining their own guests. I was in the hotel lobby one morning when I heard a distinctive voice cry 'Sue!' I turned and saw a glamorous figure. It was Carole, and she was troubled that I hadn't been in contact. 'Why wouldn't you call me? And come stay with us? What have we done wrong? We'd love to have you come and stay with us.'

And so I moved straight out of the hotel. The Hoffmans were a charismatic couple with a busy social life, living the dream. Their generosity changed my life. They moved a fair bit, but always to another huge house in the best neighbourhood with five bedrooms, five bathrooms, a gorgeous kitchen and a triple garage for the Rolls-Royce, a Jaguar and another supercar. On that visit when we reconnected, Carole made a point of saying, 'This is your room. It's here for you whenever you're passing through or you just want to come and stay for a few days.' In those days, if I lost early in a tournament, I would have had to hang around bored in my hotel in that town until the next one. But I could count on the Hoffmans as my second family and often retreated there. Their household was so much fun, on so many levels. I had a great time cooking with Carole, who would wear her monogrammed apron with 'Nobody does it better' embroidered across the top. They had a little Maltese terrier, Biffy, who would be all over me.

They would arrange for me to hit with players at Southern Methodist University (SMU), a famous tennis college in Dallas, or fix sessions with some of the pros at nearby country clubs. One of their close friends was Roger Staubach, the quarterback for the Dallas Cowboys known as 'Captain America', who might be around with his wife Marianne; their kids stayed with the Hoffmans when they went on holiday. Any time I was injured, Roger arranged for me to have treatment at the Cowboys. Once, I sprained my ankle and it was very swollen. Back home I'd have been advised to take aspirin and rest it for ten days. The Cowboys' physio put me in a compression boot and worked it until the swelling had subsided there and then; and then gave me a regimen of specific exercises. The hi-tech approach to injuries blew my mind, especially when I was back on the court in just a few days.

Whenever I was in town, Carole and Bill took me to Apparel Mart in Dallas, which stocked the fashion brand Bill represented, and he insisted I have whatever I wanted. My siblings must have been pleased to know the scraggly sister they had been so ashamed of now had a glamorous wardrobe of 'pant suits', blazers and dresses. In March 1977, I was staying with the Hoffmans for the Virginia Slims Dallas tournament, and I fell in love with a fox-fur coat. We know better now, but fur was the ultimate in glamour in the 1970s, and I'd committed to heart that image of Evonne Goolagong, the Wimbledon champion, turning up at the Palace Hotel looking like a movie star.

Bill, who was a funny man, said, 'If you win the tournament, I'll buy you that coat.' I was used to such incentives from Mr Roberts and a fur coat was a huge improvement on my first track-suit. I duly reached the final against Terry Holladay and there were Carole and Bill in their courtside box. Bill had brought the coat along in a bag. I took the first set easily but the second set went to a tie-break. Just at the point when it looked like I would win it, Bill reached into the bag for the coat, called out to me and waved the fur sleeve in my direction. I won!

They took their role of being *in loco parentis* seriously. I was staying with them once in a rented house in Los Angeles when a friend on the tour set me up with a blind date. I didn't want to go, but Carole encouraged me. This very nice guy turned up in a very expensive Ferrari. We had a lovely dinner and then went out to a show. He was great company but there was no chemistry … plus, I just couldn't stop looking at his nose. He had the largest nose I'd ever seen. When he dropped me back very late, Carole came running down the stairs to ask how my date had gone. I said he was a nice guy but he had the biggest conk I'd ever seen.

Bill had been secretly listening from the landing. At that point he came tearing down the stairs screaming, 'Oh my God, you've only just met him … your parents asked us to look after you … I can't believe what's happened …'

I said, 'Bill, what are you talking about?'

Spluttering, he replied, 'I heard you tell Carole he had the biggest cock you'd ever seen.'

I burst out laughing and had to explain that 'conk' is a slang word for 'nose' in Britain. We didn't stop laughing for an hour.

It was an art learning to put together tournaments that made a logical trail around the States, rather than zigzagging from place to place and facing the travel expenses that entailed. The Hoffmans said they would travel to wherever I was playing in the States, if I made the quarter-finals. That was another huge incentive. Over the years Carole flew to be with me in Detroit, Palm Springs, LA and New York for the US Open. She was glad to come and we would go sightseeing to break the monotony of venue, hotel, airport. We did the Palm Springs aerial tramway together, a spectacular trip from the floor of the Coachella Valley across canyons and cliffs to San Jacinto Peak. Wherever we went Carole helped me buy clothes or jewellery to send home to Mum. Her presence was a great morale booster.

Life on the tour was gruelling. At the US Open, we had to get a bus from the hotel in Manhattan at 9am and hang around to get a practice slot. I had to find someone to hit with too. In the dressing room in New York – which was the only place for Carole to wait all day – she looked across at Chris Evert, who had family and friends with her, and thought, *Poor Sue, I'm her only one …*

The tour went from city to city. If I lost, I had nothing to do for the rest of the week, except to practise … but the chief practice times and courts were reserved for players still making their way in the tournament. I didn't often lose in the first round, but if I did, I would fly to Dallas and stay with Carole. Bill would hand me the key to his convertible Rolls-Royce – the baby-blue one with the cream top – and I'd drive all over town. They gave me home comforts and freedom. In one house, they built a tennis court so that Ann Kiyomura and I could stay and practise. (They wanted the court for themselves too!) If I'd reached the quarters or the semis, I'd be devastated to be knocked out at those stages, but I'd always find Carole waiting – sometimes for hours – outside the dressing room. She wanted to be there for me. She hated seeing how much defeat bothered me. She'd say I was fun to watch, but challenging. I had a temper; I could bristle. I had this fire inside me. Like my parents, she would never talk about the game, she would just be there for me as a friend to go and eat with. It was a special time for all of us: me, Carole and Bill.

Since my move to America, I had established myself in the Top 20, but what I craved was affirmation in terms of results that my career was on the up. In January 1975, I got that. In the quarter-final of the Australian Open I beat Olga Morozova, who, the previous year, had reached the final of both the French Open at Roland-Garros and Wimbledon. In beating her quite comfortably on grass, her favoured surface, I realised I genuinely was a Top 10 competitor.

The players I was chasing were Chrissie and Martina. Without them, and their perfect rivalry, the WTA tour wouldn't have taken off. Billie started the revolution, but just as her career was winding down these two took it to a level beyond purist fans admiring Evonne and Virginia's victories. They made women's tennis front-page news, which in turn attracted sponsors. Chrissie, America's sweetheart, with her feminine demeanour – the hairgrips, the diamond bracelet and pom-pom trainer socks – was so brutal to play against. I look back at all the three-set matches with her and remember how I could hardly walk the day after each match; she made you work. We had long, intense rallies until there would be one game when I wouldn't be at my best and that would be it.

Boom, done. I had a couple of wins over her but she was always the most difficult competitor to play in my era. Glynis Coles recalls playing 'b****y well' against her in Forest Hills in the US Open and losing 6–0, 6–1 or something. Every girl wanted to be gorgeous Chrissie in her cute dresses, and every athlete wanted to be Martina, the super-talent from behind the Iron Curtain who introduced more power and aggression to the game.

Martina and I had tracked each other's progress since our junior days. She was the better player but she knew that if she didn't compete at her best, she would lose to me (which she did a few times). I was quick around the court and tried to make it hard for her to get the ball past me. We had several memorable matches. I remember playing her on an indoor court in Hollywood, Florida – somewhere between Fort Lauderdale and Miami. The line calls were so bad we were both crying. She beat me, but I definitely had the upper hand in that match. Chrissie and Martina were on another level; theirs was an incredible rivalry and the tennis they played was spectacular – the matches they had, I mean, wow! Who could break their dominance? Realistically, the most the rest of us could aim for was No.3 in the world.

CHAPTER 9

CHAMPION OF GERMANY AND FRANCE

From the springboard of reaching my first Grand Slam semi-final in the Australian Open in January 1975, I competed with confidence and picked up my first top-level singles titles on the clay in Båstad in Sweden and Kitzbühel in Austria, and on the grass of Adelaide. Mr Roberts was air-traffic-controlling my game from afar, sending me his weekly detailed letters, which I'd read, commit to heart, then crumple up and throw in my hotel bin. We'd follow up with expensive phone calls. By 1976, I was well established in the Top 10 and the deal I'd made with my parents to give tennis a go just for a year seemed a distant memory. When, in May, I beat my old junior rival Renáta Tomanová of Czechoslovakia pretty resoundingly 6–3, 6–1 in the final of the German Open in Hamburg, my confidence moved up a level, especially on the clay. In the press, I was Sue Barker, the champion of Germany. That sounded good.

I headed to the French Open in Paris, just a short hop from England, but I didn't have anyone in my box for that fortnight. Mr Roberts did not travel and my parents only watched me four times after juniors (crazy, I know, but that's the way they wanted it – they got so nervous). In the absence of Chrissie, the defending champion at Roland-Garros – she had opted to compete in World Team Tennis – I was the No.1 seed. Chrissie was the only player I feared on clay. Here was my chance to get a tally of Grand Slam victories up and running ... I backed myself against anyone. I survived a tough quarter-final against Regina Maršíková, coming back from behind to win 8–6 in the third set. In the semi-final, I took on Virginia Ruzici of Romania (who would win the title two years later) and earned my passage to the final, where I would meet Renáta.

I was anxious on the eve of my first Grand Slam final. I may have beaten Renáta a few weeks before, but she would be looking for revenge. She herself had come close to her first Grand Slam triumph in the Australian Open and she was coached by the intimidating Věra Suková, whose courtside presence I remembered from junior days. I needed distraction – and it was waiting in the form of Laurie Pignon, the flamboyant *Daily Mail* tennis writer, and his wife, universally known as the Dragon, who took me out for dinner. This would be unthinkable in modern tennis, but Laurie had this entertaining idea that we would do a walkaround of the city centre to record the 'night before' sounds of Paris. We walked around Montmartre, up the steps, in and out of restaurants, as he put his tape recorder under peoples' noses, saying, 'This is Sue Barker and tomorrow she is going to win the French Open.' We laughed and laughed. It was the best possible way to relax. Arriving back at the hotel at 10.30pm, I watched poor Laurie get a lot of stick from the rest of the British press, who asked him why he'd dragged me around Paris late at night. They all said he'd be responsible if I lost the final.

On the day of the match, ironically it was LTA coach Tony Mottram – in Paris accompanying GB junior Michelle Tyler, who had reached the girls' final – who saw me looking nervous, eating breakfast alone, and sat down to chat and ease my nerves as I ate my banana and cereal.

I was too focused to take in the build-up hullabaloo, and comfortably won the first set 6–2. One set away from victory, my concentration lapsed; I had brain-freeze and lost the second set to love. During the statutory ten-minute break before the deciding set, my thoughts were racing in the wrong direction. Looking back today, I realise that my self-belief and confidence in my game were quite fragile throughout my career. I would have benefitted hugely from a sports psychologist.

Tony kindly sat with me again and helped me reset. He was the man whose opinions had made Arthur Roberts sever his connections with the LTA, but he was a familiar figure for me on my own in the giant Philippe Chatrier show court of Paris. As a junior, I'd often stayed in the Mottram family home in a cul-de-sac in Wimbledon, throwing balls to their feisty mongrel Percy while I waited for Linda to come back from school so we could go to train at a junior clinic together. In this crucial break, Tony kindly took the time to offer me advice – and, yes, me still hitting my forehand with a bent elbow too close to my body. He knew not to interfere with my tactical game, but he said a lot of calming, positive things and told me to remember what I did well and treat the decider as a one-set shoot-out.

I went on court and put together one of the best sets I ever played. To win, having played a blinder in the final set, was a wonderful feeling. To be so in control. It ended on a double-fault from Renatá – hardly a *Grandstand* moment, but it didn't matter. I went up to the President's Box to receive my trophy and the whole occasion was so special it hardly seemed real. I had just turned 20 – and I had won my first Grand Slam!

The tournament was not televised in the UK so the plan – win or lose – had been to fly to London and drive back to Devon to see my parents and Arthur. I had two and a half glasses of champagne with the British press on an empty stomach. When I boarded the plane, I started to feel really unwell. Arriving at Heathrow, I realised I was in no state to pick up a rental car and drive to Devon so I fell into the first hotel coach that went past Arrivals, which was for the Post House. I booked into a room, put my head down and thought I'd feel better in a few hours. Well, I didn't. I woke up the next morning thinking, *Great, I've just won my first Grand Slam and I'm waking up on my own in an airport hotel with a hangover!*

When I did get home, I realised I'd lost the medal too. In all the excitement of the press reception and the champagne going to my head, I was late to call Arthur to tell him how it had gone.

I knew he'd be waiting to hear it from me and wouldn't have listened to the radio. When I had got through to his number, I was told he'd gone out, so I asked my mum to pass on the news to him. He'd gone out because he thought I'd lost, since I hadn't called him. He said he had imagined me in floods of tears in the locker room, not daring to call him.

I believed my French Open title would be the first of many Grand Slam wins. I was just 20; I'd beaten all the top players and my game was improving. If I'd known it would be my only Grand Slam win, I would have collected everything – a bit of distinctive *terre battue* dust from the court, the umpire sheet. Instead I have nothing. In 2019, Ash Barty, the newly crowned champion at Roland-Garros, spotted I had been incorrectly engraved on the trophy as an Australian. That sums it up.

It was great to be home with my parents and to catch up with my school friends. I always popped in to see Giovanna in the ice-cream parlour. We'd walk along the beach with a cornet, and I'd be interrogating her about everything she'd been up to. Or we'd meet up for coffee with Mel, who helped out in her parents' hotel. My priority really was to make the most of those precious few days with Mr Roberts. It was always grounding to return to the Palace Hotel courts. He'd watch me play and tweak a few things in my game that had gone a bit askew without his beady eye remedying me daily. We'd chat. I was bursting to share the things I'd observed from other players on tour and probe his views on how I could keep on improving. I honestly believed my French Open win was just the start of it, and I think if I hadn't lost to Martina in the quarter-finals in Wimbledon the way I did a few weeks later, my upwards trajectory might have continued.

So, to one of the two matches I hate to relive …

• • •

I arrived at Wimbledon feeling buoyant. I was the German and French champion (on both occasions beating Renatá Tomanová on the clay). Seeded 7th, I progressed to the last 16 without a hitch. I was on the cusp of reaching the second week – always a great feeling at a Grand Slam as you play your way in and the locker room empties. And the excitement just kept building. My next opponent was Maria Bueno, the great Brazilian champion who had won Wimbledon three times and the US Open four times. I was up against her when she was a veteran of 36, but she still had a strong game, anchored by a hard serve, aggressive volleying and a wiliness about the court. Most of all, she had such a presence. She was dressed by Teddy Tinling and described by the colourful American tennis writer Bud Collins as 'incomparably balletic and flamboyant'.

That morning, I'd learned, in between mouthfuls of cooked breakfast at the Mottrams, where I was staying with my old friend Linda, that our contest would be on Centre Court. So 26 June 1976 was the day I would make my Centre Court singles debut. Walking out on to the grass that very hot Saturday was an experience I carry with me to this day. The reception for both of us from the Centre Court crowd was spine-tingling. Billie Jean King says she always thought of the champions past, present and future as she entered the court, turned to curtsey to the Royal Box and settled her racket bag on her seat next to the umpire's chair – and on Day 6 of the 1976 Championships Maria and myself represented a veteran champion with a wonderful record and a 20-year-old newly crowned Grand Slam winner full of expectation.

Mr Roberts was following my progress on television at home in Torquay: 'At least that way you can bite your fingernails in comfort,' he'd say to the tennis writers. He telephoned me at the Mottrams at 8am to prepare me for the match.

'You'll think she is better than she is. Don't get upset if she starts hitting a lot of winners as she's bound to do,' he said. 'Relax and make her play the ball. Wait patiently for the mistakes and take your time.'

High drama was on the cards. The newspaper reports of that era describe the scene in language that is not appropriate for the twenty-first century. In the *Sunday Times*, John Ballantine wrote:

> Miss Bueno started by hitting a great many winners, with that magnificent uncoiling service action, the raking forehand in which she changes the direction of the stroke by angling the face at the last second, and the speed and tigerishness at the net which is still, as always, straight out of the jungle.

Nerves certainly afflicted me in the first set on this stage I had always dreamed of playing on. When I first took up position to serve, it seemed that the court was huge at my end and I was serving into a matchbox. I was so paralysed by nerves I felt that I couldn't even get my arm up to serve. But I remembered Arthur's words of caution and settled into my game plan.

As the report continued:

> Miss Barker is a very gritty competitor … and she
> began mortaring the court corners with her famous
> forehand … This match had all the spectacular ingre-
> dients: older spectators sighing nostalgically as the
> slight, ballerina-like figure of Miss Bueno, a little more
> bosomy now but walking, as she always did, as if on
> air, entered the great arena where she established her
> 'Brazilian bombshell' reputation more than a decade
> ago … while Miss Barker was out to make her reputa-
> tion by winning her very first Centre Court singles two
> weeks after winning the French championship.

I rallied to win a topsy-turvy match 2–6, 6–2, 6–1, and earned
my place in the quarter-finals. It was the second consecutive
match where I'd battled back to win after dropping a set and I
played better than usual on grass (which was never my favourite surface); I wasn't letting nerves get the better of me. The
appreciative warmth from the crowd was like nothing I'd experienced anywhere else in the world. As I bobbed down in a
curtsey on my way back to the dressing room, I couldn't help
but glance at the patch of grass where I'd picked a palmful of
blades as a young girl and think, *Yes, this was a match worthy of
my treasured grass clippings*.

My Centre Court singles debut was described by John
Ballantine as 'a match that almost had me believing in the Women's
Tennis Association's case for equal pay, for equal entertainment'.

Spectacle is one thing; a successfully implemented game plan another. The feedback from Arthur was typically blunt. 'You could have been on the next train home to Devon,' he said, before warning me to expect more of the same – in other words, aggressive net play – from my next opponent: Martina Navratilova.

Martina and I were both young players with a big opportunity: the chance to reach a Wimbledon semi-final. Martina was still 19, now self-exiled and based in California waiting for her US citizenship. She had reached this stage of a Grand Slam five times already. Twice she had reached a final – in Australia and Paris the previous year – and was primed to convert so much promise into silverware. I was just 20, with one major title under my belt, and determined not to squander my chances in my third Grand Slam quarter-final appearance. With Virginia, the No.3 seed, also through to the last eight, the pressure was building. GINNY AND SUE GO FOR THE DOUBLE, the headlines blared. The subtext to the headlines was our rivalry for the British No.1 crown. As Laurie Pignon, fresh from our Paris outing, wrote in the *Daily Mail*:

> Virginia and Sue have their personal rivalry to spur them on. Although good teammates, Sue has never hidden her ambition to take Virginia's No. 1 spot from her while she is still playing, but Virginia has no intention of handing it over until the last bead of sweat has been shed.

We were in opposite halves of the draw, so this kind of comment was irrelevant on women's quarter-finals day, especially when my next hurdle was Martina, who had beaten me 7–5, 6–3 in our last meeting in Denver. But the expectancy, or hope, was for both Virginia and me to progress.

It was a horrible match in every way. We were on No.1 Court – the old No.1, that is, which abutted Centre Court with seating for 3,400 and standing space for a further 750 spectators. You could hear the oohs and aahs from the show court next door; it felt claustrophobic. Martina was in a foul mood, furious that the crowd was so vociferously behind me. But what did she expect? She was playing a home player who had just won the French Open at Roland-Garros and had done well on the Virginia Slims tour in the States. The British press had built up my prospects and I was looking ready to fulfil them. She accused a linesman of favouring British players. She said most of the bad calls went in my favour. She groused about bad bounces and the state of the grass. We were both getting upset. Again, the press reports are almost hilariously florid.

'Confronted by the ponderously powerful Miss Navratilova, who is six months her junior, Miss Barker looked like a West Highland white attacking a sleepy St Bernard,' wrote Rex Bellamy in *The Times*. He continued:

> The 8st blonde from Paignton seldom radiates serenity when she is playing a tennis match. But on this occasion she was relatively equable, because she was sharing a court with a player whose pounding rhythms and gloomy reaction to adversity made us think of Rachmaninov and Tosca, and all those heavy musical occasions based on the assumption that we are happiest when feeling sad.

Despite Martina's protests against line calls and her irritation with the crowd, which became a bit of a farce, I acquitted myself well up until the moment I had to play out the match. Martina was visibly exhausted and demoralised. I played to my strengths and went two breaks up in the third ... and then I just threw it away. I was serving for a 5–1 lead, but lost the game. And the next one. I fought back to once again serve for the match at 5–4, but lost to love. As Rex Bellamy put it politely, I 'wilted like a flower in a parched land'.

Instead of continuing with the tactics that had taken me to a winning position, I started to play lots of ridiculous drop shots. I don't know why. Why didn't I stick with what was working? My nerve-induced capitulation wouldn't have happened at any other tournament. The pressure got to me; I remember feeling a disconnect between my brain and my legs. In my mind, that match is like an out-of-body experience. I've hardly dared look at the reports of the match until recently, but they were as harsh on the way I squandered the match as I was on myself (headlines included SUICIDE SUE and 'I'M SO SORRY' SAYS SAD SUE).

Martina and I have talked about it since and she just shrugs. 'I was losing and out, but then you just started drop-shotting ...'

I was so angry with myself. I knew I'd got under her skin and I didn't finish the match off. I let myself down. That was the first time that I'd let go of an advantage in a big game, and the psychological effect of that one painful defeat had long-term consequences.

These days, you'd say a good coach is responsible for helping a player process a setback and maintain their morale, but communication was the problem with Mr Roberts and me. He famously didn't come to Wimbledon – he had been only once since he had been a ball boy at Queen's Club in the 1920s – and I would have only stayed a couple of days before travelling back to America for the hard-court season. I just had to work it out for myself. I would have spoken to him on the phone daily during Wimbledon, and then reverted back to our weekly call when I was abroad.

Mostly we communicated by letter; he sent me his detailed missive once a week. The game has changed so much. None of us then had travelling coaches. I never thought, *Oh, I wish I had a coach to talk me through this now.* We were all so thankful that we were travelling the world to play tennis and earn a living. Prize money wasn't high enough to pay for travelling coaches. Besides, I don't know who else I would have trusted. Mr Roberts was everything to me.

While I was rueing my loss, Chrissie beat Martina in the semi-final and went on to overcome Evonne to win her second title. A new era was dawning in the men's game as Björn Borg beat Ilie Năstase to become the youngest male Wimbledon champion of the modern era (he was 20, the same age as me). And just like that, with two glamorous young Wimbledon champions, it seemed that tennis exploded, gaining box-office allure, on and off the court. Chrissie became the first woman to be named a standalone 'Sportsperson of the Year' by *Sports Illustrated* (Billie Jean had shared the honour in 1972 with fellow American John Wooden, a basketball coach). There was a frenzy of interest and it came like a tidal wave once Björn won Wimbledon, bringing his rock-star aura to our sport.

Björn was a superstar from the moment he won the French Open in 1974 having just turned 18. On one occasion that I still have to pinch myself about, I played mixed doubles with him in an exhibition tournament organised by IMG in Hilton Head Island,

South Carolina – Borg and Barker. The women's team comprised Virginia, Evonne, Martina and myself; Arthur Ashe, Roscoe Tanner, Björn and Ilie made up the men's contingent. We all played singles, doubles and mixed. I played doubles with Evonne. I'd admired Björn, as everybody did in tennis. His brilliance, coupled with his looks, gave him a status that went beyond the world of game, set and match. To play doubles with him was a dream come true.

He and I beat Ashe and Goolagong in the semi-finals 6–2, 6–2. Next up was Ilie and Martina, and if we won this tie, Björn would be guaranteed the top prize of £50,000; if we lost, then it would all depend on his final singles match. He probably went on to win that, but I recall being determined to win our doubles for him. I didn't want to let him down and we'd played really well in the semi-finals. The match started steadily. It was one game all, the men had held serve. On the American clay, Björn and I were playing it very unconventionally, both positioned mainly at the back of the court. As great serve-and-volleyers, Ilie and Martina were obviously coming in at us. It was an interesting match with a lot of lobs and attempts to pass and the crowd were on our side – because Ilie had already kicked off in the tournament. The crowd was very involved: it was the blonde Europeans against the moodier Eastern Bloc. In mixed doubles, the fans always love it when the female passes her male opponent at the net. Bizarre in this day and age, I know, but they still find that appealing. Martina was serving and on the very first point Björn, who was a man of very few words, came over to me and said something to the effect of, 'Go down his line. Wherever it comes, go down his line because he's gonna try and intimidate you.' Whatever Björn suggested was fine by me. And needless to say, Ilie tried to cross – you know, *Wham, I'll show the little blonde thing where she is* – and I managed to pass him down the line and the crowd went wild. Ilie was not happy. We were love–30 up. Björn said, 'Do it again.' So I did, and the ball whizzed past Ilie for the winner. I was so excited that I was not letting Björn down – and we broke Martina's serve.

Ilie came over to me, loomed right in my face, and said something quite threatening – the basic message was, 'How dare you? Don't ever do that to me again.'

He had a reputation for volatility and it was absolutely terrifying, it really was, but Björn came to my side and stood up to him. 'If you have anything to say to her, say it to me first,' he said.

And I thought, *Oh, he is my hero!*

When Martina served the next time, Björn said, 'Go down his line,' and I replied, 'Do I have to? I don't want to be hurt!' But I did, and we won 6–3, 6–4. It was brilliant, such a memorable match. At the end, we were interviewed by Pancho Gonzales. Talk about a legend of the game.

I remembered that match on Centre Court when he beat Charlie Pasarell over two long days with an incredible scoreline (22–24, 1–6, 16–14, 6–3, 11–9). John Lloyd alerted me to a rerun of the Hilton Head mixed-doubles match on Tennis Channel, and I was watching myself in the post-match interview thinking, *Whose insipid voice is that? Did I ever really talk like that?* Lloydie said I was visibly intimidated to be interviewed by Pancho while sitting next to Björn. I just simpered about how Björn was such a help. Oh dear, oh dear. What an impression I must have made.

Anyway I was so happy that he was guaranteed the top prize that it made my year.

CHAPTER 10

THIS IS MY MOMENT …

The best of times, the worst of times – that sums up my 1977. On court, I had a great start to the year, reaching the finals in Houston, Minneapolis and Detroit – losing every time to Martina. I beat Virginia in straight sets to win the title in San Francisco and won Dallas (and my fur coat from the Hoffmans) in early March. I'd beaten a lot of the top players repeatedly and my ranking was No.3 in the world. The two ahead of me?

You've guessed it.

Off court, I couldn't have been happier. I had recently become engaged to Syd Ball, an established doubles specialist from Sydney who was six years my senior. We met in Australia and became close quickly. He was super-nice, my first real boyfriend, and my parents liked him enormously. Mr Roberts had always warned me about 'off-court distractions', his euphemism for boyfriends, but Syd and I maintained our relationship within our tennis lives, playing two seasons of World Team Tennis on the same team (for Indiana Loves in 1977 and Phoenix Racquets the following year), which was great fun and gave us time together. I was desperate to keep developing as a player and Syd was always trying to help me improve my game, particularly my backhand. He was experienced; he'd helped a lot of other players and I listened to him. Mr Roberts wasn't best pleased about his interventions. But the tour was a lonely place and it made all the difference having someone to come back to.

I had most of my successes in tennis in America and the highlight was making the final of the Virginia Slims Championship in front of a crowd of 11,651 at Madison Square Garden. Remarkably, it was my backhand that had earned me a spot in the prestigious final. (That observation is for Tim Henman, who thinks I spent my entire career running around my backhand. On his travels to New York for the US Open in 2021, he saw an old action photo of me executing a backhand and sent it to me as a text with the caption: 'Rare sighting of the Barker backhand'.) In the semi-final, I played Martina and earned a service break for 6–5 in the first set with a backhand passing shot down the line. On match point, I struck a backhand cross-court winner that Martina acknowledged with a nod. The *New York Times* preview nicely sets the scene for the biggest match of my career to date: 'Sue Barker almost went to college for cooking, loves Mexican food, digs the Electric Light Orchestra and still calls her coach "Mister",' it reads:

> But she also hits a mean forehand, has improved her backhand and is tough when the going gets that way.

That's why the 20-year-old British blonde will play Chris Evert for the $50,000 top prize today in the Virginia Slims tennis championship at Madison Square Garden. The top-seeded Miss Evert, chasing a fourth Slims title, advanced with a 6–1, 6–1 victory over Rosie Casals, and said, 'I don't think I can play much better than that.'

I had never beaten Chrissie in our 11 previous encounters, but I was on a roll and Martina had told the press I was 'good enough to beat Chris ... It's just a question of who's strongest at the baseline.' It's interesting to look back at the reports and see how I was perceived in the American press. The preview continued:

> Miss Barker's preparation for tennis has been anything but routine. Her parents never played the game. Her coach, Arthur Roberts, is an ageing, bent-shouldered rebel, who tutored Angela Mortimer and Mike Sangster and once was threatened with suspension by the British tennis federation because he had refused to take a teaching course. Miss Barker often holds strategy sessions with 'Mister Roberts' by phone and uses rest weeks to return home and sharpen her game.

It was a showbiz occasion, with Burt Reynolds sitting courtside to support Chrissie. In a manner I'd never seen before, she was struck by nerves, double-faulting four times, hitting the ball short, not moving with her usual fluency. I took advantage of her jitters, pounded out a lot of pleasing forehand winners and took the opener 6–2. Typically, Chrissie mentally regrouped and raced to win the second set 6–1. The decider was tighter than the numbers on the scoreboard indicated (6–1 again), but I was up against the metronomic accuracy and mental strength of Chrissie that I'd seen all too often, not to mention a very engaged crowd. In her post-match press conference, she said she'd used the first set as 'a warm-up'! 'I have a drive, a burning desire to win every time I step on the court,' she told reporters. 'I'm not as physically strong as other women, I don't have Martina's [Navratilova] big serve or Rosie's [Casals] quickness. I think mental discipline is where I compensate.' It sure was.

After the Virginia Slims, it was the start of my first season in World Team Tennis (WTT). Another initiative of Billie Jean's, WTT was established as a professional league with a team format that gave equal weight to each man and woman competing for their teams. It was designed to bring the sport to cities that didn't traditionally host tennis events and ran from April to the US Open, but you were free to play Eastbourne and Wimbledon. Ann Jones was one of many who advised me not to accept a lucrative contract yet, and told me I should carry on playing the tour to get more experience, but everyone else was playing – who would be on the tour? I wanted to pay my bills! I had been signed by Indiana Loves alongside Syd, Sue Mappin, Ann Kiyomura and Vitas Gerulaitis, the charismatic New Yorker who was the star signing on $250,000 over two years. I was offered $40,000, maybe $50,000.

Teams had gimmicky names inspired by tennis terms: Los Angeles Strings, New York Sets, Chicago Aces and so on. Billie Jean herself was player-coach of the Philadelphia Freedoms, for whom her friend Elton John wrote the song of the same name. The team owners tended to be hard businessmen who expected a lot for their big-bucks investment and wanted big crowds.

Entertainment was the priority. It wasn't tennis as we knew it. The game was adapted to make it quicker: games were shorter and a nine-point tie-break was introduced because they didn't want sets going on forever. There were no lines; the court was colour-blocked to indicate the traditional service boxes (blue and green), the baseline area (brown) and the tramlines (purple). There was only one set, a shoot-out: men's singles, ladies' singles, men's doubles, ladies' doubles, mixed doubles. And you could substitute people in and out. I didn't really enjoy it. It was intense because when we went on the road, we played a match every night, travelling through the night to be in the next city for that night's match. I was absolutely exhausted. In Indiana, we were given Subaru cars painted purple with gold splodges to match our kit. It was very commercial. The only thing that I really loved about it was that I was named Rookie of the Year and got into the All-Star game held in San Diego, where I played doubles with Martina – and that was an absolute dream come true. I think we won ... but maybe we didn't. All I remember is walking on court with Martina and I thought, *Happy days*.

It was an absolute joy to play alongside Vitas. He was a lovely man, a consummate joker and a brilliant mimic. He'd imitate me, he could do everyone. He did a brilliant John McEnroe. We had very nice ground-floor apartments next to each other on either side of the main door into the block. He lived a life. I loved cooking and sometimes I used to make him a dish and tell him

I'd put something in his fridge. He'd look at me as if to say, 'Do you really think I'm going to eat your quiche Lorraine or little chicken dish?' That wasn't his style. He wanted to be out eating burgers and pizza.

One night I came home and heard music blaring from his apartment. The door was wide open and I thought, *Hmm, weird.* I rang the bell. Nothing. Knocked on the door. Nothing. All the lights were on and music at full volume. I called out: 'Vitas, are you okay?' I walked through the flat and couldn't see him anywhere and feared I might find him on the bathroom floor or something. We all knew he lived life to the fullest. He wasn't there. So I switched off the music and the lights, shut the door and left a note on it, saying I had his spare keys if he needed them. And he didn't come back for two days. The Midwest was not his natural habitat. He'd gone off to Studio 54 in New York with his mates on a private plane. It was a different life because the men earned so much more money. I would have used up all my money to charter one private plane. Vitas was so dynamic, so intent on having fun.

We had a superfan called The Gibber, a rather large man who used to sit in the front row with his legs open, sandwich-ing a massive bucket of popcorn, and abuse the opposition outrageously. After a home match, I used to drive back to my apartment in my silly little Subaru with the Indiana Loves logos splashed all over it. I started to notice that the same car followed me every night, parked up nearby and then shone its headlights right into my apartment. I would swish my curtains across, but I can't pretend it didn't scare me. Was it a stalker? Then I realised it was The Gibber. And that was fine; I knew he was harmless. I used to wave at him in his car before I drew the curtains. When one of the bosses went to talk to him about trailing me, he said he just wanted to make sure I got home all right.

As I said, he would abuse our opposition without demur. In one match against the New York Sets, I was playing against Virginia, who I had a good record against in Team Tennis. And as Virginia bent forward in front of him to serve, the Gibber shouted out, 'Watch out, Virginia, your d***'s showing.' After a few of these calls, Virginia turned and marched over to him and whacked the bottom of his popcorn bucket from underneath with her racket so that there was popcorn all over the place. I think she got penalty points or was disqualified. Virginia doesn't remember. I do, because it was one of the most hilarious moments, and Vitas thought her response was the best.

• • •

On to Wimbledon, and the build-up was hysterical. It was Wimbledon's centenary year – and I played ball by being photographed at Hampton Court in tennis apparel from the 1870s, straw hat, ankle-length petticoat and all. It was also the Queen's Silver Jubilee, which reinforced the perennial longing for an all-British final and lots of Rule Britannia sentimentality about who would be crowned the queen of tennis. All this coincided with the first time in aeons that Britain had two players in the Top 5, with storytellers ready to celebrate the 'Ginny and Sue' show.

The press bigged it up, as you'd expect. Chrissie was the No.1 seed, Martina No.2, Virginia No.3 and I was No.4. The British girls were expected to reach the semi-finals, if not win. It was a dream for both of us to lift the Wimbledon trophy. Virginia, in her thirties, thinking it could be her last chance; me, the young whippersnapper chasing at her heels. The draw worked out well for me. I'd beaten every contender in my half, as well as Chrissie and Billie Jean in Team Tennis. I'd beaten Martina at the Virginia Slims finals and I expected to meet her, as projected by the seedings, after I'd got past Kerry Melville Reid in the quarters.

Playing under the pressure of being a home player did affect me. As I told the journalists, I'd been watching matches on Centre Court since I was seven and the ghosts of past champions seemed to be in every corner. On the phone the night before my quarter-final, Mr Roberts told me to have a double brandy before I went to bed. I didn't. I didn't actually feel nervous. I was confident that the battle plan we'd discussed would work well against Kerry.

The big shock of the tournament was that Martina was beaten by Betty Stöve on No.1 Court in a testy match that ended 9–8, 3–6, 6–1. Betty hadn't featured in any pre-tournament list of the top challengers for the title. She was a formidable presence on court – 6ft 1in and muscular – but her game was erratic. She herself admitted she easily lost concentration, so you never knew what was coming from her side of the net. When she was focused and on form, though, you were on the wrong end of a serious battering. Still, it was a shock that I would be playing Betty for a place in the Wimbledon final. Quite a nice shock: I had a really good head-to-head record against Betty. I'd fulfilled the expectations of my seeding. I had nothing to lose.

It's become the custom for players to rent properties in Wimbledon during the Championship so they can walk into the grounds and enjoy the village café lifestyle between matches. In 1977, though, we all used to stay in the official hotel, The Gloucester – where Billie Jean had famously called a meeting in the early 1970s to discuss the women leaving the men's tour. A courtesy car would collect us and take us through south-west London, driving in through the gates to drop us right in front of the Centre Court clubhouse entrance. It was a very different Wimbledon then, much smaller with a more intimate feel to it. On ladies' semi-finals day, the order of play on Centre Court was Chrissie versus Virginia, followed by my match against Betty. That was problem number one for me. I always liked to be first on court. I hated waiting for the first match to be over; matches on grass are the most unpredictable. Ditto, matches when so much is at stake. Not being able to second-guess the time I'd be called on court allowed nerves to fester and, for me at Wimbledon under the huge bubble of public expectation, that was far from ideal.

This was a HUGE match. My dream. I'd had a great 1977 season. Never mind that grass was not my favourite surface, I really fancied myself to do well at Wimbledon, my spiritual home. I publicly begged Arthur to come to support me for that match. Usually he scrutinised my matches on television and lip-read my mutterings. He understood the thoughts going through my mind and we'd sort it out over the telephone. But this semi against Betty was such a momentous match because it was one I should win. Amid the mounting tension, I would have found his presence calming – and a source of pride. After all, a positive result was the culmination of my tennis dream, the goal we had been working towards together since I was 11 years old.

He had told the journalists that he couldn't bear to be in anyone's company when he watched me in a big match. 'I often have a little cry or a good laugh, depending on what mood the match leaves me in,' he'd said. 'This way, watching alone at home, no one can see what an old softie I can be.' On this occasion, he listened to my appeal and said, 'Okay, I'll come up to London.' After what had happened the year before against Martina, when I had lost such an important match from a winning position, I really wanted him there. Yet I could hardly believe it: Mr Roberts had agreed to come and support me in person. Looking back, I can see that the very fact I felt I needed him to set me up for the match and bolster my confidence meant I was in some sort of a negative headspace.

For him to agree to come was a big deal. He never travelled. His bread-and-butter job was his role as the tennis coach at the Palace Hotel – he couldn't just up sticks when one of the local players he coached for free needed him. He had travelled with us to junior tournaments in the UK, but never travelled abroad and never came near Wimbledon. He hated the hullabaloo. And it wasn't unusual for me to be unaccompanied. As I've said before, it wasn't like I felt hard done by. It was the way it was.

Arthur said he would travel up from Torquay and stay with his brother in south London. We agreed I would leave tickets for him at the gate. He phoned me at The Gloucester hotel the night before and we arranged to meet the next morning outside the main doors of the clubhouse after practice, before Chrissie and Virginia's semi got under way, to have a quiet final word about my tactics for my match.

You can't be in a semi-final at Wimbledon and not feel the magnitude of the occasion. I knew my parents would be watching on television at home. My sister was teaching in her primary school, but her head allowed her to sneak her class into the school hall to watch on the television. Carole Hoffman was on a plane, and would hear the results when she was up in the clouds.

At the appointed time, I went down from the dressing room to meet Mr Roberts, and he wasn't there. I waited for a while, then returned to the dressing room. I kept going back down the stairs to check for him, because I really wanted to speak to him. He always gave me such clarity of purpose going into a match. Still no show. By now, I was beginning to fret. The first semi was in progress and he hadn't turned up. I wondered if I'd missed him, because of course we didn't have mobile phones and there was no way of tracking him down. I didn't even have a phone number for his brother. I asked a friend to go and check whether his ticket had been collected from the kiosk – and they returned with the news that it hadn't. I could tell from the tenor of the cheers that Virginia was pulling off a surprise victory over Chrissie – a tremendous achievement because Chrissie was so dominant then and the favourite for the title. *Where was Mr Roberts?*

It reached a point when I realised I had to give up thinking about meeting him and get on with preparing for the match by myself. A Wimbledon semi-final! I remember sitting in the locker room thinking, *Oh God, there are only two people other than me left in the draw now – Betty and Virginia – and I have a winning head-to-head record against both of them this year. This is my moment.*

Billie Jean wandered past and ruffled my hair, saying, 'Go for it, Sue. You know, you can do this.' And I thought, *Yeah!* I had beaten Virginia twice that year: in Dallas in the semi-finals of the Virginia Slims tournament, and in the final in Los Angeles. In straight sets both times. And Betty, I really didn't think she would pose a problem. She had a bandaged right knee for a muscle injury that needed ice-pack treatment before she took to the court. I knew she had played well against Martina so I wasn't going to take it lightly, but I didn't think she'd present insurmountable opposition.

I remember walking on to Centre Court to the most magical reception from the crowd, exuberant after Virginia's win. She'd done her bit to make the dream of an all-British final come true; now it was my turn. I was nervous, but not super-nervous.

Normally I would start a bit shakily in a match, but this was an occasion where I grew more and more tense as the match went on ... because I found I couldn't control it. I looked up at the players' box from time to time but Mr Roberts never showed up. He had always taught me to blank out the crowd. Even when my parents came to my early junior matches, which was rare, he ordered me not to look for them. He didn't even want me glancing at him. And here I was scanning the crowd to see if he'd turned up. I don't know how much that had an effect on me. Or how much his actual absence affected me. I was used to him not being there, but I was disappointed by his no-show after we'd made such particular arrangements. I don't want to blame anyone other than myself for losing to Betty that day, but it was an unsettling background when I was playing for a place in what could have been an all-British final, at Wimbledon, the dream!

Betty played a smart game, using the weight of her shot as an intimidating weapon. She sliced the ball so much and kept hitting it low to my forehand. Because of my extreme grip, it just took my weapon away. I didn't have enough time for my backswing and it totally disrupted my rhythm. There were precious few long rallies. She played cleverly and I didn't. I couldn't find a way to combat her tactics. Until that quarter-final against Martina the previous year, I had always been able to play well under pressure; that was the cornerstone of Arthur's psychological approach. But I panicked when the momentum of the match switched in Betty's favour. Subconsciously, was I remembering my capitulation of 1976? Was I fearful of another humiliation?

Arthur said later – over the telephone from Devon – that I kept on hitting too wide to her. I should have played down the middle and blocked her. 'That's what you normally do,' he said. 'Why didn't you do that against her?' I couldn't answer. My instinct was to keep her running because she wasn't the best mover and she had a leg injury. But too often she was in control – and I couldn't forget that in the quarters she had beaten Martina, who was practically unbeatable. I knew what I had to do, I just couldn't do it. And then, when the third set started running away from me, I got very nervous. I was inhibited; I just didn't feel like myself out there. It was a horrible match, traumatising to lose in such a way on such an occasion. I absolutely should have won that match.

I was never the same player again. After that, I always doubted myself. When I got into tight situations in matches, it would creep back into my thoughts. In 1977, Syd was very much in the picture and fellow players thought he changed my game. In helping me improve my backhand, he moved me more to the middle of the court, which gave players a chance to target my weaker side. I don't blame Syd for that – I asked for help. (The following year, when I told Mr Roberts we'd split up, he said, 'Thank God, that's it. Maybe you'll get back, because you've compromised your biggest weapon.') Perhaps the campaign to improve my backhand made me feel I wasn't a complete player? I've said before, I wish I'd had some help from a sports psychologist to learn how to change the pattern of my thoughts from negative to positive in those sorts of situations. I've chatted a lot with Jo Konta, who was very much into building up the mental side of her game, and it's fascinating hearing the routine she went through.

I truly felt that was my moment. The opportunity to fulfil my dream was there … and I let it slip away. That's hard to deal with. I've learned not to consider it totally as a negative because I think if I'd won the semi-final, and maybe won Wimbledon, my life would not have gone in the same direction. I wouldn't have had to find another career, another means to earn a living when I retired; I might never have ventured into television.

And of course that's opened up the most wonderful 30 years. So it's swings and roundabouts. My dream as a little girl hitting a ball against the garage wall didn't come to fruition, but it opened up other unexpected opportunities – presenting Wimbledon to the nation, becoming one of very few former athletes to present multi-sports programmes on arguably the highest-profile channels in the world, hosting my favourite television quiz show, the one I grew up watching with my Dad. If it's possible to be at peace with yourself and yet have a smidge of regret, that's how I feel about that Wimbledon semi-final.

I can't remember anything about the rest of that day. It remains a blur. I can't remember going into the press conferences or what excuses I made. I can't remember seeking out Nuala Dwyer – then a medical student, working in the crow's nest on the outside courts as a holiday job, informing the referee's office over a walkie-talkie when matches were over from her vantage point – but she recalls me joining her up in this crow's nest and we talked for about an hour, literally immediately after I'd come off court. We were very close. We knew each other well, we travelled together; I'd stayed at her house. We were intense rivals as juniors too, but it was at a time when you were rivals and friends. She recalls us talking about our childhood, our early days with Mr Roberts. She says she said all the sort of comforting things you would say to someone in my position – there'll be another chance next year ...

To this day, I am in two minds about my views on why I didn't acquit myself well on the day. When Virginia beat Chrissie in her semi, I thought this was my moment, the Wimbledon trophy was mine, and that was my mistake. Afterwards I was devastated to feel that I'd let Mr Roberts down – he was brutal in his summary of my performance to the press. 'It was tragic really,' he said. 'If she had played not well but normally, she would have won. But if you are going to be a champion, you must learn to produce your best at the right time.' He was spot on. As always.

It's taken me a long time to acknowledge this, but I think he let me down too. He was quoted in the papers saying that he'd had a prior arrangement to drop his daughter off at the airport and he'd walked into a glass door at Heathrow. 'I was in such a state, with blood everywhere and a great bump on my head, that all I could think was to get home to Torquay,' he said. I don't know what was true, or whether he just decided he didn't want to come to Wimbledon because of the goldfish-bowl intensity. I never did get to see him because I flew back to the States after Wimbledon. And we never talked about his non-show, which is odd. Maybe he did feel he had let me down? But we did talk about the match!

• • •

My Indiana Loves teammate Vitas was very supportive. He was quick to invite me and my doubles partner Ann Kiyomura to sit in the players' box the following day to watch his semi-final against Björn. That 1977 men's semi-final now ranks as one of the all-time classics from Wimbledon, and in terms of mesmerising tennis and out-of-this-world shot-making it was a great way to stop me brooding over my defeat. The final score was 6–4, 3–6, 6–3, 3–6, 8–6, and it was incredibly close. Of a total of 353 points, Björn won 177 and Vitas 176. And Vitas responded so differently to me in losing his semi. I was depressed; he was so happy with his performance. It was a wake-up call to me to see that sometimes the result doesn't matter. For me, it was all about winning and losing. To see how joyful Vitas was that he had been able to compete against his good friend in a style that made him proud, I thought, *Wow, that's the way to deal with it.* Afterwards he said,

'Come on, we're going out!' Ann and I went out to drinks and dinner with him, and then on to Tramp, where we left him to it. We could see where his evening was going.

Vitas was such a glamorous man, a great personality, and I'm so happy I got to know him. It was sad to see him deteriorate in his thirties with well-documented substance-abuse problems. I remember walking through Wimbledon and seeing a group of three guys – one I recognised as one of Vitas's friends. I said hello to the guy I knew and then the other guy, an old-looking man who was hobbling at his side, looked up and I saw it was Vitas, and gosh, he looked ill. We had a little chat and I moved on, thinking that was upsetting. And yet, towards the end of his life, he turned it around completely. He was working in television; he was healthy and vibrant again and winning plaudits for his commentary. With his gift of the gab, I think in some ways he inspired Mac because, giving his opinion on matches as an ex-player, he was just himself and so funny. His death at the age of 40 in 1994, due to accidental carbon monoxide poisoning while staying in a friend's guesthouse in New York State, was desperately sad. Watching the funeral with all the boys there as his pallbearers ... Mac, Björn, Jimmy Connors. Only Vitas could have ever brought McEnroe and Connors together. That said everything about him. Tennis was just tennis. He loved his competitors as friends.

• • •

On the day of the ladies' singles final, I couldn't bear to watch Virginia take on Betty with the Queen watching from the Royal Box. I went shopping in Bond Street and splashed out on an expensive watch and necklace. (Meanwhile, Chrissie, upset about her semi-final exit, told Bud Collins she trashed her hotel room and stayed in her bathrobe for three days eating junk food.) This was a time when people went to a television shop to buy or rent a set, and you'd often see crowds form outside one of these shop windows watching some exciting sports action. Well, just my luck, these shops along Oxford Street were showing the Wimbledon final and big groups of people were jostling for position on the pavement. As I edged my way past I could see just how much it meant to people to have a British winner.

My flight back to America was booked for the Monday after Wimbledon, so I couldn't get away from it. I couldn't just book an earlier flight. I laugh with Virginia about it now. I spent so much money that day on jewellery I never really wore because of the bad associations.

She became Wimbledon champion and made an absolute mint. We talk about it a lot. And to Virginia I say, 'Little did I know that when you won in 1977, and I lost, I would, on joining the Beeb, have to sit down every year with you – the last British woman to win Wimbledon – and relive that tournament all over again.' She understands my pain. She's lost matches she wouldn't like to reminisce about. And in her autobiography she says she was so pleased it wasn't me she had to beat in the final.

CHAPTER 11

REGINALD PERRIN
SAVES THE DAY

I had won a Grand Slam and reached No.3 in the world rankings. I had beaten all the top players in my peer group at least once and for five consecutive years my forehand was voted the best on the women's tour. But when I look back at my career, it is our Wightman Cup triumphs that mean the most to me. This was an annual contest between Great Britain and the United States of America. Historically, it was a private match between the two countries, and between 1931 and 1973 Great Britain had only beaten the Americans three times. And yet between 1974 and 1978 we won the Cup three times. The competition was well known to the sports-following public and to be selected for the GB squad was an incredible honour. It made household names of players. Like the Ashes are to England and Australia cricket, so the Wightman Cup was to GB and the USA in women's tennis. There's nothing like it now.

I was selected for the team for the first time in 1974, when the event was to be played at Queensferry in Wales. With the Americans being so dominant and GB having lost the previous year, the organisers decided to shrink the scale of the occasion and stage it in the Deeside Leisure Centre. When on British soil, it had traditionally been played on Wimbledon's No.1 Court. The British team comprised Virginia, Glynis, Sue Mappin, Lesley Charles and myself. We were staying in a nice hotel in Chester and we really wanted to stay in our rooms because every one of us was SO nervous. At the opening ceremony, a Welsh choir sang the national anthem and we were all in tears.

The United States didn't field their best team, but Julie Heldman – one of the Original Nine – was Top 10 and we got off to a great start when Virginia beat her in a hard-fought three-setter. Glynis produced a brilliant 4–6, 6–1, 6–3 win over Janet Newberry, a Top 20 player who had been runner-up in the Wimbledon mixed-doubles final the previous summer. I had a rollercoaster against Chris Evert's younger sister Jeanne, winning 4–6, 6–4, 6–1 – opening and ending the match on a forehand winner – but I had been 0–3 down in the second. The atmosphere was terrific; the partisan vocal support echoed around the Deeside Leisure Centre and gave us a huge lift. I had never experienced an atmosphere like it. Not in Madison Square Garden, not at Wimbledon, not in Team Tennis. The crowd got behind me so much that at the end I felt that I could have gone on for another set.

In each of the first four matches, we lost the opening set only to fight back, turbo-boosted by the home support. Tennis is such an individual sport, it was the happiest time to play with the rest of the team by the side of the court. After five singles and two doubles matches, we won 6–1 and overnight became household names. In the *Daily Mail*, Laurie Pignon wrote:

> Britain's 6–1 triumph over the United States in the Wightman Cup, only the eighth since the matches began in 1923, not only brought a new life to an event that almost died of shame, but it forced traditionalists, myself included, to change their moth-ball minds.

The following year we travelled to Cleveland, Ohio. Great Britain had not beaten the Americans on home soil for 50 years, and the tennis press declared it unlikely that we would succeed on the carpeted boards of Cleveland's Public Assembly Hall – because Chris Evert was back in the side. How could the United States lose the four rubbers in which she took to the court?

But we had other ideas. Virginia set the tone, defeating doubles specialist Mona Schallau (later Mona Anne Guerrant) – who, off court, worked alongside Billie Jean King in pushing for women's rights – with the loss of only three games. There were a few selection controversies – Sue Mappin, who played so well with Lesley Charles, was left out in favour of 36-year-old Ann Jones. I was disappointed to play No.3 singles as I was No.2 in the national rankings, but Virginia explained that any of us could go out and get hammered by Chrissie, and she was giving me the responsibility of winning both my singles and doubles. We got to 3–2 up and then Glynis had the chance to clinch the trophy in the crunch singles match against Mona Schallau. Reading Laurie Pignon's report takes me right back to courtside: 'The atmosphere was an electric mixture of fear and expectation, with every member of the British team wishing they could play the strokes for her, but all glad they did not have to,' he wrote. Too right. Glynis played a blinder and earned an incredible victory for GB on her eighth match point.

Technically a dead rubber, the last match was the icing on the cake for Glynis and me. We had reached the quarter-finals in the doubles of all the Grand Slams and capped off an incredible year with a 6–4, 7–5 victory over Chrissie and Mona.

And so we'd beaten the Americans again, this time on their home soil, pretty resoundingly 5–2. For me, aged 18 and 19, those first two Wightman Cup victories were a fantastic early experience of being on a winning side. I was just discovering that life on the tour could be lonely, but here we were, all in it together, a squad of individuals with our own hopes and dreams, doing our own thing, but coming together to compete for our country's pride. The emphasis on teamwork tapped into the happy spirit of those junior forays into international team contests with the Princess Sofia trophy and the Annie Soisbault Cup. There weren't vast numbers of coaches or official entourages to dilute the camaraderie. We all recognised that the responsibility of playing for each other and our country required courage, and with that came mutual support. Those events were the happiest of times …

I felt I could get used to that winning feeling, but we lost at home in Crystal Palace the following year, and again in Oakland, California, in 1977, when the US team had all their big guns in play – Billie Jean, Rosie Casals and Chrissie. Roll on to 1978, and our ambition was to seize back the momentum.

The Wightman Cup of 1978 remains my absolute favourite moment in tennis, as I was representing my country in front of the Duke and Duchess of Kent at the Royal Albert Hall. The Americans brought another all-star team: mixing the experience of Billie Jean and Chrissie with the aggressive power-play of teenage prodigies Tracy Austin and Pam Shriver. Virginia headed our line-up of Sue Mappin, Michelle Tyler, Anne Hobbs and myself. We knew we were going to have to dig deep and raise our games. This was going to be tight, possibly down to the wire. I had the misfortune to face Chrissie in the opening singles, which predictably she won. Michelle played a blinder over three sets to edge out Pam. It took Virginia a hard-fought three-set rollercoaster to quash the 15-year-old Tracy, who was billed as a Chrissie clone with her double-handed backhand and tenacious will to win from the baseline. That was 2–1 to GB. In an intriguing partnership of youth and court-savviness, Tracy and Billie Jean took on Sue and Ann and squeezed a win. Two-all. Chrissie, in dominant form, then gave Virginia the same treatment I'd received, which left us 2–3 down, and me next up in a crucial match against Tracy. If I won, the tie was still alive.

Lose, and we were out.

I took the first set 6–3. She responded by taking the second by the same score. I was tense and nervous going into the decider.

I think I lost my serve in the opening game and sat down at the changeover in a bit of a state. I was worried I wasn't going to be able to turn it around. Sue Mappin was sitting on court next to me as captain, as Virginia would play next in the doubles. Sue and I go back a long way, since I'd squatted in her house as a sometime lodger. To this day, I call her Nag and she calls me Barker – we can't be bothered to call each other Sue. She knew me well and could read the signs: I was tightening up. She leaned over to me and said in her no-nonsense way, 'Just remember, Barker, you didn't get where you are today …'

'Oh, Reginald Perrin?!'

Then we were laughing. It must have looked so inappropriate to be laughing at that stage of the key match, but her intervention helped. The Reggie Perrin sitcom – starring Leonard Rossiter as a bored, middle-aged, suburban executive for Sunshine Desserts – was so big on television at the time, spawning all sorts of catch-phrases. There was Reggie's pompous boss CJ's 'I didn't get where I am today by …' and the 'Great, supers' of his fawning colleagues. It snapped me out of a negative mindset and I went on to beat Tracy with a satisfying 6–1 final set. That was a huge win. It seems fitting that we evoked the very British spirit of Reggie Perrin in this tense scene of sporting drama in the Royal Albert Hall. Nag and Barker – both in giggles.

That left the score poised at three-all. The pressure was on. Virginia and I had to win the final match, the doubles, and we were playing Chrissie and Pam. Pam had just been in the finals of the US Open and Chrissie had smashed us both in the singles. We started with a bang, taking the first set 6–0, then the Americans came back at us in the second. Virginia and I both played shakily. The battle for honours went into a third set. And it was the Royal Albert Hall. The atmosphere was simply amazing. My parents and my brother and sister were there – far enough away for me not to hear Dad's oohing and ahhing. We reached match point. Pam was serving. Virginia whispered to me, 'If I get this return in, just cross,' and I was thinking, *Virginia, just hit a winner!* I was so nervous. You know, *Just win it for us, Virginia!*

Needless to say, the old Virge hit a fabulous return right at Pam's feet, the ball came up towards me and I thought, *I'm going to go for it.* I remember hitting it. And it was the sweetest shot I ever hit. A winner. The Albert Hall erupted. There were embraces all around and silly plastic Union Flag hats to wear. Victory signified more to me there than winning the French Open, because representing my country meant so much to me. I can't believe players now want to be paid for the time they spend competing in the GB kit. To me, just to hear 'Game, Great Britain' was amazing. I was the proudest I could be. I hit the winning shot in the Albert Hall, with the crowd going mad, and we were up against a heck of a US team: Billie, Chrissie, Pam … Tracy, in her pigtails, obviously so young, but always so hard to beat.

It was amazing. Mr Roberts always said, 'Just do the best you can and just do it.' Well, we played the best we could. And that's what you want in these moments, which don't come often in life. You want to make the most of it and we did. It was an amazing feeling. The press declared that Britain hadn't beaten a stronger US team since 1930. We didn't know it at the time, but that was to be the last year that Great Britain won the Wightman Cup before it was discontinued 12 years later.

A week or so after our jubilant moment, Dad was sitting on the sofa at home watching the Royal British Legion Festival of Remembrance at the Albert Hall on television. A procession of military bands representing the different forces walked through in the presence of some members of the royal family and struck up a performance. As Dad told it, one splendidly moustachioed bandleader announced, 'This time last week Sue Barker was hitting the winning shot for GB in the Wightman Cup here, so we're going to play this in her honour.' And the musicians started to play, 'If You Knew Susie (Like I Know Susie)'. Dad was in tears. He always loved watching this national tribute to the military personnel who dedicate their lives to protecting Britain, and the unexpected tribute to his daughter made it for him.

Over the years we had a lot of fun representing Great Britain in the Fed Cup (now named the Billie Jean King Cup) – Virginia, Glynis, Lesley Charles and the younger members, Anne Hobbs and Jo Durie – guided from 1978 by team manager Sue Mappin and her blunt Yorkshire sense of humour. At one stage we had seven British players in the Top 20; we were a strong tennis nation.

In 1980, the tournament was held in Berlin at the Rot-Weiss Tennis Club. Virginia and I played Argentina in the second round. The LTA hierarchy were in the stands to support us for each match; I'd won my singles, Virginia was defeated in hers. The tie stood at 1–1 and so a place in the quarter-final against the host nation hung on our performance in the doubles. It was a tight match – they won the first set 6–7, we won the next 6–2 – and I remember we were 3–2 in the final set when we noticed, at this cliffhanger of a moment, the LTA officials get up and leave to go to a cocktail party. We played on without our support group and were euphoric to take the final set 6–4 and earn a place in the next round. The next morning, Sue and I were coming down the lift; the doors opened and in walked one of these bigwigs.

'Oh, hello, how did you get on?' he asked breezily.

If you could have seen my face. To think they'd gone off to a party and not bothered to find out our fate seemed so rude. Sue and I rearranged a few letters in his surname, which happily spelled out a popular slang term for an idiot.

Laughs were guaranteed on these trips. During the 1981 Fed Cup finals in Japan, there were a lot of cocktail parties and receptions, almost one every night it seemed, and players were obliged to attend. We'd get bussed over to the venue from the hotel. We played Belgium, France, the Soviet Union and Australia to reach the final – GB's first final since 1972. Virginia, Sue and I always seemed to be clambering on and off the player buses for yet another compulsory official party attendance. At a reception on the eve of the final, Virginia told Sue she wanted to go back to the hotel right then and there. She didn't want to wait for the bus to slowly fill up to capacity with players and then set off. We had an important match to play and needed sleep. Sue said she thought we'd have to wait for the bus. She asked me what I felt about the situation and I said I definitely wanted to leave too. We slunk out of the room and Sue was so funny – she'd noticed the officials travelled to these receptions in limos driven by chauffeurs in white gloves. Each limo had a number on a card on the windscreen. At the front of the hotel, there was no sign of the bus, but there was a line of numbered limos. Sue held up her arm and boldly shouted, 'Number Three!' The driver of limo number three duly leaped out of his seat and politely opened the doors for us and whisked us back to the hotel. Sue was terrified she'd be found out and reprimanded but she got her two singles players home for a good night's sleep.

The final was a huge event – on clay – and we tried our best, but our efforts to beat Chrissie and Andrea Jaeger were fruitless. And when Sue checked out, she was shocked to find the bill for physio massages was higher than the cost of four rooms in the hotel over that week. We left with lots of good memories – including sumo wrestling impersonations in the dressing room … there was no TV or Netflix to watch. Sue was the best sumo wrestler for sure.

Virginia and I get on so well now. In some ways I regret that we didn't get on better when we were both playing at our peak. But we were both competitive and rivals for the GB No.1 spot. It's interesting, because the Americans don't have rivalries – there are just so many American players – but Virginia and I were the only two Brits consistently ranked in the Top 32, which made up the Virginia Slims draws. The tension between us was evident in March 1977, when I played Virginia in the semi-finals of the Dallas tournament. A big British press contingent was there, invited by the wonderful tournament director Nancy Jeffett. In those days, the requirement was for both players to attend the post-match interview together. How bizarre is that? I beat Virginia 6–3, 6–4 to reach the final, and Virginia was furious, so infuriated that she refused to attend the press conference with me. I understood her anger; it was the same feeling I had when I lost to her. And I lost to her so many times I don't remember them. I just remember the matches I won.

How could I aim to be world No.1 or No.2, if I was still the British No.2? It wasn't a nasty rivalry, because we were members of the Wightman Cup and Fed Cup teams together, and we had a great doubles record. But the British No.1 status was important to both of us. She went into the press conference at Dallas on her own and said I just went for everything and I was so lucky because all my shots hit the lines for winners. When I went in, Laurie Pignon, John Parsons and company put Virginia's line back to me.

'Virginia said you just hit the lines.'

My response was, 'I didn't realise that wasn't legal! Am I supposed to hit down the middle of the court back to her? Or miss the lines? No, I didn't think so.'

She didn't like that. It caused a bit of a stir.

Another time, in Chicago, we were playing a nine-point final-set tie-break. Whoever is receiving serve can choose which side of the court they want to return from. And so it's one point to decide the winner. I loved it. It's brutal. I lost a few of them, trust me, but I loved the adrenaline of these final-set tie-breaks. I was playing Virginia in, I think, the semi-finals. She was to serve and I chose the left court. She missed a first serve and off the second serve I hit a glorious winner. Beating her was so important to me then, I can remember to this day just how wonderful that shot felt.

Now we laugh so much over our reminiscences. Even about her winning Wimbledon. One of the best anniversary chats we had about that match was filmed on the beach at Eastbourne. She suggested we sit down. We saw a couple of deck chairs and the two of us decided to try and work out how to put them up. Neither of us had a clue because they're so damn difficult, and in the end we laughed until we cried, and then we stuck towels on the end and sat like a couple of old ladies with our arms straight by our sides. We used to giggle about how the old people sat at Eastbourne watching the tennis and here we were, a couple of old biddies reliving our glory days.

CHAPTER 12

NOT SO HAPPY
EVER AFTER

In the late 1970s, the tour was a small bubble of players drawn from all over the world, though not yet Asia. For each of us from our very different backgrounds – Chrissie from her father's tennis academy in Florida, Virginia from a childhood in South Africa, Evonne plucked from her indigenous town to train in Sydney, Mima Jaušovec from Slovenia (which back then was part of Yugoslavia), me from Mr Roberts's stable in Torquay – our racket was our passport to a fulfilling life, earning a living while travelling the globe. Naively, I assumed that, once on the tour, we were all playing out a version of 'happy ever after' … until the mysterious disappearance of a lovely Russian girl called Natasha Chmyreva taught me otherwise.

Natasha was two years younger than me and destined, I thought, to be No.1 in the world. She had won the 1975 and 1976

Wimbledon girls' singles title and the 1975 US Open girls' singles championship. She had a terrific serve and was a fabulous volleyer, and her instinct was to play a high-risk offensive game. She wasn't the best mover, but that would have come. She and I joined the tour at about the same time and started playing doubles together. I didn't really know anyone and nor did she.

She hardly spoke English but we were put together by Olga Morozova, the senior Russian No.1 who used to play with Virginia. She and I did well in the doubles – we beat Olga and Virginia once, which pleased us both immensely – and we became good friends. In the course of hanging out together, I observed that a group of men followed her around, keeping an eye on her. 'That's because she's from the Soviet Union,' I was told by others.

Natasha had an exuberant presence: she was tall, with a great swish of long auburn hair and a smile that would light up a room. She loved everything about America. As her English picked up, she told me she had been trained hard for glory by her parents from the age of seven. Her mother was the coach of the Dynamo tennis club in Moscow; her father, an athletics coach. I was fascinated to listen to her. It was clear she was bright and strong-minded. As a young child she had wanted to go into gymnastics but she had been assessed physically and sent to the tennis academy; it was the path chosen for her. She just loved everything tennis now brought her, travelling around America.

In the nicest possible way, she was a bit nuts – a big personality with a tremendous sense of style. On court, she wore striking dresses designed for her by Teddy Tinling and she held back her hair with a sweatband. Off court, she liked American culture and going to the disco with friends. She enjoyed the money she was earning (at least, the percentage she was allowed to spend). One day she came back to the hotel in a beautiful new fur coat, flared jeans, a big-buckled belt and cowboy boots embellished with turquoise beads. I said, 'Wow, Tasha, what are you wearing?' It was a bit over the top but she was so proud of it. And she looked a million dollars.

We became established as a doubles partnership and we were flying. We had high hopes of winning the Grand Slams. I'll never forget turning up at our next tournament and signing up for singles. I told the organisers I'd sign up for doubles with Natasha as soon as she arrived. 'She's not down for this tournament,' the organisers said. 'Or for the next tournament.' That was the first I heard of it.

So I sought out Olga and said, 'Where's Natasha?'

'She's not coming,' she said brusquely.

'Why isn't she coming?'

'She's not well.'

'Okay, well, when is she likely to be back?'

'I think that's it. She's not well.'

End of conversation. I never saw her again. I tried to write and get in touch but she never wrote to me. There are no results recorded under her name after 1979. She played the Fed Cup that year in Madrid; her last match was a singles contest against Tracy Austin, which she lost 6–0, 6–1. And it was baffling, because she was at the top of the game. She had beaten Chrissie twice in World Team Tennis; she had lost a tough semi-final in the Australian Open to Martina; she had reached the quarter-finals of the US Open. She loved life and we had plans to conquer the world in doubles.

I never got to the bottom of her disappearance until I read an article not long ago that revealed she had been living in an apartment in Moscow. She had never left Russia since her withdrawal from the tennis scene. The article quotes her former hitting partner, Michael Chesalov: 'Natasha never fitted into our system. Unlike the disciplined Olga Morozova, Natasha could never keep within the bounds.' That's what I feared: she became too westernised. She was an individual talent who wouldn't conform.

Just before the Winter Olympics in 1996, I went to Russia to do a report for BBC *Grandstand* – a sort of 'Where are they now?' segment about great Soviet athletes. Listening to their stories of how they were treated made me wonder again about Tasha. They spoke about the difference between those who defected and flourished and those who had remained loyal to the Soviet Union and, in some cases, had to sell their medals to survive. We filmed in the apartment of one of the players from the 1980 USSR hockey team that lost to the USA in the game dubbed the 'Miracle on Ice' – I think half of the team defected and half went back – and this guy, a bulky, big-shouldered defender, had a huge cardboard cut-out of himself in the corner. He said he regretted not defecting; he had ended up with very little and any money he makes he gives to three former teammates who are living in an asylum with no means. He gives what he can, though he has nothing. I wondered then if Tasha was living a life like this.

Tasha's disappearance came on the heels of Martina's poignant defection from behind the Iron Curtain. It seemed incomprehensible to me that Martina had not been able to see her mother after she left Czechoslovakia as a 19-year-old in 1975 – despite her being just a two-hour flight from London. She was the first of us who travelled with people around her and I'm sure a lot of that was to do with her needing to have a close-knit circle nearby because she couldn't see her family. We were young and vulnerable when we joined the tour – 16, 17, 18. With no internet or mobile phones, and maybe just two channels on TV, we didn't know anything about the world, let alone its geopolitics. I felt like I was being brave leaving Devon, where I had so much to keep me there ... but for Martina, to go to this new world and never return to her family and homeland must have been beyond daunting. Her father encouraged her to leave because he wanted her to live her dream, but she never said goodbye to her mother because she couldn't bear to. We all sacrificed a lot of normal family life and teenage friendships to pursue our careers. In the 1970s, we had to go to America to follow our dream. But for Martina, the sacrifices were just way, way more painful.

Her parents were not allowed to leave Communist-controlled Czechoslovakia to watch her play and she couldn't travel to visit them because she wouldn't have been allowed to leave. She didn't even know if her parents were able to see her first Wimbledon victory in 1978 on TV (as it turned out, they did watch it, on German TV) – and it was thanks to the intervention of the Duchess of Kent that her mother was able to get a special visa and witness her daughter's 1979 triumph on Centre Court.

CHAPTER 13

PLEASE DON'T TALK
ANY MORE

In October 1981, I was playing in the big WTA event in Brighton and happened to be staying in the same hotel as the Shadows, who had been the backing band for Cliff Richard in the 1960s. Hank Marvin and Brian Bennett were midway through a UK tour and on their evening off they wanted to come and watch me compete. They were big tennis fans. I was playing well and had beaten world No.1 Tracy Austin in the quarters. I gave them tickets and they watched me win a close match against Barbara Potter in the semis. They seemed to bring me good luck, as they then came to watch me win the final against Mima Jaušovec. I was on cloud nine, so thrilled to win a title again (my last win had been in Sydney at the end of 1979) and the home crowd was so appreciative. The lads had cheered me on and I gave them a hug at the side of the court after shaking hands with Mima and the chair umpire, before revelling in every minute of the trophy presentation with Barry Davies. I'd almost forgotten how good winning felt.

At home the following night, I was tucking into an Indian takeaway when I got a call from someone calling himself 'Cliff, Cliff Richard', and I just giggled. I have a lot of practical jokers in my life, and I thought a friend must have seen me with the Shadows and was having a laugh. The guys in the takeaway who'd handed me my chicken tikka masala were always playing pranks on me, and I thought this was another one. It eventually became apparent, though, that the voice down the telephone line genuinely was Cliff, who had been watching the Brighton tournament from home as he was also a huge tennis fan. He'd been surprised to see me celebrate so warmly with Hank and Brian.

I had told Hank and Brian that I would come and see them in concert in London the following week and gave them my number. They had passed it on to Cliff. So there he was, asking me if I'd like to go to the Shadows concert with him. I panicked … I'd never met the guy! I said I'd love to go to the concert, but I already had plans to go with my friend Sue Mappin. Cliff suggested we make it a four and Sue and I could join him and his friend Bill Latham.

I then rang Sue and said, 'I don't know if you have plans for this weekend but you'll have to drop them and come with me!' We had a really, really nice night at the concert at the Hammersmith Odeon. Sue and I joined Cliff and Bill to go backstage to see the boys and then we all went out for dinner. It was fun and we decided we would meet up again.

The next day I was flying to Japan for the Fed Cup – Virginia and I in economy, the LTA officials in first class (and Virginia had a real go at them about that: 'We are the ones playing tennis the next day…'). En route, we had a four-hour stopover at Moscow airport and Virginia took me to the caviar and champagne bar so I could try caviar for the first time – I hated it! When we arrived at the hotel in Tokyo, I received a telegram from Cliff wishing me all the best in the matches and hoping we could meet up again … so I knew he was keen. This was during our terrific Fed Cup campaign, when we made the final only to be thumped by the USA.

From Tokyo, I flew on to Australia and then to the US hard-court circuit. Cliff and I had a few chats on the phone, mostly about tennis. When I was staying at the Hoffmans in Dallas, Carole and I were watching *Morecambe and Wise* on TV and Cliff was on as a guest. I pointed him out and Carole said, 'He's too old for you!'

'Ah, but he's ever so nice,' I replied.

In March 1982 I was due to play an exhibition match in Denmark before coming back to the UK. On the phone, Cliff said he liked Copenhagen and asked if he could come and watch. I was shocked and felt a bit unsure about it – six months had passed since our only meeting – so I asked my brother Neil to come over too so that I wasn't on my own. I was the aperitif match to Borg playing Vitas Gerulaitis. I won my match in straight sets and then Cliff, Neil and I flew back to London together.

Bizarrely, the snappers were out in force. Even though we got into separate cars at the airport in London and went back to our own homes, the newspapers reported that we left together.

I'd been given flowers and gifts from the event organisers, but of course it was written that these were presents from Cliff.

We started dating then and saw as much of each other as we could, but with him recording an album and me playing the European tour before Wimbledon, it really wasn't that frequent or serious. We were, as he later said repeatedly, 'close friends'. He and I played tennis – he was a good standard, and I took him to play at Wimbledon. I was just feeding him balls and letting him have a good time. He struck the ball well. In return, he invited me to the studio where he was cutting an album. It was a lot of fun listening to him singing and meeting his fellow musicians. He had very famous friends and it was a refreshing change from my sporting life and my previous relationships. Cliff is warm and engaging and funny. We both enjoyed being introduced to each other's worlds of work and started to spend time together.

The press picked up on our ongoing friendship and went crazy. I hated the attention. Following my split with Syd Ball towards the end of 1978, I'd gone out with Greg Norman for just under a year and never experienced the media frenzy that accompanied Cliff. In my eyes Greg is more famous worldwide than Cliff, but the press virtually ignored our romance. He hadn't yet won a major but he was being billed as 'the next Nicklaus' so there was a focus on him as the next big thing in golf.

The age difference had scuppered my relationship with Syd: at 28, he wanted to retire and start up a tennis academy, but I was 21, 22, and determined to see where my career would go. Syd was one of the loveliest people I'd ever met but the timing wasn't right. Similarly, with Greg, we bonded over our respective ambitions in sport and eventually agreed to go our separate ways in order to pursue them. There wasn't much synchronicity in professional tennis and golf schedules. We travelled the world when we could be together and had a lot of fun, but it started to go wrong when Greg flew in to surprise me when I was playing in Boston in 1979. I needed to make the semi-final of that tournament to qualify for the tour final in Madison Square Garden.

I'd missed two tournaments because of injury. I knew I'd have to face Chrissie in the quarters and I was determined to stay focused and work hard. The phone rang early one morning in the room I was sharing with my doubles partner Ann Kiyomura – it was Greg, in the hotel reception! I went downstairs, not happy, because this was such a big week for me. I explained I had to put my tennis first and of course he understood.

Compared to the click-click-click of cameras that seemed to ambush Cliff and me, there's probably just one photograph out there of me with Greg. But I have to say it was a lot of fun being in Cliff's company. Although the press spotlight bothered me, I put up with it. Cliff got on well with my family and friends. They were impressed by his behaviour to fans – he never flinched when approached in public. He was always gracious and wrote admirers a personalised autograph. Everyone liked him, but my parents were wary. They didn't like the age difference (16 years, it was the same as theirs). I was 25, Cliff was 41. Dad warned me that an age gap becomes a problem as you get older.

I played badly at Wimbledon that summer, losing in the first round, troubled by a knee injury. I flew to Dallas to see the Hoffmans, who put me in touch with a surgeon in the hope that I could play in the US Open. The surgeon wanted to operate on my swollen knee, but he warned that the ensuing recovery programme would mean I'd miss the US Open. For a second opinion, I called 'Fingers Matthews', a fantastic physio back home, who told me, 'Get yourself back here.' Thank goodness I did because, sure enough, the knee issue was a knock-on effect of a hamstring problem and didn't need an op. So I was back in the flat I'd bought in Wimbledon in 1979. As I had been expecting to be in America in the build-up to the US Open, I had agreed to let a girl called Jill stay there. She worked in South Africa and was dating Cliff's housemate Bill Latham. The arrangement was that she could stay in my flat while they went on their annual two-week guys' holiday to Spain or to Cliff's house in Portugal.

But now I was receiving treatment on my hamstring and trying to get fit enough in time to fly back to the States, and Jill was in my flat. I was depressed, injured, really down, and I kept calling Cliff for a chat because I was upset and wanted to talk to him about it. He was, I thought, my boyfriend. With Syd and Greg, we'd make the effort to be there for each other on the phone even if we were in different parts of the world. But Cliff wasn't replying to my messages. Meanwhile Jill, in my flat, was chatting happily every day to Bill, who was holidaying with Cliff. I knew something was strange. I asked Jill to ask Bill to ask Cliff to get in touch. He didn't. Forty-eight hours later I got a call from one of Cliff's friends, on Cliff's behalf, saying Cliff just wanted to cool it. Our 'relationship' was over.

Really? He had asked his friend to pass this message on over the phone? I flew back to the States, upset and angry. During those five months, we hadn't been seeing a lot of each other – I was doing the tour, he was doing an album – and, from my side, it didn't feel like we had reached a point that merited being dumped. It felt to me like a friendship that had the potential to develop, rather than a significant romantic relationship, because we had not taken it far, and I'm not just talking about sex. When my previous relationships had ended, we'd talked it through, explaining why it wasn't working or couldn't work. I was absolutely floored. It was so odd. And Cliff didn't speak to me for weeks.

Eventually he did make contact and said he'd missed me, and could we be friends? I said yes, and we started to go out for dinners. There was a brief stage when I hoped something might be rekindled but I soon realised we were just going to be friends. The press, of course, continued to focus on us as a couple whenever we were seen out together, but from that time onwards, we were always with other people, never *à deux*. And this sort of friendship continued for a year or so. We might have dinner with family and friends. When Giovanna mentioned she was going to Florida, I asked her to bring back some peanut butter and jelly – the kind that comes rippled together in a jar – because I knew Cliff loved it and couldn't get it in Britain. That was the extent of it and we have remained friends ever since.

The only thing we have fallen out about is the fact that he kept harping on about me in interviews – 'I didn't love her enough to propose,' and so forth. This went on and on. I'm very private and it really upset me. It wasn't as if I was pining for him or still held a torch. I was desperate for Cliff to meet someone else and take the focus off me but that never happened. Jill Dando, who I used to see at BBC Television Centre and who was a sort of mentor in the early days of my broadcasting career, approached me one day in the canteen and asked if I'd mind if she tried to make a go of it with Cliff. I couldn't have been happier to give her my blessing. But that obviously didn't come to anything either. And still his interviews kept mentioning me, turning our brief close friendship into a long-running saga. Six years later, when I'd married Lance, we woke up to the headline: WHY I COULDN'T MARRY SUE – BY CLIFF. I said to Lance, 'Bad luck, mate, you've just done it!'

It was bizarre how Cliff leaped from putting an end to our friendship casually via a mate on the phone to declaring to the world that he couldn't propose to me. I never felt that it had reached anywhere near the stage when you're thinking long term. It felt like the early days of a relationship. It was romantic, but not that affectionate. He was very Christian. Syd and Greg were much more important in my life than this brief time with Cliff, and yet this relationship has always been hanging around my neck. It's the one that just won't go away. The press coverage it spawned totally changed my life and put me off any unnecessary interaction with the media. It's frightening not to be able to control your own truth.

I begged Cliff to stop mentioning me and to have some respect for my marriage, and for Lance. It would have been so easy for him to say to any inquiring journalist, 'Sue is happily married to Lance now, let's leave it.' I have a cartoon framed in my loo at home of me having wrapped a racket over a reporter's head with Cliff lying on a sunbed in the foreground. The caption reads: 'I'm sorry, Cliff doesn't want to talk to you at the moment'– a nice allusion to his chart-topping hit, 'We Don't Talk Anymore'. I think it looks silly now that he's still talking about a relationship that was never really more than a friendship 40 years later, but it came up again on Piers Morgan's *Life Stories* in 2021.

Piers asked Cliff outright: 'Did you love Sue?'

And Cliff said, 'I loved being with her, but it wasn't something that was going to lead to our marriage.'

No, it wasn't!

When I think about my time with Cliff, I think – if you forget about the press attention – there was nothing unusual about two people meeting and giving the relationship a try but reverting to just being friends pretty quickly. What was unusual is one party to the relationship still talking about it decades later to anyone who would listen and then framing it as a near miss in terms of marriage. Twenty years later, I would read statements such as 'I didn't love her quite enough to marry her', and I'd think, *He can't be talking about me, surely? It never got to that level.*' Or: 'I was seriously considering marriage, but a friend told me it's not whether you can live with her but whether you can live without her.' Another of his comments was: 'She asked me what I was doing next Saturday and I didn't like that, it was a bit intrusive or serious.'

Really? I don't ask my husband what we're doing next Saturday … I tell him. It seems ridiculous to me that someone who is apparently considering marriage doesn't like being asked what he is doing next Saturday.

I never spoke about our relationship. I kept quiet throughout, but it painted a picture of me just waiting at the altar, waiting for him to say 'yes'. Yet this relationship didn't enter a universe where I was considering marriage to him.

Lance and I still see Cliff now and again. We went to his fiftieth-birthday party, and joined his sixtieth-birthday cruise. We also went to support him at the Royal Albert Hall a few years ago after that horrible BBC/police raid. There's no animosity there. And it will come as no great surprise that I say all of the above, because I spoke to Cliff in person about this many times and made a direct request to his agent and his manager to stop bringing up our time together in interviews. It's been frustrating. I really enjoyed our early friendship, but the hurt that came with all his talk, not just for me, but for Lance – who's been constantly reminded why someone else wouldn't marry his wife – is something that is just not fair. It's not respectful. I've hated the Cliff-Sue storyline played out in the press. If I had my time again, I wouldn't go out with Cliff. If someone had told me that the relationship would last a few months but I would still be hearing about it 40 years later, I wouldn't have gone near it.

I learned to try and laugh it off. Des Lynam was all for me going to interview Cliff on that rainy Wimbledon day in 1996 when he was asked to entertain the Centre Court spectators while they waited for play to resume. There Des and I were, yet again trying to come up with topics of conversation to fill the time between reruns of old matches, when the All England Club's secretary invited Cliff to give an impromptu concert. You have to hand it to Cliff, he is the consummate performer.

'I never thought I'd actually play on Centre Court,' he quipped, as he got the crowd clapping, swaying and singing along under their umbrellas and rain ponchos. Des saw all the girls behind Cliff standing up, singing and waving their arms as if they were his backing group – Pam Shriver, Liz Smylie, Andrea Jaeger, Virginia, Martina, Conchita Martínez and Gigi Fernández – and, full of mischief, he said. 'Come on, get down there, Sue!'

I said, 'I'm not doing it, Des. It will be on the front page of the papers tomorrow … "Sue and Cliff reunited at Wimbledon".'

Des was so funny. 'Come on, you've got to do it for the programme. And we'll just have a laugh about it.' And I thought maybe we could have a laugh about it, you know, because it was that far down the line, 15 years on and I'm very happily married.

So I agreed to Des's playful request and went down and stood at the bottom of the stairs, waiting to be allowed entry by a steward. All the while, Cliff, in a pastel-checked jacket with his AELTC member's badge on the lapel and mint-green tie, was giving it his all, belting out 'Singin' in the Rain' and 'All Shook Up', and his own hits, 'The Young Ones', 'Bachelor Boy', 'Summer Holiday', 'Living Doll' and 'Congratulations' to an audience that included a rather bemused Joanna Lumley and Prince and Princess Michael of Kent. He christened his new backing singers 'the Supremes', as in 'supremo tennis players', and said they should have brought their rackets to play air guitar.

As Des said, 'Who needs tennis, the man is an absolute star … The only thing that worries me is that Cliff didn't know it was on television and we might get one hell of a bill!'

In 2021, I embellished the story on our farewell *A Question of Sport* tour and said that as well as 'Bachelor Boy' and 'Living Doll', Cliff was also singing 'We Don't Talk Anymore'. The truth is, I didn't join him because just as I was about to go up the stairs he started singing 'Bachelor Boy', so I thought better of it. The steward looked at me and said, 'Sue, I'd give up now if I were you.' And I nearly cried with laughter.

CHAPTER 14

DOWN A BLIND ALLEY
IN SPAIN

A long-term injury is an athlete's greatest fear, but the nature of an accident is that it happens when you least expect it. That was the case when in August 1980 I met up with my parents, who were visiting my aunt in Spain, for a break from the tour. The four of us went to visit some friends of my aunt for lunch. It was a lovely, long, relaxing meal, but because I was keeping to an athlete's regimen and my parents were having a drink after lunch, I said I'd go and help clear up. In the kitchen a couple of ladies were washing up and I said, 'Do you have any tea towels?' They indicated the laundry room next door.

I opened the door and saw a dog there. It was a mongrel that looked a bit like an Afghan hound – quite tall, slim, with a long, pointy nose. I've always loved dogs and as this dog looked up at me from its basket and went 'Gggggrrrrr.' I said, 'Oh, don't you be silly,' and I leaned across it to reach the tea towels on the side. The dog launched up like a rocket and bit me twice on the right side of my face. It had its teeth right inside my mouth. All I remember is being in total shock and seeing blood everywhere. I wet one of the towels with cold water from the utility-room tap and held it over my face. Without looking in a mirror, I knew I'd been comprehensively savaged, cut through my eye, my cheek and my lips. Even the inside of my mouth was bleeding.

I went and found my parents and said, 'I've got to go to the hospital.' My poor aunt's friends were absolutely mortified. There was a chorus of shocked exclamations and, because they'd all been drinking, one of the ladies in the kitchen said she'd drive me to the hospital. That offer was vetoed as everyone wanted to accompany me. They all ended up piling into a couple of taxis while the kitchen help drove me and Mum to the front of the hospital. My mum kept wanting to see my wounds. And I said no, no, no. And I kept holding this thing over it because I didn't want it bleeding everywhere.

She said, 'I want to see the damage before you go in there.'

I put her off. I knew it was bad. We'd pulled up outside the hospital and she made me remove the damp tea towel – and then promptly passed out. Honestly, you couldn't make it up! I said, 'Dad, you look after her. I'll go to the hospital.'

An A&E medic came out and saw Mum. 'Is she all right?'

Dad said, 'She'll be fine,' and pointed to me. 'But can you take her in?'

I remember sitting in the waiting room in the Spanish hospital trying to swat away the flies buzzing around my head. The doctor ran a lot of tests because it was soon clear I couldn't see out of my right eye. The dog had ripped off the lower eyelid, and it was hanging down. I asked if I would be blind and the doctor was reassuring. He said my eye was in trauma and I should regain my sight within a day or two, but he couldn't absolutely confirm that. I realised the wait to find out would be agonising.

And with sight in only one eye, I'd never be able to resume my life in tennis … the implications were starting to sink in. The doctor said he'd stitch it back up, but warned that he was going to have to do it with the stitches they had in his A&E unit, not the really fine cosmetic ones.

'I want to make sure that I put the lower lid back correctly because the fine ones can break. And I want to make sure that your lid is put back in one piece.'

The tear duct, which had been ripped away, he said he'd try to restore as best he could. And then he stitched up the cheek, and the upper and lower lip. He predicted the inside of my mouth would heal quickly. I had 25 stitches in total. The suturing process and subsequent inflammation hurt like hell.

Potential blindness was not the only problem, nor the only terrifying prospect. The owner of the dog had confirmed that it had not had a rabies shot. I was not allowed to leave the country for three weeks while I was monitored for potential symptoms.

'And if rabies develops, what's the treatment?' I asked.

'Not very pleasant,' the doctor said. 'Needles in the stomach.'

So I went back to my aunt's place in a state of shock. I was trying not to panic, trying to think positively, trying to shrug off the pain. We were staying in a nice little apartment beneath her house. My mum came into my room and sat with me and sweetly tried to comfort me.

'Never mind,' she said. 'All things happen for the best and I'm sure something good will come from this.'

And I said, 'Get out! What possible good can come from this? Not only can I not see out of my eye, I'm going to be scarred for life and I may never play tennis again. What good can you possibly see coming out of this?'

To be fair to myself, even today I can't see any good that came out of it. I was distressed and in pain, and I genuinely thought my tennis career was over and that I was going to be disfigured for life. Within 36 hours, the sight in my right eye returned just as the doctor had hoped, though I was told I'd have to have multiple surgeries in the future to sort out the scar tissue. My aunt bought me these massive Jackie Onassis sunglasses so that I could go to a restaurant and no one would stare at my balloon face. I looked like I'd gone ten rounds with Mike Tyson – battered, dreadfully bruised, and so puffy. I remember someone said something funny over dinner in this restaurant and as I laughed, a torrent of pus flowed down my face. It was awful. I put everyone off their meal. Fortunately, I didn't develop rabies either.

I had further surgery later that year because the stitches that were used left entrenched marks, which thankfully could be fixed. I had all 25 stitches redone with finer thread and the sutures remained visible across my face for five weeks. I was told

I'd need another procedure in about ten years, because the scar tissue would make my eye sag and the lower lid would be pulled down. I returned for that eight years later and that doctor tried to move the tear duct a bit … but I'm so lucky to have all the elements of my eye. I can never wear lipstick because it bleeds into the surrounding skin – not that I ever want to wear a huge amount of make-up anyway. When I look in the mirror I can see a big bulge of hard scar tissue under my eye.

My face was very sensitive during recovery. I didn't play the US Open. The most difficult aspect was dealing with the tear duct and the trauma of the whole incident. It made me terribly fearful of dogs. When I returned to the UK, the press pack were waiting outside my home in Wimbledon, trying to get pictures of me, and my face was still blown up like a balloon. What was I going to do?

At night, I drove up to my brother's because no one really knew I had a brother. He was running a pub in St Albans and I asked if I could come and stay to escape and recover in peace, even though I knew the pub had a resident dog called Murphy. An Irish wolfhound, he was the size of a miniature pony. But Murphy loved me and I loved Murphy. He was the friendliest dog, absolutely wonderful, and as I walked down through the gate of this pub, Murphy spotted me. In fright, I flattened myself up against the car park wall as Murphy came hurtling towards me, a million miles an hour, and jumped up and put his paws on my shoulder, licking me to death. I was screaming, 'Murphy, get off,' and the more I screamed, the more he thought I was playing and the more excited he got. But he absolutely won me over and I felt secure again with dogs.

Although I don't remember any of the pain of the actual dog attack, I do recall the pain of the stitches and the throbbing that came with them. But if I cut myself now with a little knife when I'm dicing the carrots, I forget I once had my face ripped open and needed 25 emergency stitches. As for the pressure in television to maintain a youthful appearance? It's never been an issue. I'm not the sort of person who would choose to have cosmetic enhancements or invasive procedures – and Lance wouldn't want that either. With all my scar tissue, it's no Botox for me!

CHAPTER 15

GORDON BENNETT, YOU'VE RETIRED!

In 1983, I started to get terrible pains in my shins and my Achilles tendon. I played my entire career in Green Flash plimsolls, which had no padding like the shoes of today. We didn't have shock-absorbing cushioned soles and bespoke orthotic trainers. My game relied on me running a lot and I was now suffering the inevitable wear and tear. We now know that one hour of intense fitness training is far better than four hours, but I was brought up with the idea that the more miles you put on the clock, the better you're going to be. I'd probably overtrained. By 1984, I had a shin splint down both legs and a torn Achilles tendon that wouldn't heal. I went back and forth to physios and had a lot of treatment but I was forced to miss tournaments. I constantly came back too early and suffered another setback. It was frustrating.

Medical experts advised me to avoid playing on cement and indoor hard courts. This took up a lot of the tour and most of my time in the States. Finding clay, grass and some indoor carpet (although doctors didn't like that surface either) was difficult. Besides, grass was my least favourite surface. I found myself playing fewer and fewer events and my ranking started to drop, which meant I could only qualify for the main tour events by being awarded a wild card. I was lucky to receive many of them in the States, but then came the Australian tour.

My friend Karen Scott was the tournament director of the New South Wales Open in Sydney. We'd met as teens when we both dated an Aussie doubles team (Syd Ball and Bob Giltinan). The dating didn't work out but our friendship has lasted for life. Karen gave me a wild card into this pre-Aussie Open event but was criticised for doing so by the Australian tennis association. At that time, two conglomerates, IMG and ProServ, represented and managed players. Karen ran ProServ Australia and they presumed she had given me a wild card because I was her best friend and a ProServ client. She took on the critics in the press, revealing that first, I was an IMG client, and second, I had an established role in bridging the gap between the players and the tournament sponsor. These were the early days of corporate hospitality in sport, and Karen would ask me to pop into the sponsor's lunch and give a talk and meet the guests. I was happy to do that – but I hated being the centre of a public row.

A public debate then began about whether I should be awarded a wild card for the Open itself. The head coach of Australian juniors, Ray Ruffels, expressed the view that wild cards should not be given to older players who had slid down the rankings, no matter what they'd achieved in their careers. If I'd been in his position, I'd have agreed. I didn't want to be taking places in the draw away from young people, trying to live the dream. I decided to decline, regardless of an offer.

I was now ranked 63 in the world. There were 64 places in the Open draw, but take away the places for qualifiers and wild cards, and I didn't make the cut. I was staying in Karen's apartment in Sydney and, against the fabulous backdrop of that city, I had a long, hard think about my future. Where could I play? When could I play? Could I string enough tournaments together to raise my ranking? With the American indoor season scheduled after the Aussie trip, my prospects looked bleak. If I couldn't play often, and particularly if I couldn't compete on the American indoor circuit, life in the second tier beckoned and it wasn't appealing. As I was in Melbourne, I decided to play the qualifiers to try and earn a berth in the draw for the Open. Needless to say, my heart wasn't in it and I couldn't wait to get off court.

I'd had enough. It had been a two-year downward spiral. I'd had a real resurgence after winning the tournament in Brighton in 1981 – beating Tracy, who was world No.1, in the quarters – but from then until 1984, my love of competing waned. I had tried to tap back into my love of the game in order to improve my form. In 1982, when I'd had a dip, I invited Sue Mappin to come on tour with me for company. We entered a couple of tournaments in Italy, then decided to drive to an event in Austria and on to France. It was like a road trip and we had a fabulous time.

At the Italian Open, the women's matches were either early in the morning or in the evening – the men's singles were scheduled at primetime. It was hard to get on the practice courts too. It was very much a two-tiered system. Sue and I had lots of time to kill and we sat in the stands watching the men's matches, rating the players for best legs! (Adriano Panatta won.) It wasn't all about playing big matches; sometimes we looked up somewhere to play, got out the road atlas and tried to get there. It was hilarious, trying not very successfully to map-read across the Italian Alps. On court, my results did not please me. I used to think there was something to learn from losing a match, but I was beyond that stage. The more losses I had, the more depressing and hurtful they became.

I spoke a lot to Mr Roberts. I spoke to my parents. They knew I wasn't happy. Arthur's point was that if your body's gone, your body's gone. You're not going to get it back. If I was playing today with those injuries, I would have been back at 100 per cent fitness in a few months, but it was a different era. Even the Dallas Cowboys and their fancy hi-tech machines couldn't put me back together.

And so, in January 1985, I made the decision to quit.

Although we admire the longevity of Roger and Rafa, Serena and Venus, few players of my era played beyond the age of 30 (Billie Jean and Martina being the honourable exceptions). Borg's retreat from the sport at 25 was considered young, but only by a few years. In the women's game, we started to see this incredible conveyor belt of young American talent roll in: Tracy Austin, Pam Shriver, Kathy Rinaldi, Andrea Jaeger. We sat in the locker room like sixth formers assessing the impact of these 14-year-olds. Gosh, get the popcorn out!

It was a fantastic era. Tracy, so quick around the court, was phenomenally driven and drilled her groundstrokes with unerring accuracy. Pam arrived like a meteor, reaching the US Open final when she was just 16. Andrea was such a clever competitor. Pulling on her bunches, she moped around on court and looked like she would rather be anywhere else, all the while making you look an absolute idiot. Rosie Casals and her partner Connie Spooner, the tour trainer, always cheered us up. We were all rivals but we banded together whenever we lost to one of 'the kids' and went out for consolatory piña coladas – the cocktails didn't taste like alcohol but you felt you were drowning your sorrows. I remember Wendy Turnbull losing to either Andrea or Tracy and us all clubbing together to take her out for dinner.

It didn't take long for these youngsters to dominate. With them, the locker-room atmosphere started to change. They were accompanied by coaches and parents. Entourages were coming in. With more money in the game, players could afford to have travelling coaches and hitting partners. Martina even had a dog walker. (She had a chihuahua-type dog called KD; I think it was named after the Canadian singer k.d. lang, but we nicknamed it 'Killer Dog'. Trust me, it was an apt name. It used to sit in her bag, and if anyone approached, it would growl and prepare to launch itself at them. Not a scenario I wanted to revisit.)

The tight-knit camaraderie that sustained us in the late 1970s was diluting, but for a good reason. Billie Jean's initiatives, consolidated by Chrissie and Martina, had turned women's tennis into a blockbuster show, inspiring these young girls who started to emerge from all over the world. I'm grateful to have played in an era when tennis was a fun way of earning a living, rather than for making money. I remember dining in San Lorenzo during Wimbledon in the mid-1980s with four mates. We were having a great time. On a nearby table of eight a young Steffi Graf was sitting with her parents, her coach, her agent and so on, and I thought, *How sad, there is not one person her age with her.* The new generation would have more lucrative careers than I had: more tournaments, more prize money, more sponsorship options. But I wouldn't change a thing about my time in tennis – even though I knew when I retired that I would have to work for the rest of my life.

Following my announcement, I received more than 30 consolation messages, mostly from media outlets. I ditched the majority, keeping just three: from my parents, from the Hoffmans and from someone called Gordon Bennett, who I presumed was a friend having a laugh and ringing up to say, 'Gordon Bennett, you've retired!' I called 'Gordon' back on the number he'd left, wondering which friend was taking the mickey. Gordon Bennett turned out to be the boss of Channel 7 in Australia, and he saved my life. There and then on the phone he offered me a job, suggesting I fly over next year on an eight-week contract to work as a commentator and tennis reporter. I'd done the odd bit of guest punditry for Channel 7 when I'd been on the sidelines with injury or been knocked out early. I was aware of how they worked.

John Barrett was involved in the set-up too. Evonne came in for the long fortnight of the Open. The plan was I'd go from tournament to tournament during the Aussie season – Hobart, Brisbane, Perth, Adelaide, Tasmania, Sydney and, of course, the Open in Melbourne. What a glorious thought: two months in Australia, just talking about tennis. I agreed enthusiastically, and Gordon called a week later to talk finance. Thank goodness he was called Gordon Bennett. If he'd been called Gordon Smith, I'd have ignored his message ... and might never have got started in television.

Meanwhile I had a glorious month with Karen in Melbourne and Sydney. We went to the cricket, had days out on Bondi Beach, enjoyed dinner parties at the home of John Alexander, a member of Australia's 1977 Davis Cup-winning team, singing along to Roy Orbison songs. It was a hoot. Karen and I have called each other 'Toss' since an early occasion at Wimbledon when Karen, who was managing two young Aussie players, referred to an official as a 'f***ing idiot'. I fixed her with a steely eye and said, 'Karen, we are at Wimbledon. You do not call someone in that position a f***ing idiot.' Dramatic pause. 'You call him a tosser!'

The last time Karen and I had lunch together, when Lance and I were on holiday in Florida, we were in a restaurant called Turtles. The pair of us were laughing so hard that a complete stranger walked over and said, 'You two must have known each other for many years, because you can only laugh that hard with a long friendship.' We told him he was most correct.

Anyway, while we were gallivanting around the beaches and bays of southern Australia, Karen said I must contact 'Hilly' – David Hill – a top TV executive I'd often met for the odd lunch and dinner with Karen. He had helped media mogul Kerry Packer revolutionise the way cricket was broadcast with innovations for the one-day games of the World Series Cricket competition in 1977. One of his initiatives was to introduce former players as presenters, rather than pundits. Years later, he would become a boss at Sky Television in the UK and give me my big break. With my experiences co-commentating alongside Gerry Williams and my guest appearances on Channel 7, I was mulling over the possibility of a secondary career in television. I needed to find *something*. My total prize money in tennis – US$878,701 as calculated in 1985 (which equates to about $2.5 million today) – wasn't going to stretch a lifetime. I was just 29. I needed to earn my living.

I flew back to London via a solo holiday in Fiji, arriving in a biting-cold, grey drizzle, and headed to my flat in Wimbledon. That's when it hit me. I woke up the next morning and realised I didn't know what to do. I didn't have to go for a run, I didn't have to train or play. I didn't have a schedule to plan, courts to book or flights to arrange. I didn't have friends to go out with in the evening. All my friends were on tour or in the States. I had nothing and no one, except my family and friends down in Devon. I felt utterly miserable. Life as I had dreamed and planned and known it since I was 10 or 11 was over. I had spent 11 years travelling the world, playing tennis and having an absolute ball. I thought, *That's it; the best part of my life has gone.*

I could look back with pride on my achievements. I was a Grand Slam winner and a Wimbledon and Aussie Open semi-finalist. I'd been ranked No.3 in the world behind two supreme champions who shaped the women's game. Throughout my entire career, Chrissie and Martina had juggled the top two spots in the world rankings (a remarkable dominance of the No.1 perch that was broken only for two weeks by Evonne, and 21 weeks by Tracy). My forehand had earned a reputation of its own. After an injury-plagued year in 1978, I'd fought back and reached six finals, claiming three titles, and was named Comeback Player of the Year by my fellow players. I'd been a member of the Wightman Cup squad in an unparalleled mini-era of success for the GB team. In total, I won 15 WTA singles titles and 12 doubles titles and played my heart out. I think I met Billie Jean's requirement of leaving my guts on the court to beat the likes of Chrissie, Martina, Evonne, Tracy, Virginia, Rosie Casals, Andrea Jaeger and Pam Shriver.

What would that 11-year-old girl pocketing blades of grass on her first visit to Wimbledon say? I think she'd be pretty amazed. I may never have beaten Billie Jean in a Wimbledon final 7–5 or 6–4 in a deciding set in the manner I visualised as I pounded balls against my garage wall, but I did beat her ... on the carpet at Houston in 1982 with a score of 6–2, 6–1, even if she was 39! I could also point to my crucial role in setting up the deciding tie in our thrilling Wightman Cup triumph over the US team Billie Jean had captained in 1978. I'd had to draw on a spirit of feistiness I'd always admired in her. Talking about going down to the wire.

For 11 years as a pro player, I'd woken up every morning with a goal to strive for and had an absolute ball. On paper, I was, and am, very proud of my tennis career, and thankful that I loved the whole adventure. But the next page of my life was blank, and that was terrifying. I hadn't prepared myself for this. Tennis had enabled me to pursue my dream in a parallel life to the real world. Tennis had structure, rules, referees. If you lose, you don't die; you can come back tomorrow and have another go. (A thought Boris Becker expressed so memorably after losing to Peter Doohan at Wimbledon in 1987: 'I lost a tennis match. I didn't lose a war. Nobody died.').

Without that secure construct to my everyday life, what would I do?

The series of tournaments leading up to the 1986 Australian Open that Gordon Bennett had engaged me for seemed a long way off. I couldn't just kick my heels until then. I still loved playing and I couldn't just drop it, so without pushing my Achilles too much I started to play tennis at the David Lloyd Club in Heston. David asked me to join him and his other coaches to hit with his newly formed Slater Squad.

David and businessman Jim Slater formed a squad of young boys to train away from the LTA. They would receive coaching every day at the club and otherwise go to boarding school at Reed's School in Cobham. The squad included Tim Henman (aged ten), Jamie Delgado and James Davidson, who all played pro tennis and are still involved today, two other boys who are now pros at Reed's, plus a former Australian junior champion in James Baily. I loved working with the youngsters, they were so enthusiastic and incredibly talented. By then I had moved to Esher so I was asked on many occasions to leave my car at the club and drop the boys back at school in the minibus as the school was so close to my home. This was when I introduced naughty treats into Tim's diet – hamburgers, chocolate and cola – for which he berates me in jest to this day.

• • •

Mr Roberts remained a part of my tennis life until the end. Having set me on my path in his selfless idiosyncratic way, he saw my career out. I went to visit him in early 1986 when I was down with my parents and we talked about all things past and my possible future projects. He knew I had the tennis commentary role for Channel 7; he knew where I was heading in my post-tennis life. I never stopped looking up to him and I desperately wanted him to be proud of me. I really cared about what he thought of me. He was 82 then, and I heard he wasn't well a few months later – he was far too private to let me know personally. I phoned to ask if I could come and visit. He was bed-bound by then and he told his wife to tell me to remember him as he was. That frightened me, but I knew never to cross him. I called often to see how he was but he didn't want his wife to give me too much information. Then I got the call to say he'd gone. I asked about the funeral, but he had requested family only. That was so him. No fuss.

Mr Roberts was such a huge part of my life and I owe him everything. We had the most incredibly strong bond. He totally understood my character, my nature. We were more like father and daughter than coach and player. He was uncompromising and tough when I was young but, as Giovanna remembers, he was also kind – he'd always buy us Orange Maid ice lollies after training if she came to watch me. It took a lot of getting to know the man behind the cranky exterior. When the tax laws changed in 1979, I'd moved back to the UK and our coaching relationship relied once again on regular telephone calls, not weekly airmail letters. By then he was 75, and he wasn't taking on new kids to coach. He did less and less, but he was there for me. He always answered the phone.

At various stages, he found two people he trusted to work with me when I needed support on the tour. There was Bob Howe, a former Grand Slam mixed-doubles champion from Australia, and the former player Joyce Williams. They both knew not to change my game, just to encourage me and be there as moral support. That was fine by me. And of course, Mr Roberts had never travelled with me. As he said, 'I can't help you when you're out on court, so what's the point?'

I just wish he had lived long enough to see some of what I went on to do outside of tennis, because in some ways, although one Grand Slam win and a world No.3 ranking is good, I would have loved to have been more successful for him. The matches I lost hurt deeply because I felt I'd let him down. I wish he had seen that the values he taught me set me up to go where no female former athlete had gone before – to sit in the famous *Grandstand* chair, to front the coverage of BBC Sport's 'crown jewels' for more than 25 years, to interview live on Centre Court the first British Wimbledon men's champion since Fred Perry. He would have had a quiet smile about that, and perhaps a tear in his eye.

CHAPTER 16

HUSBAND, HOMES AND HOUNDS

My husband doesn't want to be in this book. When he read Roy Keane's autobiography, the only thing he learned about Roy's wife was her first name, and he likes that approach. But I want to say a few more words about Lance. After all, we've been married for 34 years. He's my best friend, my rock, and he makes me laugh every day. He has the best sense of humour and I can't imagine my life without him. So bad luck, Lance, here's a little bit more on you.

We met soon after I retired from the tour when I was working in a specialist coaching role at the David Lloyd Club in Heston, where Lance was a member. I was there to bring on three very talented young girls and also to work with the boys in the Slater Squad – Tim Henman, Jamie Delgado and Co – who were hoping to become professional players. It was a fun set-up; I knew all the other coaches and got to know some nice people who were members. I didn't know Lance to speak to but we seemed to have a few mutual friends. I confided in one of the head pros, Donald Watt, that I wanted to know more about Lance. He said he was great fun, a very nice guy, fit and athletic, but obviously a self-taught player. His forehand was okay but his backhand looked like he was using a machete to fight his way out of a jungle.

We got to know each other better on a members' tennis holiday in Portugal when I was one of the coaches. One evening when we were back in the UK, I stayed late at the tennis club to get supper because I was having a new kitchen fitted in my house in Esher. Lance was also there and it turned out he was fitting a kitchen in his new place. We had supper together and decided to go out the next night to a restaurant instead of eating again at the club while our kitchens were out of action. Pretty soon we were a couple. We kept our relationship quiet for a long time; no one was aware except our very close friends. When we got engaged, the news crept out and he hated the attention it brought from certain parts of the press. He was a detective in the Metropolitan Police at that stage, and it shocked him when reporters doorstepped him at the station for a photo. Incredible, really. We ended up giving the press a photo of us to send them on their way.

Stuart Higgins, then a senior reporter on the *Sun* (he would go on to become the paper's editor), wanted to buy pictures of our wedding. No chance. Stuart thought I was saying no to negotiate a better deal. 'Oh, you're driving a hard bargain,' he said as he kept putting the money up.

I said, 'Stuart, you're not getting this. We don't want to sell our wedding.'

'Everyone's got a price,' he said.

'Honestly, we don't,' I insisted.

This put Lance off so much that we decided that he might come down to Australia when I was working on Channel 7 and we could just go and get married there, as we had lots of friends in Melbourne and Sydney. I didn't want a big wedding in a church. We were planning to do that when Stuart called and said, 'I hear you're getting married in Australia.' Argh! In the end, Lance and I decided we'd just slip into a registry office. We learned that to have a civil ceremony, you have to marry in your borough. We didn't have much choice of venue.

There was a rather obscure place near Ashford in Surrey, above a butcher's in a row of shops and opposite a pub. That seemed to be ideal. We gave the registrar our notice of intention to marry – a legal requirement – and thought if news got out, we'd do something else, but no one twigged. In those four weeks before the ceremony, we didn't tell anybody other than our parents. On the day of the wedding we were obsessed with doing it without the press finding out. No one was present except for two of our friends, Hugh and his wife Serena. Hugh turned up with a new camera and had decided that he now knew all about shutter speeds and exposure and would move off auto and set up the camera manually. He rattled off a few shots at the registry office. These were the days when you sent off your films to be developed at Boots or Snappy Snaps. We have just one photo of our wedding (tail between legs, Hugh). It is completely black from the bottom of the photo to the head and shoulders of two smiling faces. We were signing the register but we could be anywhere. Credit to Hugh for not just saying the photos got lost in the post. We have it framed, it's hilarious.

At the last minute, we invited a group of friends to come away with us for the weekend. The instructions were to join us at our house at 3pm, then we would drive up in convoy to Wales. And they all came on the honeymoon: 20 of us took over one hotel. We had an absolute blast for three nights.

I couldn't resist sending a piece of wedding cake to Stuart Higgins with the message, 'Sorry you missed it.'

Stuart sent us back a message: 'You beat me. Well done! Congratulations.' He sent us a bottle of champagne and then took us out for lunch later to celebrate in person. That was a nice ending to the story.

When we met, I lived in a modern detached house in Esher and Lance lived in Pinner in north London. On a night out with a crowd of friends, the debate on where we should live got heated as the beers flowed. He lost the toss and Esher became our home. Very soon I realised I had married someone who had an illness, a compulsion. He couldn't stop knocking down walls and moving front doors. My parents often visited and loved my modern home. Within a year, Lance had moved us into an old house that had been lying empty for eight years on a private estate called Burwood Park in Walton-on-Thames. It hadn't been updated since it was built many years previously.

The exterior was lovely and so was the location, but inside … oh, my word! Off Lance went, tearing the place apart in order to rebuild it. My parents came for Christmas and my Dad's face was a picture. He kept walking around the bare bones of the house, shaking his head as he questioned Lance, 'Are you sure you know what you're doing, son?'

I have two huge regrets when I think of my Dad. The first is that he never saw that house finished, because it ended up being wonderful. The second is that when he came to stay, I had lost my job with David Lloyd and was unemployed. The unfinished house and my lack of an income worried him. I was always very close to my parents and that Christmas visit in 1989 stands out as an emotional milestone. Dad came with me one morning to walk my Rottie CoCo around the beautiful woodland of Burwood Park. Midway along our stroll, he stopped and took my hand and said if anything happened to him, would I make sure I looked after Mum. I told him of course I would. 'No,' he said with feeling. '*Promise* me.' And I did. On their way home to Devon a week later Dad had a stroke in the car and died in hospital. He must have known his time was nearly up.

Dad never saw my second career in television kick off and that's a huge shame. He would have been so proud. I'm sure he could never have imagined that I would go on to do the things I've done in television. He loved sport and he would have been beside himself to see how my career panned out at the BBC, much more so than my mum, who just wanted me to be happy. Dad was 84 when he died, leaving Mum a widow at 68.

I honoured my promise and took care of her. She came on at least two holidays a year with us, and to Florida when we had a home there. She was one of the most well-travelled pensioners you can imagine, and still had a BA silver card at the age of 93. We went to the fjords, to Barbados, Mauritius, LA and New York. She was great company to have around. When I was working in the States on one occasion, she flew out with Lance. The plan was that I would finish my job and meet up with them for a holiday. I'd asked Lance to pack some extra clothes for me and, of course, that would be the occasion he got stopped at Customs and had his suitcase searched. The expression on the face of the Customs official was apparently quite something when he looked up from the lingerie he'd found in Lance's suitcase, eyes flicking between my mum and Lance. They both fell about laughing. My favourite trip was a round-the-world journey Mum and I made alone, taking in Hong Kong, Sydney and New Zealand, where I'd set up a reunion for her with her brother John. It was such an emotional journey to the other side of the world as they hadn't seen each other for more than 40 years.

I was thrilled that Mum reached her hundredth birthday in 2021, still living in her own home. I have a treasured video of her opening her centenary birthday card from the Queen. That footage ensures I will always remember her voice. Sadly, her health deteriorated and she needed to move into a care home, where she contracted Covid and died of a chest infection shortly afterwards.

Friends ask what was Mum's secret for a wonderful life of almost 101 years. I'm not sure her example was one to follow. She smoked 60 cigarettes a day until she was in her fifties, only ate white bread, never drank water ('rots your boots') and loved Spam, ham and corned beef. One of her nicknames was 'Betty Six Gins'.

I don't have the words to say how much I miss her.

• • •

Once that first dilapidated house in Walton-on-Thames was rebuilt and refurbished, it was put up for sale. I was then moved from house to house: buy, sell, buy, sell. Walls down, front doors moved, extensions built. Friends were called in to help out. At weekends there would be four or five of Lance's burly detective colleagues hanging off the scaffolding while I mixed the cement; each day's work was celebrated with a barbecue in the evenings. After a series of renovations, we ended up in St George's Hill, a private gated estate in Weybridge with security guards at the entrance. Off we went again, this time doubling the size of a lovely old 'Tarrant' house, one of the original homes constructed in the 1920s by Walter George Tarrant, the builder who developed St George's Hill into a secluded enclave for celebrities and wealthy entrepreneurs. We always lived in the houses we were doing up. Lance, the 'tight git', wouldn't rent us a place while we did the hardcore demolition and stripping out of the old interiors. He would build a stud wall to create a private area for us – great, in theory, except for the dust, which gets everywhere.

By 1996, I was losing patience with this way of life and under a lot of work pressure with Wimbledon starting, followed by the Atlanta Olympics. I remember leaving the house on the Sunday before the start of the Championships; I wanted to check out the studio and bring in some outfits. All the boys were up on the scaffolding. As I got to my car in the driveway, I looked at the clothes on their hangers and they were covered in a thick layer of dust. I started shaking them out in the driveway and was soon enveloped in a thick cloud of dust particles. I heard someone cry, 'Oh, s**t. Everyone duck!' I looked up and all of them had hit the scaffold boards, hiding as best they could.

I see the funny side now but at the time I was furious. Lance knew he'd gone too far. After Wimbledon I was happy to get away to Atlanta for three weeks and stay in a lovely, clean, dust-free hotel. When I got home the progress was remarkable but I announced that this time I wanted to sell up before it was even finished. I hated the private estate; it wasn't for me. I wanted to move to the countryside. The house sold in minutes and the profit was astonishing.

But we didn't stop investing in property. We decided years ago that investing in the stock market wasn't for us; instead, we have built up a portfolio of houses that we rent out. I like to think that we are good landlords; we concentrate on acquiring nice tenants rather than seeking the most rental income. Some people have been with us for years. Lance runs the business and deals with the day-to-day management. He sometimes tests me on what I know about the houses and I'm clearly not paying enough attention.

•   •   •

Before we got married, we decided that we wanted to get a dog. I'm not sure how it happened but we ended up with a female Rottweiler puppy called CoCo. I do remember Lance showing me photos of Rottweiler puppies and I thought they were delightful, black-and-tan Labrador-type dogs, which I suppose they are. Back then, they didn't have the reputation that they seem to have today.

Our puppy was only six months old when we started to read all sorts of newspaper articles about Rotties being feared for their aggression. The internet didn't exist, so research was difficult. Dog books don't allude to any innate aggressive traits;

they just describe the breed as loyal, strong-willed and in need of firm guidance. There's nothing I can say to anyone who has had a bad experience at the hands of a bad-tempered Rottweiler, but over the course of 30 years, we have owned seven. People always seem surprised that I would have Rotties! At one time, we had three on our 20-acre home in Surrey. We loved them: ours were the most calm, wonderful pets you could imagine. They loved people, but a few wouldn't tolerate being jumped on by dogs they didn't know. If you own this type of dog, you owe it to other dog owners to have them under control and well-trained.

As we got older we reluctantly changed breeds to cocker spaniels and rescues. I started to feel less confident about controlling a couple of Rotties. When we moved from Surrey to a very small village in the Cotswolds, we had a male and female. Bosley was our boy. He had a head like a grizzly bear, but he was the softest, sweetest dog. After an initial period of people crossing the road when they saw us approaching, everyone in the village loved them. One lady, Pam, used to keep dog treats in her pocket especially for them. They would spot her across the road and make their way over to see her with great determination. Holding both of them on their leads, I was almost water-skiing behind them, with sparks coming off my shoes. I was in my fifties then and you do lose strength as you get older. I knew then that the game was up, but my husband took some persuading.

Our next dog was Charlie, a cocker spaniel from Battersea Dogs and Cats Home. I had been sent a photo of him but as we were in the States, Battersea said they would find him a different home as they don't like to keep dogs in kennels for too long. When we got back from the States two weeks later, I called Battersea and they told me Charlie was still available because the vet had needed to operate on his eye, so we could have him after all. In the meantime, Lance had heard about an old street dog that had been rescued from a kill shelter in Romania by a wonderful charity called K-9 Angels, and registered interest. The charity saves stray dogs that have been rounded up and held in terrible conditions before they are killed. K-9 Angels had looked after this dog until a new home could be found. He didn't photograph well and he'd been waiting for many years in Romania with no prospect of being re-homed. He was eight when we said we would have him. It was a big gamble for us. He'd never had a home, never had a collar on – he really was a street dog. His given name was 'Baiatu', which was a difficult name that we kept having to spell out loud for people. When we learned it simply meant 'boy' in Romanian, we changed it to Batty. We had him for about six years and he was the most wonderful, loving dog you could imagine. A bit on the ugly side, but so gentle and sweet. When we got him he was frightened of just about everything, but he seemed to learn from Charlie. The only thing we didn't manage to do was to get him to play. He had no concept of fun and games. Tennis balls would just bounce off his head. Food, safety and affection were his priorities. I'm a patron of the K-9 Angels charity and most of their work involves neutering the street dogs to try and put an end to the problem. They do outstanding work.

CHAPTER 17

WHERE'S BANANARAMA?

M r Roberts always said tennis would give me a career when I retired, and he was right about that too. For the next few years, I juggled my work as a commentator for Australia's Channel 7 with coaching the Slater Squad. It was a nice balance, and a gentle way to ease away from the tight-knit circle of locker-room camaraderie. The Aussie tennis season was the best possible way to switch camp from competitor to commentator. Initially, it was tricky. I could be criticising match performances of players who were recently my peers and who I might want to go and have dinner with that night. As I knew only too well, even if you know it's true, you don't want to hear it – especially from a friend. The first few times I held a microphone up to one of my friends was awful. They wouldn't stop laughing. But that meant there was always good banter and I made a point from the outset of calling a match as I saw it, with honesty and the understanding that comes from being a former player.

Reporters criticise players for losing without fully appreciating what they were up against on court. I know what they've gone through; I can see that their tactics weren't right or that two points made the difference or that luck played its part on crucial points.

There have been moments when I've made an observation about a player from my understanding of the game, and that player has expected more loyalty from me. I can only say what I see. I had a run-in with Mac at Wimbledon in 2019 when Jo Konta, our British No.1 and the No.19 seed, missed out on a semi-final against Serena Williams by losing 7–6, 6–1 to Barbora Strýcová, then ranked outside the Top 50. In the heat of the moment, Jo ranted at the press about the nature of their questions in the post-match conference. She felt she'd given her all and there were people asking her if she had coped well enough on the key points.

'You're being quite disrespectful and you're patronising me,' she said. 'I'm a professional competitor who did her best and that's all there is to that.'

Mac said, 'Well, I can identify with that,' but I knew that getting into a spat with the media wouldn't help Jo down the line. Once the press knows it can push your buttons, they'll carry on. I told Mac I didn't think she was right to do that. You have to rise above the fray. I admire Roger Federer's attitude. He is a master of the media, so savvy even when he's disappointed or angry about the outcome of a match.

'No matter what interview I am doing, I'm not doing it for the channel or the reporter, I am doing it for the fans who will see it,' he says.

The Channel 7 team of presenters included John Barrett, the veteran BBC commentator who is married to Angela Mortimer and who had followed my career from the start, so I couldn't have had a more familiar mentor in my first stint of a new career. I learned from the best, and my early mistakes were thankfully soaked up by the Australian viewing public a good 9,000 miles from home. I have a fabulous picture of Evonne and me working at the Australian Open, glass of champagne in hand. It's not like that any more. They were great people to work for and I continued in that role until Wendy Turnbull retired in 1989. I understood why they would want her to step into my shoes. When a player from a home country who's a Grand Slam finalist and Top 10 player retires, it's right to introduce her fresh perspective for the viewers.

For me to work six or seven weeks away in Australia covering tennis seemed perfect. I'd just married Lance, who was not interested in the limelight at all; he thought his new wife had retired from a life of press scrutiny. He accompanied me on one of my eight-week Australian stints for Channel 7, and as far as he was concerned, that was a nice little sideline for me. But I'd caught the broadcasting bug, and once Wendy had inherited my headphones and microphone, I thought I'd see if I could get a job at the Beeb.

'No, thank you,' was the response. 'We have two Wimbledon champions in Ann Jones and Virginia Wade.' They didn't need a semi-finalist! They had their quota of been-there-got-the-trophy pundits.

And then dear old Gerry Williams came to my rescue. He was working for Eurosport, which was briefly part of BSkyB, alongside John Barrett. Gerry asked if I'd come and work with them for the Australian tournaments as I'd been doing for Channel 7. I agreed. A year later, my Aussie mate David Hill took over BSkyB, which launched the Sports Channel in 1990, and then formed Sky Sports. I was one of the first calls he made. We went for lunch and with typical Aussie frankness he said, 'Do you want to be a lady of leisure or do you want to work for a living?' Within a month of being married, I was embarking on a new high-pressure career, learning a new set of skills from scratch, honing my craft as the anchor of BSkyB's live tennis coverage.

This was at a time when Bob Wilson, the former Arsenal and Scotland goalkeeper, was probably the only retired sportsman who had made a high-profile transition into broadcasting as a presenter rather than a pundit. Just as Bob had switched from competing to hosting *Football Focus*, *Grandstand* and *Match of the Day* for the BBC, David Hill thought I could make a similar move from tennis, and bring my knowledge and personal insight of the game to viewers. He had put ex-cricketers in front of the camera with the Packer series in Australia, and he made a good case for it being a relatively straightforward transition. As a tennis player, I was used to performing in front of a large audience and under pressure. I had been drilled to keep my focus by Mr Roberts and to take it one ball at a time, learning to adapt to any curveballs that came my way in the course of a match. As tennis is both a team sport and an individual effort, I knew how to work with and alongside people, and I could handle the spotlight. I saw the logic.

I knew myself that I had an unusually good recall of matches and scores. If I think of a particular match, I can remember almost every shot, how I played the big points, what I did well and badly, every detail of the action. That would stand me in good stead. I'd always fulfilled Billie Jean's desire for us to sell women's tennis by talking engagingly in detail to the press. And I'd been on the other side … I knew how I'd responded to media questioning and I knew how not to interview an athlete. There was a type of reporter who'd come with a list of set questions in their notepad. I would answer the first question at length, according to Billie Jean's mantra.

It might be, 'What happened at the beginning of the second set?'

I'd explain: 'I got off to a slow start, but I managed to get that break back and the really important game for me was at 5–4 because she had the chance to take the set but I managed to level.'

The next question would be, 'Was one of the key games at 5–4?' Well, I've answered that.

They hadn't taken in my reply. I would bail them out, of course. 'As I said before …' and all that, but it happened time and again, and I vowed that if I were ever in the interviewing seat I would listen very carefully to my interviewee's answers. If you have the knowledge, and you've done your homework, an interviewer doesn't need any more than a few prompts or facts written down on paper. On live television, it's got to be a natural exchange, a conversation, not a stop-start interrogation. And you have to listen closely because sometimes someone can give you a nugget, and if you don't pick up on that, if you just revert to question number three on your pad, you've lost the story.

So I started all over again, learning the hard way. I thought it very odd when David Hill told me to treat the camera like my best friend, but I did. He gave me a solid grounding. I started with continuity work, filling the gaps between programmes every after-noon, five days a week. I had to keep an eye on the news, write my own scripts and do two- to three-minute hits between the programmes. It was pretty intense, and I struggled at first to hit the hard counts. As soon as I heard 'ten seconds' in my ear, I was trying to get to the end of the sentence as quickly as I could, and then there'd be an awkward three seconds when I just stared at the camera in a way in which I certainly wouldn't have stared at a best friend.

Des Lynam lived around the corner from where I parked my car before work, and I'd sometimes bump into him. I'd tell him about not getting the timing right on the hard count and 'Oh my God, I'm looking at the camera for three' – and he would laugh and say, 'We've all done it. That's part of learning. And you won't do it again. Don't give up!'

Trial and error was the best way to learn. I was the only female presenter at BSkyB and my hiring was not a popular decision. It wasn't a sexist resentment; it was more a journalist-versus-athlete thing. There was some ill feeling that I'd been given this opportunity when I hadn't paid my dues on local newspapers, radio or TV. I understood that, but I felt my years on the tour gave me an equally important perspective. I'd been interviewed by representa-tives of all forms of media around the world – surely that counted as knowledge? I appreciated there are various skills that contribute to good journalism – and I hadn't been trained to write or piece a story together – but I did have first-hand knowledge of being on court, of losing and winning at the highest level. I brought different strengths, not better strengths. One presenter openly questioned my motives, asking me why I wanted to present the tennis coverage when 'female sports stars are studio guests'? I'd be excluded from little gatherings. I was used to someone wanting to eliminate me for the duration of a match on a tennis court before a sporting handshake at the net. This felt more personal – and alienating. I was used to being a bit of a loner on the tour, but never being shunned. I brought it up with Hilly. He told me to 'man up' and carry on.

Mr Roberts's motto of 'do the best you can and just get on with it' served me well.

David Hill and my superiors had no problem with me. I wasn't going to give up. I had a great producer, Nicola Cornwell, a no-nonsense Aussie who wouldn't let me get my head down. There were three other women on the team and collectively we were known as Bananarama in the office, which was typical of the attitude. We weren't individuals, just a nameless female group. 'Where's Bananarama?' we'd hear them ask on the other side of the office. We just laughed along. I never felt my position was under threat. But it did make me even more determined not to make a mistake. On one occasion I messed up and 'compensation' came out on air as 'pomcensation'. There wasn't time on the hard count to say, 'Sorry, I meant compensation.' I could sense that everyone was laughing at me.

I went to David's office and said, 'I'm not sure I'm cut out for this.'

He said, 'I never sack anyone after one mistake. Come back when you've made three.'

I went back to him again a few weeks later after I'd messed up the timings a few times and told him I was now on three. He burst out laughing and said, '*Sue!* Carry on!'

And I did, because of course you learn on the job. You learn under pressure.

The launch of Sky TV a year later was an exciting time. I remember posing for a publicity shot with a giant Bart Simpson mascot (*The Simpsons* launched on the network too) alongside Scott Chisholm, Richard Keys, Alison Holloway and Andy Gray. The editorial team were based in a big open-plan office and were all great for a bit of banter. All sportspeople love banter, so that kind of ribbing was fine by me. I presented the tennis coverage, but in 1990, when BSkyB broadcast from Wimbledon, I was gutted to be pushed aside for the main hosting role even though I'd been the anchor-presenter through the calendar year. That role went to Garry Richardson and I was given the breakfast show, running around as a back-up reporter the rest of the day.

In 1992 David Hill wanted a Saturday sports magazine show, a bit like BBC's *Grandstand*, but in those days, Sky couldn't afford Formula One, Test cricket and so on. So we were following sports such as arm-wrestling, truck-racing and darts. The programme was called *Sport Saturday* and aired for about five hours, dropping into a variety of sports and rounding off with the news of the day's football action. I co-presented it with Paul Dempsey, who is still a friend today. That's where I learned the craft. Rik Dovey, another Aussie, taught me more about television than anyone else. *Sport Saturday* was a fast-paced show. Interview X, pick up on Y, back to Z, read the football results. We didn't know where we were going, we'd respond to whatever was thrown at us. We had Sunday off, and on Monday morning Rik would sit down with Paul, then me, with clips of the programme. First of all, he'd say what worked well, and urged me to do more of it. And then he'd bring out the longer VT (video tape) – and tell me don't do *this* any more.

'Why did you say that?' 'You should have approached it this way.' 'You said that twice.' 'You've got to think more.'

It was just brilliant coaching and I absorbed it like a sponge because it was like Mr Roberts working with me, telling me how I was going to get better. And I don't think there's enough of that kind of constructive feedback in television – there's so much gush. I know myself whether I've done well or not. When I walk away from Wimbledon each day during the Championships, I give myself marks out of ten. I think, okay, I didn't do that well. When you're doing that much live television, it can never all be perfect. But I know when I should have been sharper. It's like, why did I hit that drop shot? I can equate it to a tennis match. Why did I lose my concentration? It's exactly the same thing.

We used to invite sporting guests in for a chat as part of the mix in the five hours we were live on air each week with *Sport Saturday*. One afternoon, Ken Bates, the chairman of Chelsea FC, came in. There was a buzz in the studio as he arrived – he was a huge name for our little programme. As we outlined our thoughts with Ken about how the interview would go, I noticed his wife Suzannah standing by the door. I offered her a cup of tea and found her a seat at the back of the studio: it turned out we were both from Devon so we had a nice chat about our favourite places. The interview went ahead, with Ken being his usual self … cheeky and challenging. A few days later I received a beautiful hand-written letter from Suzannah, thanking me for looking after her that day, and inviting me and my husband to a game at Chelsea and a drink beforehand. That was in the early 1990s and we are still friends today.

Suzannah is the sweetest lady you could ever meet … and Ken is Ken. You have to be on your toes when you meet him. We visited them recently in their home in Monaco. It won't be a surprise to hear that most of our conversations are not repeatable, but he's very entertaining. I'd like to say that Suzannah keeps him on the straight and narrow, but that would be stretching it a bit.

It was through Ken that I met Lord Richard (Dickie) Attenborough. He was a great friend of Ken's and a devoted Chelsea fan. I got on well with Dickie and we often spoke about young people in sport, and this led to him telling me about a charity he had been involved in since the early 1960s, working on behalf of youngsters with muscular dystrophy. He had met some kids at a fete who had muscle-wasting conditions and he was moved to get involved to help promote medical research and to offer families support. Dickie had been the long-standing president of Muscular Dystrophy UK when he called me one day on my mobile.

'Hello, Sue, it's Dickie here. I have a favour to ask,' he said. 'Can I take you to lunch? Are you free next week? I'll book a table at The Ivy.'

He was already sitting at his favourite table when I kept our appointment. He stood up, gave me a warm hug and sat down opposite me. Taking my hands in his, he leaned forward and asked if I knew why he'd invited me. 'I'm hoping you're going to offer me a part in your next movie,' I joked. He laughed and then told me, with tears in his eyes, that he would like me to take over the presidency of the Muscular Dystrophy charity. He was so emotional about it, and I was honoured to take it over. That was in 2004, and I represented the charity in that role for 14 years. Towards the end of my time as president, I felt my public profile was slipping and the fundraising team could do with a fresh face. I decided it was time to 'do a Dickie' and pass the baton on to somebody capable of pushing it forward with renewed impetus. I could think of no one better than Gabby Logan. Young, sporty, incredibly bright and a presenter whose profile was very definitely on the up, Gabby was at the top of her game and a great fit for the charity. I remain honorary life president and, lucky for us, Gabby accepted the presidency.

Rik Dovey at Sky was brilliant at teaching me, and a few years later I felt I let them down when I left for the BBC. In 1992, I was approached by John Rowlinson to see if I'd be interested in joining the BBC Wimbledon team as a presenter. I was gobsmacked. Sadly, I told him I still had a contract with Sky for another six months, so we decided to leave it for a year. He suggested I didn't sign a new contract. When my contract was up, I didn't re-sign and Sky said they would keep me on a rolling monthly contract. The next year, John contacted me again so I went to David Hill to ask his advice. Football was now king at Sky so he wasn't against me going to Wimbledon on loan. My good friend and tennis producer Claire Michel, however, was furious.

She had a feeling they'd poach me on the long-term, and she wanted me to stay. But I was allowed to go. To my amazement, my role was to co-present the evening highlights programme with the legendary Harry Carpenter and to be a guest of Des Lynam during the daytime coverage. I'd met Des through my occasional work with Gerry Williams, when I was still a player, and he had been a calming, casual advisor when I started at BSkyB. It was a magical opportunity but terrifying to work alongside these two titans of TV. I hadn't been so nervous since my first singles match on Centre Court against Maria Bueno …

I understood from the start that to do well in my new career, I needed to bring with me the key things I'd learned from tennis, and fundamentally that was a work ethic. Training, preparation, research for the programme ahead. With that groundwork, you can rely on your instinct and innate skills. Being 'on loan', every-thing and everyone was new. I was keen to learn how the BBC worked and asked a lot of questions, probably annoying every-one, as I wanted to understand what each person in the operation did and how it all came together. Outwardly, I seemed calm, but inside the butterflies were fluttering. I was determined to acquit myself well, and I have to say performing on a global stage in tennis gave me the courage to just go for it.

I was intimidated by Harry and Des's reputations – Des was known as 'God's gift to broadcasting' – but they couldn't have been more welcoming. Harry and I hit it off and from day one we got some great publicity. At the end of the first highlights programme, the producer Dave Gordon turned to the director and said, 'Wouldn't it be great if we could work with Sue after this fortnight is over?' There was a feeling that this could be the start of something. I found it a very different way of working. Harry liked to script everything and have it on autocue. I wasn't using autocue at Sky, but I thought if that's the way it was done at the BBC, that's what I would do. But I didn't like it. I wrote the scripts and input them, but I found it really awkward answering Harry's question while looking at him, then swivelling to the camera to introduce the next item using autocue.

We had a running joke about Harry's pronunciation, especially the names of players from the Balkans. He called Goran Ivanišević 'Iv-an-i-say-a-vitch'. When it came to Slobodan Živojinović, he gave up and called him Bobo. We always had a bit of banter about those names. Harry made it good fun; he was so generous. On the final day he presented me with some beautiful flowers and said how much he'd enjoyed working with me. I was beyond thrilled ... and the feeling was mutual. To have his acceptance meant the world to me.

Des was equally welcoming. I used to sit in during his daytime show just to observe him and learn. One rainy day, I was there in the background in my jeans and a T-shirt and I was told that Des didn't have any guests. Would I mind joining him on air? I said I couldn't, indicating my jeans. I had my outfit for the highlights show hanging up ready for the evening, but there was no time to change. They insisted, so I sat on a little sofa and chatted with Des through the rain break. The next day in the papers it was all about Sue Barker turning the BBC upside down, as if I was a rebel who was not treating Des with respect.

On the day of the men's final, Harry fell ill. Throughout the afternoon, I could sense that he wasn't going to be well enough to broadcast. I was scared about being left to host it myself, as Harry had done most of the hard work in the programmes. He opened the show; he closed it. I was involved in the bits in between. After much debate about whether he'd get through the programme, he left the studio with five minutes to go before we were live on air. We had to scrap the autocue, because it had been scripted for Harry and Sue. I was told to ad lib from start to finish. There I was, on my own, in charge of the men's final highlights on BBC1. It was terrifying. I thought, *This is where I get found out.*

But Pete Sampras had defeated Jim Courier 7–6, 7–6, 3–6, 6–3 to win his first Wimbledon title in a flurry of aces and volleys with two tense tie-breaks and the fear of losing hanging over him. Pete wasn't everyone's favourite but I was a huge admirer of his shot-making artistry. He'd finished second best to Stefan Edberg in the 1992 US Open and said that was the wake-up call he needed to work out how to become the world No.1. Never mind Harry's absence, I had plenty to say! At the end of the show, I was still shaking. Trying to hit the hard count spot on for the first time on BBC1 ... I'd done it time and again on Sky for 20,000 viewers, but it's very different when you're doing it for an audience of five million. And I did do it. Daz, the floor manager, put his hands on my desk and said, 'Well done, Sue. Next stop, *Grandstand.*'

On the middle Saturday of that Wimbledon, John Rowlinson and the then-head of BBC Sport Jonathan Martin took me to lunch. A lot was discussed, and they offered me a three-year deal. It would include Wimbledon plus all tennis, *Grandstand, Sports Personality of the Year,* the Olympic Games, the Winter Olympics, Commonwealth Games and figure skating. When Sky learned of the approach, they announced they would sue me for breach of contract if I went to the BBC. I'd left IMG when I hung up my racket and I didn't have an agent any more. I was ready to turn down the BBC if I was in the wrong.

Mark McCormack, the founder and chairman of IMG, phoned to ask if he could help me. He was in the country for the Open at the Royal St George's Golf Club in Sandwich. Mark told me to meet him on the Tuesday after the Open, at 10am. When I was a client, I'd read his book *What They Don't Teach You at Harvard Business School*, and remembered his advice about always arriving on time – never early, never late. I made sure I was there bang on ten o'clock, and he was there and greeted me with pleasantries. I considered him a good friend. I'd been to dinner with him and his wife Betsy, who was a top junior and a very successful doubles player. I told him I was nervous about the Sky situation. I'd never been threatened with legal action before. The BBC said they could not get involved in the contract fight when Sky declared to the press that they were suing me, and I didn't want to end my time at Sky with this cloud hanging over me. I was eager for Mark's advice. We talked about the lawsuit and he said I hadn't got a valid signed contract with Sky; they were just trying to pressurise me into staying.

'We won't let that happen,' he said, and we talked about my history with IMG and how the company had given me my start in tennis. 'But why did you leave us?' he asked.

And I said, 'You don't know why I left you?' And I told him that an adviser had discovered that my pension fund had not been invested well towards the end of my career. Mark stared at me as I told him this, narrowing his eyes and nodding his head. 'Give me a moment,' he said. He got up and walked out of the room. And I never saw him again. After an uncomfortably long break, Bill Sindrich, head of TWI (broadcasting), came in to see if he could make things work for me to rejoin IMG. But I decided no.

I hired my own lawyers, who simply wrote to Sky saying I was not under contract. Sky accepted this and I paid my own £13,000 legal bill. They then offered to triple my money, which was a lot more than the BBC fee, and suggested I could front a new 'big interview' show. Before deciding I went to see David Hill, who was under pressure to persuade me to stay. I showed him the BBC contract. After studying it for some time, he looked up at me and said, 'You know which deal to accept.'

I also sought Billie Jean's advice. She's been a mentor in tennis and in life, and very early on she picked up on my interest in all sports – she loves a variety of sports too, and her brother, Randy Moffitt, played professional baseball. From my family's involvement, I was immersed in golf. I'd been able to get to know a lot of the players on the England and Australia cricket teams from my stints down under. I went to Torquay United with my brother (until I came back with blue spray paint over my jacket and my mother banned me from games for a month). My brother also supported Arsenal and, because Liverpool were their big rivals at the time, I became a huge Liverpool fan. I could recite the whole team and carried my keys on a club keyring that had a concertina pull-out of photos of all the players. Billie knew how much I enjoyed doing a bit of work in the media. When we were playing Team Tennis, she asked me what else I liked doing besides tennis. I'd been working on the radio with Gerry at the odd tournament, so I told her about that. And she encouraged me to keep that going. So when the Sky/BBC dilemma blew up, I asked if I could talk to her about employers. I told her I had this opportunity with the BBC, but that Sky, and the people there, had been very good to me and I wasn't sure what to do.

Billie Jean's first question was, 'Could you do both?'

I said, 'No, that wouldn't work. They're in competition.'

She said, 'Well, this BBC thing, it's your dream.' And she told me that I had to do it.

I felt particularly disloyal to Rik, who had come up with a great idea of an interview-style programme I could host, and we would have had so much fun working on it, but the thing that swayed me was Wimbledon. Having presented the highlights with Harry Carpenter – and with it having gone so well – how could I just sit back and watch Wimbledon in the future, when I had it in my hand to continue working there? I knew that Harry would be retiring soon and the plan was that I should take over his role on the highlights show. A year later I received the most lovely letter from David Hill, saying how proud he was of me. I was in tears reading it. Without his help, encouragement and guidance, I would never have had the guts to go ahead with broadcasting. He left Sky shortly after I left, as he had been promoted to be head of Fox America. That made me feel less guilty. And over the years he often popped into Wimbledon to say hi.

CHAPTER 18

SKATING ON THIN ICE

If I owe my tennis career to luck and timing, I can say the same about my second life in broadcasting. Luck comes in threes, so they say. If my family hadn't been living in south Devon in the orbit of Arthur Roberts, I would never have had the opportunity to receive top-class coaching free of charge. If I had been born seven or eight years later, Arthur would have effectively retired from talent-spotting and no one would have picked me out from a PE class. If I hadn't emerged as a top junior in the early 1970s, just a few years after the formation of the women's tour and the Battle of the Sexes, I wouldn't have been in a prime position to benefit from the pioneering work of Billie Jean King and the Original Nine. It was all meant to be, wasn't it?

It's a similar story in my life on television. If I hadn't responded to that phone message from Gordon Bennett in the aftermath of my retirement, thinking it was a prank, I'd have deleted the dream offer of working on Channel 7's television coverage, which gave me an early, addictive initiation in broadcasting. If I hadn't taken up my Aussie friend David Hill's bold suggestion to go in front of the camera at BSkyB and then Sky, I wouldn't have embarked on a steep trajectory to become a live sports TV presenter. And I emerged from the school of hard knocks at Sky just when the BBC was actively looking for more female sports presenters.

Times were beginning to change. Helen Rollason had joined BBC Sport three years earlier and become the first female presenter of *Grandstand*, but she didn't want to take on the role. She loved her BBC2 *Sport on Friday* programme, which covered live racing, snooker and bowls as well as previews for the weekend's sport. So John Rowlinson and Jonathan Martin, always forward-thinking, were seeking a suitable female to join their presenting line-up. And my loan to the BBC for the Wimbledon highlights programme came just when Harry Carpenter was on the cusp of retirement. It wasn't as if I was fighting to get a role at the BBC. I was invited on board. Again, I was in the right place at the right time.

My experiences at both Channel 7 and Sky stood me in good stead for my start at the BBC. I was thankful to have amassed my air miles in broadcasting experience out of the limelight and on the other side of the globe. Sky was lower profile in those early days. I'd survived my initiation years and next up – just months after my first Wimbledon with Harry and Des – was the adrenaline rush of covering Torvill and Dean's extraordinarily dramatic comeback at the Winter Olympics in Lillehammer in February

1994. Steve Rider and I had flown to Norway to record a preview programme the week before – Steve having arrived at the airport straight from hosting *Grandstand*. His luggage failed to arrive and all he had were the clothes he was wearing. On the second night we went out to dinner and a man came up and said, 'I was only watching you on *Grandstand* yesterday', and Steve said, 'Yes, and I was in this very same lounge suit.'

For our opening link to the Olympic coverage, he and I were filmed in a chairlift coming down from the mountain, saying 'Welcome to Lillehammer' with big smiles on our faces. The camera crew filmed us just as we approached the bottom, but they said, 'We'll keep filming until we get the best shot with the most dramatic backdrop.' The 1994 Winter Games were the coldest Olympics on record; temperatures dipped to –11°C. We must have gone up and down in that chairlift about 20 times until the sub-zero temperatures paralysed our eyelids and mouths – and Lillehammer is not the easiest word to say when your lips are frozen. It was all good fun, and we flew back to present the Games from Television Centre.

Presenting an Olympics is an endurance test. First, it's a smorgasbord of sports – some mainstream like the figure skating, Alpine skiing events and curling; some fairly niche such as luge and biathlon – all of which require focused homework; and then there are the 18-hour daily schedules across 16 days, moving from one venue to another. I absolutely loved it – the timespan is similar to a Grand Slam and I just thrived on that treadmill. Towards the end of the first week, with the Torvill and Dean story set to explode, Dave Gordon decided to send me back out to

Lillehammer on a 36-hour mission to report live from a rinkside position. How lucky was I?

After ten years as professional performers, a change in eligibility rules meant that Jayne Torvill and Christopher Dean, the British, European, World and Olympic champions, could compete in the Games. Other champions of the past, Katarina Witt of Germany and the American Brian Boitano, also returned to the rink to perform for their countries. I've always loved watching skating (whenever I was in Bristol for a junior tennis event, our team went to the rink, though all we did was speed-skate around as fast as we could). Torvill and Dean were my era. Every time I went to *Sports Personality of the Year* as a tennis player, I sat with Jayne and Christopher and chatted. I considered them friends. To follow their comeback was an amazing experience: I was almost living with them during the build-up, starting from Sheffield, where I presented the action from the British Ice Dancing Championship, which they needed to win to qualify for the Europeans in January 1994. And I got on well with their long-standing coach Betty Callaway, who had come out of retirement, too, to act as confidante and sounding board for their comeback.

Ten years after Sarajevo and their perfect-scoring 'Bolero' routine – a time when everyone could hum along to the military marching tune of their paso doble – Torvill and Dean's return lit the public imagination. Their rumba original dance scored highly; in the free dance they put together a compilation of dance steps and sequences called 'Let's Face the Music and Dance' in the spirit of Ginger Rogers and Fred Astaire. Two weeks later, at the European Championships in Copenhagen, they brought the house down, beating the Russian pair Oksana Grishuk and Evgeni Platov, who had topped the points table until Torvill and Dean came back. They won, but only by a slim margin. We were live on BBC1. The show overran because we were waiting to get rinkside interviews with Jayne and Christopher. It was one of those moments that united the nation.

We got very high viewing figures for the BBC coverage of the Europeans, and Torvill and Dean's success caused such a stir going into Lillehammer. The charismatic duo seemed to be a shoo-in for the gold medal – the big British focus of interest at the Games. This was an incredible story and I was so fortunate to be given it so soon after joining the BBC. Dave Gordon led a concerted effort to ensnare interest in the Winter Olympics by throwing heart and soul into bringing to life the human stories. What we didn't know was how the politics would play out within the sport. How can this pair come back after ten years and win? It seemed people were looking for ways to prevent them from topping the table: if these oldies come back and beat the newbies, this isn't great for the sport. That's what I felt. Jayne and Christopher tweaked their free-dance routine to add a few more athletic, light-hearted elements to the technical programme, incorporating steps from older dances such as 'Barnum' and 'Mack and Mabel'. They were perfectionists and didn't respond to critics who had started finding faults in their routine, with whispers that one move – an assisted lift that had prompted no red flags from the European Championships judges – was deemed to be above the shoulder, too high, and would lead to a deduction in marks. There's no one who knew the rules better than Chris and he was confident it was a legal move.

At the last minute, the BBC production team managed to get me a rinkside position for those fervent few days of the final competition on the ice. It was a one-camera operation and I had Robin Cousins as the expert; I was directed by Dave Gordon and Martin Hopkins in my earpiece from London. On the night, it was hard to hear anything down that dodgy piece of wire. When Chris flipped Jayne, the crowd just went bananas, stamping, cheering, throwing flowers, whistling. The ovation went on and on. Barry Davies and I both said, what an amazing night. The atmosphere was electric. They were the people's champions, without question.

The judges thought otherwise – and then it all kicked off. The crowd booed as they were classified a dismaying third place. The judges wanted to humiliate them. The gold and silver medals were awarded to the Russians Oksana Grishuk and Evgeni Platov, and Maya Usova and Alexander Zhulin. I scurried around and got the wonderful Canadian figure skater Tracy Wilson, who was working for American television, to talk to us on camera. She said Torvill and Dean's performance was not only the best skate she'd ever seen, but technically the most accomplished. The saga was growing by the second. I tried to talk to the judges but they obviously wouldn't comment. (It was after this Games that they stopped showing the judges' nationalities because almost every Eastern Bloc country voted low on Torvill and Dean while the American and British judges voted high, and a controversy arose about the political divide.)

They were robbed, there was no doubt – and I had to get them to respond live on air. It was hard to hear the directives coming down the wire into my ear. But Dave was so calm and measured. He'd never panic or shout. He helped me through it by methodically suggesting I try this or do that. That's when the adrenaline kicked in and I went into sportsperson mode. I knew what losing felt like, though at least my pain on tennis courts was self-inflicted, not judge-inflicted by this subjective scoring. Our coverage overran, but it was such a huge story we stayed on. It was very moving. They were really down, Jayne particularly, because they felt they'd skated their best. It was such a shame for them because it should have gone down in history as the most uplifting, triumphant return. It was certainly one of those office water-cooler moments, and earned viewing figures of 23.95 million for the programme; audience figures for the Olympics have only ever been higher for the London Games in 2012. I felt so privileged to play my part in relaying one of the most dramatic stories of British Olympic sport.

· · ·

It was at Lillehammer that my pronunciation of names beyond East European and Balkan tennis players was further sharpened. Barry Davies was the figure-skating commentator and his son Mark, who is now the chairman of British Rowing, studied French and Russian at Cambridge. Barry was getting corrected by Mark, and I was reaping the benefits. Martina used to try and correct my pronunciation of tennis players, too. She would point out that we put the emphasis on the wrong syllable of names like Navratilova and Sharapova. It should be 'Navra-TEE-lova' and 'Sha-RAP-ova', but I said that after 35 years, if I started pronouncing her name as it would be in her original language, no one would know who I was talking about. We've had Björn Borg wrong from the start too: his surname should be pronounced 'Bor-ay'.

But as Monica Seles said on becoming a US citizen in 1994, 'I'm in America now, I'm Seles.' In her native Yugoslavia – she was born in what is now Serbia – her surname would have been pronounced 'Sel–esh'. I work hard to learn the names of athletes and enunciate them as they would themselves. The WTA and ATP now have many of their players introducing themselves with audio on their websites, which is such a good idea. I do practise them a fair bit. When a new player arrives on the scene, I keep saying it over and over again, and I sometimes write it phoneti-cally so I can see it at a glance. But Des used to make me laugh. When I saw there was a new Slovakian name, I asked him if he'd like me to find out how it's correctly pronounced. He'd say, 'No, no, I don't need that.' I was so impressed. And then the result came up and Des proclaimed, 'Arantxa Sanchez Vicario beat … the Slovakian,' and winked at me.

My first year, 1994, was a hardcore initiation. I also presented *Sunday Grandstand* on BBC2. Sitting in the chair for the first time, listening to that famous theme tune, I was terrified. This was a programme I had grown up with and it seemed scarcely credible that I was in the hot seat. The first time I was asked to present *Grandstand* on Saturday on BBC1 was even scarier, but I was saved by the wonderful producer Martin Hopkins. As the last few seconds of the music were playing, he said in my

ear, 'Sue Barker! First time in the chair presenting *Grandstand* …
Good luck!' and chuckled wickedly as only he can. That made
me laugh. It was a producing master class as I went on air saying
'Good afternoon' with a big smile on my face rather than looking
like a deer in the headlights.

Nerves don't affect me any more, but in the beginning I
did suffer quite badly. Liz Thorburn, who I've worked with for
more than 25 years at the BBC, will say she's seen me evolve from
someone whose hands were physically shaking when I conducted
an interview to being as solid as a rock. For me, *Sports Personality
of the Year* was the most nerve-wracking show to present as it's
highly structured, tightly timed and all on autocue, which I never
use. You've only got two minutes for three questions, with any
one of the live interviews potentially a minefield (hello, Bradley
Wiggins). Walking out there in front of all those people isn't that
easy. You've got all the BBC top brass in attendance as well as the
great and good of the sporting world, and an audience of 10–12
million at home. There's no place to hide if things go wrong.
When Clare Balding first joined the presenting line-up, I told her
I always wore trousers so no one would see my knees knocking.
And that wasn't a joke.

I joined Des Lynam and Steve Rider for my first *Sports
Personality of the Year*. If I was jittery beforehand, my nerves
quadrupled 40 minutes or so before we were due to go on air.

Over the years the *Sports Personality of the Year* line-up
changed. Initially it was Des, Steve and myself; then Des left, and
Gary Lineker came in. Then, following Steve's departure, first
Adrian Chiles and then Jake Humphrey joined us. Now it's Gary

alongside Clare Balding, Gabby Logan and Alex Scott. Whatever the presenting team, the show was always an easy target for TV sport critics. They'd take a pop at what we wore, things we said. I'm all for accepting criticism where it's due, but not gratuitous insults. One year it went too far. One journalist wrote, 'Lahore came up as a caption on the screen and quite fittingly it cut to a close-up of Sue Barker.'

My husband called the newspaper to complain. He was put through to the on-call editor and asked to speak to the journalist who'd penned the column. The editor said he didn't think he was in the office, to which Lance said, 'Well, if I don't speak to him now, tell him he'll find me on his doorstep later.' Needless to say he was put straight through. Lance asked why he felt that comment was appropriate and the hack admitted he had gone too far. We all decided to move on. You can't dwell on these moments, but you can call them out.

CHAPTER 19

THE BEST SEAT IN SPORT

For many years I had the *Grandstand* theme as the ringtone on my phone. This slightly defeated my desire to live anonymously away from the cameras because every time it rang, people would home in on me – the upbeat tune remains a siren call to two generations of sports fans, me included, who grew up with the multi-sport afternoon show wallpapering our weekends. The *Grandstand* chair represented the pinnacle of sports broadcasting. From that studio perch, the presenter's challenge was to share a kaleidoscope of the best sports action – football, golf, Formula One, rugby league, racing, Test cricket, athletics, snooker and so on – on any given weekend, with certain shows dedicated to the 'crown jewel' events, the FA Cup final, the Boat Race, Wimbledon, Olympics, the Grand National … The show was flat-out, fast-moving and stressful, delivering the breaking stories and results over four or five hours of action. Des and Steve made the job look easy, but it wasn't. You can never be complacent about a live broadcast.

After Des left, Steve pushed for *Grandstand* to go on the road more often, parachuting into major events in rugby, golf, tennis, snooker, racing and so on to convey the atmosphere of the event. The technology for outside broadcasts wasn't as advanced then, which added another layer of complication. Anchoring *Grandstand* was tense, always a challenge; I had to know my stuff and deliver – and that's what I absolutely loved about it. I was pushing myself out of my comfort zone much as I did every time I walked on court for a key match. Tennis was my home territory, but I felt I could only prove I was any good at broadcasting if I could bring the same depth of knowledge and rapport with competitors across all the sports we followed.

I was most worried about racing – it's such a world within its own world – but I had a great relationship with Frankie Dettori and it was a huge compliment when Clare Balding, then the racing presenter, said I got things out of trainers and jockeys through asking questions it wouldn't have occurred to her to ask. Clare probably wondered why I was needed on a big race day, but the prevailing view was that the Grand National, the Derby, the Prix de l'Arc de Triomphe and Royal Ascot were bigger national occasions than just race days. At the 2005 Derby, I left her effectively anchoring the coverage next to the parade ring and I took on a roving reporter's role. Motivator, a beautiful bay with a white star, was favourite to win the richest flat horse race. I started by interviewing representatives of his well-heeled owners, the Royal Ascot Racing Club, a 230-strong group that included Simon

Cowell, in grand surroundings. Next, I ventured into the middle of the Downs, where admission is free of charge, to meet the pearly kings and queens. At one point I was interviewing a man in a string vest with a knotted hankie on his head in a queue at a burger van. With a mouthful of fried onions, it was back to the exclusive winner's enclosure to pick up the chat with the winning jockey, trainer and the very happy, very numerous members of the Royal Ascot Racing Club. All in a day's work, as they say.

Des had perfected the art of appearing totally relaxed in front of the camera, almost nonchalant, with his down-to-earth, witty quips. His style was deceptive: that breezy manner was underpinned by a daily refresh of his bank of sporting facts and fables. 'One tip, Sue,' he said. 'Buy all the papers, read everything, keep abreast of all sports and all the different points of view.' Knowledge is power; on live television, it is also confidence. The facts, opinions, background stories and stats you absorb then fall naturally into a conversation or interview on air. These days, of course, you can google something in the 30 seconds the viewers are watching a piece of VT, but I've always liked to keep myself thoroughly informed. Des and Steve thought I was a bit of a swot, with all my research notes, but I was determined not to let anyone down. It was my competitive instinct; I wanted to be good at this. What's the point in not trying to be the best you can be?

From *A Question of Sport*, and particularly from Ally McCoist's brand of quick wit, I learned that sometimes it was best to act as a foil, rather than pepper an interviewee with too many questions. Peter Kay, the stand-up comedian, did a star turn at the Grand National in the days when John Smith's sponsored the

Aintree meeting and he had been starring in a series of very funny advertisements for the brewery. I literally put the microphone under him, got him under starter's orders and he was off – he was scheduled for three minutes but Carl Hicks, the producer, kept him on for a quarter of an hour. We had a similar comedic turn from Johnny Vegas, after he'd finished a short stint training to be a jockey. I simply had to laugh along with him and he produced television gold. Being game for a laugh became an occupational hazard. Carl always said I was a comedian's best audience.

One night at the European Athletics Championships in Gothenburg in 2006, we faced a dilemma. Unusually, Great Britain had no athlete in any of that day's finals. There was next to no patriotic interest for viewers at home. The production team hit upon the idea of 'Swedish night' and, to make it work, we had to take it all the way. The make-up team painted Swedish flags on my cheeks; I had my script translated into Swedish; I opened with words to the effect of, 'It's Day Five in Gothenburg and the terrible news is that no GB athletes have made it to a final, so we are going to join our hosts tonight and support the Swedish medal hopefuls: Carolina Klüft in the heptathlon, Stefan Holm in the high jump and Susanna Kallur in the 100-metre hurdles ...' It was just a different way to deep-dive into the battles for the medals with some human-interest angles.

It was a great privilege to be the first regular female anchor of BBC Sport's flagship programme and I remain immensely proud that I was entrusted with delivering for its huge audience. The pressurised, on-the-hoof nature of the show meant it was considered the best training ground for presenters and the technical crew for the multi-week Olympics and Commonwealth Games. Everyone was under pressure; everyone had their own way of dealing with it. I like to sit quietly with my notes for a good half hour before we go on air. Clare, by contrast, will say she's like an excitable puppy. Her energy levels go up the closer we get to broadcast time. Co-presenting *Grandstand* for the Arc at Longchamp Racecourse in Paris on one occasion – and I was especially on edge when I was presenting racing – we had a Winnebago as our green room, equipped with a French espresso machine. Clare was talking too much, being too loud, and I had to say, 'Look, Clare, I'm really sorry, but could you please go out?' Sorry, Clare!

During one major event, Steve was finishing off *Grandstand* and I was coming in to present the latest action from the Commonwealth Games. We had one minute for the handover. I was standing out of shot, ready to leap into the chair as he vacated it, when I noticed his talkback had detached from the connection so he couldn't hear anything from the producer and editor, let alone the hard count. Luckily, they went to a short voice-over piece and I crawled on my hands and knees, out of shot of the cameras, and clipped his talkback back in. He looked down and gave me a thumbs up as I reversed backwards out of view. When it came to the handover, I put my notes down and plugged myself in, and Steve disappeared with his stuff. Just as we went live, I realised I was staring at Steve's notes and he had scarpered with my script. For the first three minutes, I had to busk it and then motion to someone to catch Steve before he reached the car park and drove home.

Live television calls for a repertoire of hand signals and body language. The trouble is, they are open to misinterpretation. At one Winter Olympics, Steve and I were sitting either side of Robin Cousins in the studio. I was interviewing him when urgent word came through our earpieces that the way Robin had crossed his legs was blocking a camera: could Steve somehow get Robin to cross his legs the other way? The only way to do that was for Steve to nudge Robin on the thigh under the desk and try to indicate what needed to be done. Tricky.

The first year Mac worked with us full-time at Wimbledon, we had to fill 15 or 20 minutes before going to the *Six O'Clock News* and we had him on because he's such a good talker. I was told to leave a minute free at the end so we could show a couple of ten-second clips to dot the i's and cross the t's – you know, Steffi Graf is through, Andre Agassi next faces so-and-so, and we've got more tennis for you over on BBC2 – so I was timing the last question for Mac to allow for this summing up. Then I gave him the hand signal to wind up. He carried on talking with a new burst of energy. I gave the signal again, and he carried on talking. The clock was ticking down. I cut in, 'Mac, sorry, we'll have you on BBC2, but we have to go now to the news … Goodbye.' We didn't have time to show the clips. Mac looked at me questioningly with a furrowed brow.

'I was giving you the winding up signal!' I said.

'Ah,' he replied, 'But in American TV, that signal means "keep going".' He made a cut-throat gesture. 'Why didn't you just do that?'

CHAPTER 20

BY ROYAL APPOINTMENT

The spring and summer of 1999 marked shifts of many kinds in my role at the BBC. I was pottering around at home one day when I received a phone call from Dave Gordon. 'Guess what?' he said. 'You're number one on their request list.'

He was referring to Prince Edward and Sophie Rhys-Jones, who were to be married at St George's Chapel, Windsor Castle, on 19 June, and he went on to say the couple wanted me to conduct the official interview with them to air five days before their royal wedding. I couldn't be more honoured. I'd been there on the day they met in 1993 and played a part in introducing them. The serendipitous meeting came at a Real Tennis Summer Challenge event at the Queen's Club in London, which I was reporting on for Sky Sports. Prince Edward was taking part to raise money for local charities around Britain and I was due to interview and play real tennis with him. After the interview I was asked to pose in different baseball caps and T-shirts emblazoned with the names and logos of TV and radio stations around the country and to stand alongside Prince Edward in our tennis kit at a photocall. For commercial reasons, Sky wouldn't allow me to promote other media brands so we suggested that the bubbly PR girl who was organising the promotion stand in for me instead.

Sophie was reluctant and took a lot of persuading, but the rest is history. The first ever photo of the pair is there for all to see: the prince in a crisp white polo shirt and white trousers with a smiling Sophie Rhys-Jones – a racket slung over her left shoulder and her right arm on the prince's shoulder. I followed up the following week and learned she'd already been invited to Buckingham Palace to discuss the event with Prince Edward over dinner.

Prince Edward was also a great supporter of the Commonwealth Games so I'd had the occasional five-minute chat since then, but an eve-of-royal-wedding interview seemed out of my comfort zone. The more I thought about it, though, the more I thought, *I fancy this.* I could hardly refuse as they were so lovely and I come from a tremendously royalist family; the Queen was my mother's hero.

Mum came with me the following year when I was awarded an MBE in the Queen's 2000 New Year Honours List for services to sport and to broadcasting, which was presented by Her Majesty herself, and it was one of the proudest days of Mum's life. Out of the blue, I had received notification that I was to be offered an MBE – an honour I had never thought I would be considered for, bearing in mind I had won my Grand Slam title

24 years earlier. Times have changed: Virginia and I were not honoured instantly for winning Grand Slams in the way that sports achievers today seem to be. The award meant so much to me, but it meant *the world* to my mum and I so wished my dad had been alive to see it. I took Lance and Mum to Buckingham Palace and afterwards we went to celebrate at Mosimann's, a restaurant in a converted church in Belgravia, near Buckingham Palace. Anton Mosimann, a tennis fan, was there to make his special bread and butter pudding, which I loved. The rest of the day is a bit hazy, as the champagne flowed; Mum wasn't slow in coming forward with her glass either. Lance was driving and remained totally sober. As he went off to get the car, a nearby table heard of my award and ordered another bottle of champagne to share with us. The damage was done. Lance said that when he saw me and Mum stumbling out of Mosimann's, clinging on to each other with our hats in our hands, he thought, *Shall I just drive on? Am I really with them?!*

Following my MBE, I was invited to join the honours committee for sport. I spent ten years in that role. I cannot talk about the deliberations or the other committee members, but it was a privilege to review the outstanding achievements of other British athletes on and off the field. I only left when, in the spirit of openness, the government decided that they should publish the names of their committees. I met so many sportspeople in the course of my life on television and I didn't want them to know that I had an involvement in the decision-making in the process of awarding honours. I was asked to put forward my name to be chairperson of the committee but I declined

... I have since gone on to receive an OBE from the Queen at Windsor Castle and just last year a CBE from Prince William, again at Windsor.

These three awards are my prized possessions.

• • •

But back to 1999. The set-up for the pre-wedding interview was relaxed. We filmed on a sunny June day sitting around a table on a terrace overlooking a large pond in front of their future marital home, Bagshot Park, in Surrey. Prince Edward and Sophie couldn't have been more welcoming and were fully prepared to give a candid, conversational interview for what became a half-hour documentary.

Compared to my usual sports-based interviews, I was well off-piste. We reminisced about the day when they'd met on the real tennis court and Sophie had to change in and out of different T-shirts for the photocall while Prince Edward diplomatically turned his back to practise some shots in a corner of the court. That first meeting was clearly etched in their memories – I later learned that they'd chosen to top their seven-tier wedding cake with decorative tennis rackets to commemorate the occasion. A working couple, with their own businesses in public relations and television production respectively, they emphasised how keen they were to continue to earn their own living while supporting the Queen whenever called upon. Sophie, with her English rose looks and blonde hair styled short, revealed she was sometimes mistaken for the Princess of Wales. Their wedding day fell less than two years after Diana's death.

They talked openly about trying to move into a new era of press cooperation and were frank about not wanting to encourage comparisons. 'We don't want to even begin to fill that gap,' Edward said. They came across as a lovely, normal couple looking forward to an exciting new future. 'Contrary to public opinion, we have never lived together before, so, you know, we want to get used to living with each other,' Prince Edward said. 'There still will be an awful lot of things to do in the house and garden, and with our respective businesses, and to go straight into – you know – extending the family, we are not intending to do that immediately, so I think everybody can wait patiently.'

The interview went down well so the BBC then asked if I'd be part of the team for the coverage of the royal wedding. I'd recently snapped my Achilles while playing tennis at home with Lance (who had to cart me to the car in a wheelbarrow that had just been emptied of manure to get me to the hospital because I was in agony) and I was just out of my orthopaedic boot. My foot was massively swollen and I couldn't put a lot of weight on it. I didn't think I could be part of the wedding presentation line-up because I couldn't wear heels – and 20 years ago, no one wore trainers with smart clothes. I'd hidden my feet under the table of the pre-wedding interview.

'Don't worry,' I was told. 'We'll make sure we don't shoot your feet.'

So I agreed, and on the day I sat alongside Michael Buerk and Fiona Bruce. But honestly, I felt out of my depth, because there was an assumption that I was a close friend of the royal couple and that I went shopping and things with Sophie. I felt embarrassed, as if I was assuming this role of being a best friend. It wasn't the easiest thing to do. I knew nothing about her favourite colours and all these things I was being asked live on air. I just tried to get through it chattily without trying to embarrass her or myself.

I'd had a little chat with them on the day before the wedding when they came down to the chapel for a walkthrough. I thought I would be brought in like a pundit now and again, talking about how they met, but there was a lot of filling when the guests were arriving and then, at the end, there was supposed to be about 20 minutes when the married couple left the chapel and posed for photographs on the steps. On the day, the wind was getting up and Sophie's veil was flying all over the place and they cut the photo session short, leaving us with 15 minutes to fill. Everyone went into panic mode – what could we talk about with no image to comment on? It was only Michael and me in the studio and, the next minute, the wide-angle camera comes in and shoots my trainers – and I'm on the front page of the Monday paper for being disrespectful to the royal couple. It was a rerun of when I was dragooned into going on with Des when he had no guests and I was wearing jeans. They'd promised they wouldn't shoot my feet! I was mortified. I went back to Queen's the next day to present the tennis and waggled my foot about on air to remind people I was recovering from an Achilles operation, but of course we only had about 500,000 viewers, not the 12 million that were watching the royal wedding the day before.

●　●　●

Out of the blue, Des Lynam walked away from the BBC in August and announced he was moving to ITV. He was essentially God at BBC Sport and his departure left everyone agog. Immediately, it presented two issues: one was the football programmes, which was easily solved by Gary Lineker stepping up to present *Match of the Day* and to anchor the big live matches and international tournaments. The other was that Des had been about to fly to Seville to present the BBC coverage of the athletics World Championships in the last week of August. Dave Gordon, who was on holiday in a *gîte* in France and climbing up hills to find a decent phone signal, put me forward and I couldn't have been more excited to be heading a presenting team with my mentor David Coleman and Brendan Foster in the commentary team. I literally got a call from Jonathan Martin, head of BBC Sport, and Christopher Bland, chairman of the board of governors, saying, 'Can you do the athletics on Saturday?' I cancelled a holiday and flew to Seville.

They also asked me to pick up Des's other gigs – the Grand National, the Derby and the Prix de l'Arc de Triomphe – and said I'd now be the anchor host at Wimbledon. I was also asked who I thought would be best to take over my highlights show and I suggested John Inverdale.

I get many letters and requests from youngsters asking my advice on how to get into sports broadcasting. I have to be honest and say I have no idea. I was lucky enough to be invited in. I didn't have a strategy; I didn't try to take anyone's job. I have never had any ambition to take over another person's role or replace anyone. All of this just seemed to land in my lap.

I was in awe of David Coleman; I found him terrifying yet was grateful for the way he'd taken me under his wing and, three years earlier, entrusted me with *A Question of Sport*. He was tough; he wouldn't hold back in his appraisals. He also told me I didn't need an agent to negotiate contract renewals. I just needed him. 'You come and tell me when you're due a renewal and I'll tell you what to ask for,' he'd say. 'And I'll tell you what they'll give you.' He was old-school in that he made the point that women weren't going to be paid the same as men. I wasn't offended. It was the way it was in the world then, not just television. I was just happy to have a job I loved.

We had worked with each other quite often when I was presenting *Grandstand* from an athletics event. So much so that he had nicknamed me 'Blizz', short for blizzard, because the weather was dependably awful whenever I turned up. Just a year before, we'd travelled to Scotland to cover Paula Radcliffe in a five-mile road race around Balmoral Castle in Aberdeenshire. Needless to say, the start had been delayed by bad weather. The studio was a temporary structure on a platform erected on the grass in front of the castle, standing about 25 feet high. To get up to the platform we had to scale a rickety old window cleaner's ladder and duck beneath scaffolding poles. Liz Thorburn, the floor manager, thought I'd absolutely freak out.

This was after an incident when I was presenting a racing festival at Ascot amid skittish horses, hooves, stable lads, photographers and other journalists all trying to get close to the winning jockey. Racing was the one sport I never felt 100 per cent comfortable with so I was on edge, and Liz and I were both new to outside broadcasts. She was trying to protect me as best she could, but I was getting jostled and couldn't hear what I was being told by the editor on my talkback. Once I'd finished the interview and *Grandstand* had gone off to another event, I turned and let off steam at her. *Woah*, she thought. *Sue's really scary.* But she says it was a pivotal moment; she realised her job really mattered, that a presenter absolutely relies on a floor manager to make sure a broadcast segment goes smoothly, and from then on she said her mission was to prove that I would never have reason to shout at her again.

So there we were at Balmoral in the bleakest of weather and she came to meet me at the TV compound. She painted a grim picture of the platform and the ladder and admitted the producer had said we'd just have to cope with it. Apparently I grew paler and paler as she regaled me with the horror of the situation. When we emerged through the trees and I saw it, I said, 'Oh, that's not too bad at all!' After the exchange at Ascot, I could see she was relieved. The weather was freezing so when I wasn't required to be in front of the camera, we'd scurry down the wobbly ladder and sit in the Land Rover or scamper back to the athletes' zone to keep warm. As the snow continued to fall, the platform also became as slippery as a skating rink. Every time the light went red, snow would fall or, rather, come in at horizontal angles.

Paula won the race, setting a new world-best time, and we were all pleased to have been there to capture it. News came through late in the day that she had to do a random drugs test. David Coleman and I had been chatting to her and wondering where everyone had gone. The officials who would normally oversee formalities had left. Paula was keen to do the test, which had to be witnessed, otherwise the result wouldn't stand, and she was so passionate about ensuring athletes were all seen to be competing on a level playing field. None of her team could witness the test, obviously.

'Well, one of you has got to do it,' she said, looking over at our BBC crew. 'David, you're not doing it.' We all burst out laughing. Dave Gordon was vetoed too. 'Sue, will you do it?'

'Well, yeah, I don't want you to lose this title and this record or whatever,' I said.

So we went into the ladies' Portakabin loo. We were the only ones there. She said, 'Right, I'll just piddle in this cubicle.'

I said fine, I'd keep a watch outside, and I pulled the door to, saying, 'Tell me when you're done.'

'No, no, no,' she said. 'You have to watch so that you can see that I'm actually piddling into the bottle and that I'm not pouring it in from a different bottle or something.'

'You're kidding. Look, I trust you 100 per cent,' I said. 'I know you won't do that, so I don't need to see this.'

She was adamant. 'You don't get it; you have to witness it, otherwise I can't sign this form.'

So I had to watch her fill the little bottle and put it into the package to go off to be tested. When we rejoined the others, DC asked, 'Did she do it all right?'

Honestly, the things I never thought I'd be called upon to do!

• • •

David, Brendan and I had first worked together as part of the BBC Olympic team at the Atlanta Games in 1996, but we formed

My wonderful American 'second mum', Carole Hoffman, and my real mum, Betty, enjoying Wimbledon hospitality.

Early eighties, still with a wooden racket and sponsored by a tobacco company. Whoops!

My first ever singles game on Centre Court against the great Maria Bueno. Lost the first set 6–2, but stormed back to win in three. A glorious memory.

I took my brother, Neil, to Dallas to meet Carole Hoffman at her home. He died in 2016 of skin cancer. Please get checked.

When I retired from tennis in 1985 and returned to the UK, I made sure I spent as much time as I could with my wonderful parents.

With my great mate
Andrew Castle, who I have
worked with for decades.
We started here at Sky
Sports in a portacabin.
I love his commentary.

My good friend Cliff.
We should have just
stayed as friends.

SPOTY 1999. I wasn't
going to miss out on this
photo and squeezed
in next to the greatest,
along with two legends
of broadcasting
Steve Rider and
Harry Carpenter.

London 2012 and a royal visit to the studio. On camera, just delightful. Off camera, so charming and friendly to every member of the crew.

On a speedboat outside our Florida home. Such happy memories.

Wimbledon 2022. The colourful trio of Wimbledon presenters. My good friend Clare Balding and I were joined this year by the lovely Isa Guha.

© PA

'Now, Susan.' The very dapper Bradley Wiggins was a cheeky chappy that night. I loved it.

Ten years later, HRH The Duke of Cambridge presented me with a CBE at Windsor Castle. How many 'proudest days of my life' can I have?

This basically says it all for me.

The Grand National, before going on air. Clare Balding hard at work as I gossip with Richard Pitman.

Sacked and straight out to lunch. Cheers, Daws and Tuffers, and here's to many more get-togethers. I love these boys.

The Covid non-Wimbledon with Tim Henman and Heather Watson. Still smiling, whatever the weather.

I worked with so many legends at Wimbledon. Here with two of the best, Martina and Billie Jean. Proud to call them friends.

What a line-up. What an era. Connors, McEnroe and Borg. Reunited on Centre Court with yours truly.

How can anyone be frightened of Rotties? My little Bosley aged 10 weeks.

What was I saying! Bosley coming in for a kiss, aged six, with Nina our new rescue.

After 30 years of Rotties, our two rescue boys arrived. Batty from Romania and Charlie from Battersea.

Our latest addition, a Newfiedoodle. The beautiful Bella.

A Dawson selfie on our last night of the farewell QOS Tour. With four of our favourite guests, Dion Dublin, Martin Bayfield, Denise Lewis and Tim Henman

I lost my dad in 1990 and my mum in 2022. A special day on her 100th birthday. I was so lucky to have them as my parents.

Wimbledon Centre Court centenary, 2022. A special word for the amazing John McEnroe. What a privilege to work with him for so many years. Thanks, Mac.

And it's goodbye from her.

an instant, tight bond as a trio in Spain for the 1999 World Championships. I've always loved following track and field, but I didn't have the level of residual background knowledge required to present the World Championships to the nation at a few days' notice. I made sure to run the scripts for my links past David. Every morning we'd go through the day's events and Brendan would add his expertise – look out for X, mention Y, don't worry about Z, keep an eye on so-and-so.

David was the ultimate professional, with one blip to his record that mortified him. I'd witnessed this myself in Atlanta, where I was presenting the early morning shift while Des was in the chair for the evenings. I came in on the morning of the Olympic marathon at 6am, an hour ahead of the race start, and by 6.30am we were wondering where David was. He was never late. We tried ringing his hotel room. No answer. We presumed he was on his way. Brendan had turned up, so it was just the two of us counting down to the start of the marathon. David's reputation was such that it was unthinkable the race could start without his distinctive excitable tones at the microphone, but Brendan was given the alert that he'd have to start the commentary on his own.

Meanwhile, we phoned Penny Wood, the BBC coordinator, to tell her that David was missing. She was still in her nightie, but said she'd go and knock on his door. She did, and he answered, clearly having just clambered groggily out of bed to see who was at the door. He was startled and furious to learn that he'd over-slept. His alarm hadn't gone off and he'd slept through the phone calls. He would have done the athletics late into the night before and was probably still shrugging off jet lag, but he was appalled. The athletics commentary booth was next to my studio, with a camera to capture the stadium atmosphere. There was Brendan on his microphone, watching footage of the marathon, adding his commentary, when David walked in. I watched in mock-horror as Brendan switched off the mike and David started bashing him around the head with his wad of papers – and for a while there was no commentary at all.

When he retired, I picked up the baton from him by presenting the London Marathon and the Great North Run. The producers were keen to broaden these events to include the stories of the ordinary entrants running for charity or a personal goal, as well as to focus on the athletes in the elite competition. Logistically, the London Marathon was a problematic outdoor broadcast as I had to introduce the programme – watching the wheelchair entrants shoot off, then the elite runners and finally the nervous fun runners before the mass start – and be at the end of the course to talk to the first finishers.

In the early days, we'd have chaotic rehearsals as we weren't guaranteed to get consistent signals from the ground-level cameras or establish steady radio links. On one occasion a member of the royal family was going to be at the start and royal protection shut down all the communications. Talkback would regularly just pack up. Sometimes I would be talking live over images I couldn't see. It was all wing-and-a-prayer stuff but we always got through it. And I loved the challenge of thinking on my feet: it was like feeling my way through a rollercoaster tennis match, and I'd had my share of those.

Dave Bedford, the somewhat mercurial race organiser, drove me from the start to the finish in his estate car. Much of the road system was closed, as it formed the race route, but he knew the twists and turns and shortcuts. My floor manager and I would be crouched in the boot, right over the spare wheel hub, getting thrown around as Dave drove like Lewis Hamilton to get us to the finish. Cars would beep-beep as he tried to weave through, but we always fell out of the back of the car in time to interview the first finishers.

I always returned home an emotional wreck after the marathons. I met the most awe-inspiring people raising money for charity, heard their poignant stories and witnessed the selflessness of people helping each other get to the finish line. One man's tale really stuck with me. He was a heart-transplant patient who was running his fifth marathon since he'd received his new heart and his story just poured out of him. He described how he'd been a couch potato for years and he'd been driven to lose ten stone because the surgeon said if he was going to receive a new heart, he had to earn it for the family of the man it came from. He wrote to the family, and they'd kept in touch. He described his determination to adopt a healthy lifestyle for his 12-year-old daughter. 'My goal is to walk her down the aisle in years to come,' he said. I was in floods of tears. So many stories each year lift the marathon beyond being simply a wonderful sporting occasion into a showcase of the best of humanity. At the finish people would pass and always wave to me as if I was part of the finishing protocol. It was always a moving day, but incredibly uplifting.

The Great North Run, an annual half-marathon from Newcastle to South Shields, was another highlight. Founded by Brendan in 1981, it's become a hugely popular event, bringing the North East together with plenty of famous faces to spice things up. We'd go up there a day or two before and sit in the hotel lounge discussing the stories and scoping them out to include in a programme. They were fun Saturday afternoons, fleshing out some ideas, and then on Sunday morning I'd be at the start before racing to the main production hub at the finish in South Shields. We always used to catch up with the late Chris Chataway, who helped Roger Bannister run the first four-minute mile in 1954 – I interviewed him many times when he ran alongside his son, Adam. His son had lost his fiancée, and they were running together for WaterAid because it was her life mission to help get water for people in Africa.

Like the London Marathon, I met so many fascinating people from all walks of life. I've lost count of the times I've interviewed newsreader Sophie Raworth. She first competed in the London Marathon in 2011 and then got the bug, competing in marathons around the world, including the Marathon des Sables, a six-day, 156-mile endurance feat in the Sahara Desert. Running has become a drug for her. It never was for me!

CHAPTER 21

NUMBER SIX, PLEASE, SUE

1984 was the year in which I would play my last professional tennis match, but it was also the year I received one of the most exciting invitations in my life – to join Emlyn Hughes's team on the 150th edition of *A Question of Sport*. Gareth Edwards of Welsh rugby fame was also on our side and we were up against Bill Beaumont and his guests, the golfer Sam Torrance and jockey Willie Carson. It was surreal to imagine my parents now watching me participate in our favourite family quiz on the television at home in Paignton in the very same room we'd gathered together for glorious entertainment when David Vine was the presenter.

'Home or Away?'

'Definitely home,' was my nervous answer in the key round during my debut, opting for the easier one-point question, which was a nice nerve-settler.

'Last year Martina Navratilova won the one title she'd never won before. Can you name it?'

Before I had time to say, 'The US Open,' David Coleman was saying, 'Don't dash in. Take your time. Team game.' He was so good at putting guests at ease with his calm authority. Everyone involved made me feel at home on the show I'd watched addictively for as long as I could remember. I even got the classic Emlyn squeeze of a hug for my correct answer. This was three years before Emlyn's infamous touchy-feely royal cameo. In one show, he had guessed a mud-splattered rider in the Mystery Guest question was John Reid, the Irish flat-race jockey, when in fact it was Princess Anne. 'Don't put that out. You can't put that out. They'll hang me,' he pleaded as everyone cried with laughter. Two weeks later, the good-humoured HRH was a guest on the show herself and teased Emlyn remorselessly, threatening him with her handbag when he went overboard with his hugs. An incredible 19 million people tuned in for that classic moment of the show.

Not long after my appearance as a panellist, I was zipping myself into a ridiculous outfit to be the Mystery Guest myself. There weren't that many prominent female sportspeople to call upon at the time and I had long blonde hair that was hard to disguise. What better way to carry out the subterfuge than for me to dress up in a large chipmunk costume? The production team had borrowed a giant furry outfit from the comedian Tommy Cooper's collection in Ealing. When it was shown, the studio guests stared and stared at the footage showing tantalising glimpses of me in this garb and suggested the concealed person was either … Alan Minter, the European middleweight boxing champion … or Ray Clemence, the 6ft 4in England goalkeeper. Thanks, chaps! So everyone thought I was a bloke. It made for a good laugh. That's the spirit of the show.

Twelve years after my first appearance, I was working at the BBC and still obviously a huge fan of the show when at the 1996 SPOTY after-party I was approached by the *Question of Sport* executive producer Mike Adley and asked if I would step in to present three episodes the next day as David Coleman had lost his voice. I couldn't have been more thrilled. What an honour! The show had a simple magic formula: a fun quiz between two teams of super-competitive sports stars with an (in those days) unchanging format. Dad and I used to enjoy pitting our wits against the panel of guests as they mulled over the Picture Round, the Individual Round, Home or Away, Mystery Guest, What Happens Next? and the One Minute Round, before going back to the Picture Round at the end. In those early days there were sometimes as few as eight programmes a year – and a summons to feature as a guest ranked as an accomplishment in itself. I'm told British medal-winners at the Olympics would be given a special letter practically as they were stepping off the podium inviting them to be on a future edition of *A Question of Sport*. With only four guests appearing with the captains on each show, you had to be a superstar to be on it. Now there are 36 shows a year.

When I was starting off with Mr Roberts, I used to turn to Dad while we watched it in our living room and wonder out loud if one day my tennis would get me to a level where I'd be asked on the show. That was my pipe dream, and it came true in a way that was even better than I could have possibly dreamed. The show has been a huge part of my life, from watching it avidly to presenting it, a constant that much like Wimbledon has brought such good fun and so many great friends along the way. I had a special relationship with David Coleman. Perhaps it was because we had that early *A Question of Sport* connection and he could see how much I respected the show as an institution of entertainment, but when I joined the BBC David really took me under his wing. He told me always to run things past him, so I sought him out for advice on all sorts of matters. He was my TV mentor, a father figure and – very like Arthur – brutally honest. I was flattered to be entrusted with holding the fort for three episodes until his voice recovered. Little did I know that this was, in fact, an audition, as David was planning his exit.

In 1997, I inherited the quizmaster's chair for what turned out to be an incredible 24 years. Did I have my work cut out or what? Phil Tufnell might say, 'It's three people against three people with a couple of buzzers having a little chat about sport and a laugh,' but my job was to control the proceedings with humour, and I was a stickler for the rules. I felt strongly that I was the guardian of something very precious that David Coleman had handed on to me; it was my duty to maintain the integrity of the show. With captains like John Parrott, Frankie Dettori, Ally McCoist, Matt Dawson and Tuffers, that was a tall order. Particularly with Ally – the archetypal naughty boy with a cheeky grin who constantly tried to push the boundaries. There were more than a few occasions when I had to give him 'the look'.

We were all giving each other a surreptitious 'look' when George Foreman, two-time world heavyweight champion and Olympic gold medallist, was a guest. We were thrilled to have such an international legend on the show – a participant in the infamous Rumble in the Jungle of 1974, a fight many consider to be the greatest moment in sport of the twentieth century. George had been the undisputed and undefeated heavyweight champion until one billion viewers around the world watched underdog Muhammad Ali knock him out in the eighth round. It's hard to think of a bigger legend – and perhaps a bit naive of us to think he'd keenly have his finger on the buzzer. George's agent said he was in London for five days (on a promotional tour to sell his George Foreman Lean Mean Fat-Reducing Grilling Machines) and he would come on the show. We all agreed to put him alongside Matt, who was marginally more reliable than Ally.

On the day, George arrived in a chauffeur-driven limo and waltzed into BBC Television Centre with his bodyguards, his sons, all bigger than him, which is saying something. He declined to go into the green room so he waited in his dressing room until called and didn't speak to anyone, just a smile and a nod to other guests. It became obvious quite quickly that George didn't know he was coming on a quiz show; he thought it was going to be an interview. The first round was the Picture Round, which had two boxing images behind the numbers and we breathed a sigh of relief when George chose one of them under number six. This was the perfect way to get George off to a flying start, but he looked at the picture and said, 'I don't know who it is.'

Matt, being a good captain, put a reassuring arm on his and said, 'Yes, sure you do, George. Look, he has a middleweight belt and the Mexican flag on his shorts. Name some famous Mexican middleweights, George … You've got this.'

George shrugged and said, 'I don't care who it is.'

Unperturbed, Matt put an arm round him to cajole him into an answer, at which point George said in a menacing manner, 'Don't ever touch me again!'

Matt recoiled and, for once, was lost for words until Coisty piped up: 'Eh, Matt, ask him if he's got any grills in the boot of his car!' It didn't go down well and let's just say that was a long, frosty hour.

So many legends of sport passed through the studio. The fun of it was meeting the guests at the lunches beforehand, all great achievers in sport, and seeing them in a different light. You don't get that cross-pollination of sports in the form of family entertainment anywhere else. You could have a Wimbledon champion and a rugby World Cup winner with a cricket international and an Olympic gold medallist all sitting down for a chat. Rather like me being slightly incredulous to find myself in the company of Emlyn, Bill, Gareth, Sam and Willie back in 1984, we'd see high achievers, stars in their own right, in utter awe of each other.

A Question of Sport's green room was a very special place. I wanted everyone to feel at ease and enjoy their time on the show so I was adamant that the green room should be restricted to the inner circle of presenters and guests so that we built up the sort of jovial camaraderie that was the show's trademark. I loved my hours of homework; I wanted to be able to congratulate guests on their most recent feat or wish them luck for their next competition. Panellists included the likes of Shane Warne, Martina Navratilova, Jonah Lomu, Seve Ballesteros, Evander Holyfield, Jason Kenny and David Coulthard. Often we'd find that these globally famous figures, who'd watched the programme since they were kids, would be incredibly nervous. They were confident performing in front of 50,000 people in a stadium or on a sports field, but felt totally out of their comfort zone in the alien environment of a television studio. Mutual respect was always evident; guests would react to each other like fans meeting their heroes.

A notable few treated the programme with the extreme respect I feel David Coleman would have appreciated. When Nico Rosberg won the Formula One World Championship in 2016, he flew over at his own expense on his private jet, and brought his Mercedes car on the show. It was a bit of a blow when he realised his team had packed his title rival Lewis Hamilton's car instead.

We had many great Wimbledon champions on the show over the years, including Martina, Mac, Boris and Ilie Năstase. Andy and Jamie Murray accepted an invitation with the stipulation that they were on opposite teams. Ultra-competitive and proud sports nerds, each wanted to earn the bragging rights at home (Jamie won, so Andy had to foot the bill for dinner that night). Tim Henman was our number-one guest. He only ever got one home question wrong. To reveal a little bit of a trade secret here, we always made the home question fairly easy for a guest's first appearance on the show. You don't want to embarrass a big name. We never let anyone know in advance what the questions would be or give them the answers; I was a strict enforcer of making sure it was all above board. But after a few appearances, it transpired Tim was a walking encyclopaedia of tennis. His knowledge is such that he can not only tell you who won Wimbledon in a particular year, but will say, 'It was so-and-so and they beat X, Y and Z along the way ... and do you want the scores?' We used to try and think of some absolute stinkers to catch him out, but we flummoxed him just the once. Eventually we framed this question: who were the other Wimbledon semi-finalists in the year Richard Krajicek beat MaliVai Washington in the final? You could almost hear Tim's brain whirring, *Todd Martin and ... er ... er ...* He couldn't get it. It was Jason Stoltenberg. He was furious with himself. To this day, every so often at Wimbledon we talk on air about well-known Aussie semi-finalists and I make a point of saying, '... and of course, Jason Stoltenberg' – and Tim looks daggers at me.

Laura Davies, the golfer, was also sensational. Gary Speed had fantastic knowledge on all sports. Adam Jones, the Welsh rugby player; Nick Matthew, the squash champion; and Michael Jamieson, the Scottish swimmer, were also on a different level. You expect people to get their own sport's questions right, but it was great when they knew about all sorts of other weird and wonderful sports as well. If they weren't elite sportspeople, they could easily have had a job as question writers on the production team.

The fun started with the competitive rapport between the captains, and the dynamic between me – the Boss, as I liked to be called – and the two captains. With John and Ally in one 1999 show, I was on the wrong end of pantomime hilarity. As I mentioned in an earlier chapter, I had snapped my Achilles tendon while playing tennis at home with Lance. Two days after an emergency operation, I was due to be in Manchester to film *A Question of Sport*. The surgeon said I couldn't travel but I had only recently taken on the show and I didn't want to let the team down. The studio had been booked, the audience invited. The surgeon relented and said I could do it if I could keep my foot elevated for a minimum of eight hours a day. So I was tipped from my wheelchair into a taxi and driven up to the studio with my plastered foot raised high. The plan was for Ally and John to wheel me to my desk as the announcer intoned, 'Please welcome … Sue Barker.' On cue, we moved forward but the pair of them rammed the wheelchair into a line of television cabling on the floor, the idiots, and I went flying forward like I'd been catapulted on to the set – which certainly set the tone for the show.

John Parrott departed quite suddenly in 2002, leaving Ally and I scratching heads about a replacement. It had to be someone he would have an instant rapport with; it had to be a big personality. We were lucky to have Frankie Dettori for two years. He was loved by everyone and always smiled and laughed through every challenge we threw at him. It seemed incredible to me to have that much wit and understanding in a second language. He was a pleasure to work with but, two years later, he had to leave when his racing commitments in Dubai didn't fit in with our busy timetable. And once again we were scratching our heads. England had recently won the Rugby World Cup, so Matt Dawson's star was high, plus he had performed on the show regularly over four years and proved himself to be a stand-out guest. He came up with correct answers quicker than JP and Ally. He knows his stuff!

And he had gone the extra mile for numerous Mystery Guest appearances: shaving his legs to dress up as a woman, transforming into a vampire in a coffin, lying in a beauty-salon treatment room with cucumber slices on his eyes. He was an easy choice. Up against Ally, who was risqué and borderline rude, the comedy dynamic was built on competitiveness and challenges. With Phil, four years later, the interaction was more sitcom humour.

What can I say about Daws and Tuffers? It's the question I'm most often asked when I am out and about in public. What are Matt and Phil like? Are they given the questions and answers beforehand? People think they can't know all that they do, but their sporting knowledge is truly amazing. Facts, stats, dates, facial recognition – they really, really worked at their research. And the knowledge they needed on the buzzer doubled when women's sports quite rightly began to gain a much higher profile. As the Boss, they'd expect nothing less of me than to acknowledge that Tuffers was a worrier and Daws knew how to exploit that ... very entertaining! The synergy between them – technically rival team captains, but brothers in arms – was a joy to work with. With a combined 57 seasons between us, and 14 years with the three of us together, we can almost second-guess each other to a hilarious degree. It's been an absolute ball. The memory of some of Tuffers's sprint-finish charades has me in stitches now.

'Where athletes go for a shag?' The Olympic village.

'Scottish golfer with boobs?' Colin Montgomerie.

'Man United right-back nobody likes?' Gary Neville.

Tuffers is the most naturally funny guy. By the end, when we were shooting blocks of ten shows across three days, we learned he was mildly dyslexic and by the fourth show at 8pm on the final night couldn't be expected to know his White Hart Lane from his West Ham United. He wasn't great at dates either until Matt let him into a secret – that the Olympics are on a four-year cycle, while World and European Championships are biennial events. And he was a great bluffer (or maybe not).

Turning to a guest, he'd say, 'You're in rugby, you should know this …'

The stunned riposte from his team member would be, 'Yes, I was the captain and we won this game.'

Hats off to the boys. They put their heart and soul into each show. Physically, they were called upon to try pole vault, volleyball, high jump, judo and so on in the confined space of the studio. Tuffers claims to have pulled his hamstring more often on *A Question of Sport* than in his entire cricket career. He even managed to stab himself in the leg with a pencil while sitting behind his panel. As for stunts involved in the Captains' Challenges, they were game for anything. They endured bucking broncos and wakeboarding all for the sake of family entertainment, while I smugly looked on. Judging by his face when I breezed up at an airfield after they'd wing-walked on acrobatic stunt bi-planes and asked sweetly if they'd do the loop-the-loop one more time, that was a stunt too far for Daws.

I've often said *A Question of Sport* has given me more fun than anything else in my career. It's not a scripted comedy quiz: we would ad-lib, ask questions and hopefully our panellists would know the answers. Of course, it was even funnier when they didn't. We had Frankie Dettori struggling to unscramble his own name in the anagram TRINKET RIDE OAF or Ally failing to recognise himself when dressed up as a showjumper from a previous episode. There was the extraordinary moment when Paul O'Connell, the Irish rugby union player, correctly guessed Borussia Mönchengladbach with only two letters – I and G – on the board, earning himself a standing ovation and reducing me to throwing a clutch of my question cards over my shoulder.

At the end of filming the Christmas edition in 2014, Daws interrupted proceedings to say he had a little present for me and an important announcement to make. On walked an official from the *Guinness Book of World Records*, who duly presented me with an award on behalf of *A Question of Sport* as the World's Longest Running Sports Quiz. That was a very proud moment for everyone involved.

I miss my *A Question of Sport* routine. On a typical studio day, we would record three shows at three o'clock, five o'clock and seven o'clock in Salford. I'd get to the production office to meet Gareth Edwards, the producer, at ten in the morning, armed with the scripts I'd been emailed earlier in the week. We would go through the scripts for that day and I'd have notes and questions. I'd nail the pronunciations of, say, a Sri Lankan cricketer or a Hungarian weightlifter and ask why we were posing this question to this guest. Fail to prepare, prepare to fail, as the saying goes. I would have done a huge amount of background research so if, for example, a question involved a footballer who had scored against Scotland, I would want to know who the goalkeeper was, where the game was played, what stage of the tournament it was, what the stakes were and so on. The more knowledge you have, the easier it is to be natural on camera.

As a viewer, I'd always loved the actual quiz. The only frustrating aspect of being the host is that you don't get to compete. So, I built in a little bit of fun for myself in these production meetings. There were certain rounds in the scripts that I wouldn't look at, because I wanted to play them myself. One was the Mystery Guest. Gareth would get a video screen up, I'd settle back in my chair, and we'd play the clip. I would verbalise my thoughts throughout and I was always dreadful. Even when it was someone like Andrew Castle, who I've known for years, I couldn't get them. The team took almost sadistic pleasure in watching me tear my hair out – 'I know this person. I know them. I know them. I know them!' When we went on set later, and the teams were puzzling over that same Mystery Guest question, I could empathise with them and, hand on heart, say, 'I can see why you're struggling.' I took all the opportunities I could to not look at the answers prior to the morning meeting so I could enjoy my own little quiz in the office. Once we were happy with the scripts, I'd challenge Gareth to sports quizzes on Sporcle, the quiz trivia website. The number of times there'd be a knock on the production-office door and the call, 'Sue is needed in hair and make-up *now*!' or 'Why is Sue so late for hair and make-up?' And we're going, 'Hold on, we're midway through a 1980s Davis Cup quiz.' That was a highlight, almost my own version of *A Question of Sport*. We'd do tennis, golf, football, American football, all sorts of sports. That was my studio ritual to relax before we would walk out and record three or four episodes in one long session.

In October 2016, *A Question of Sport*, along with *Songs of Praise* and *Holby City*, was one of the first BBC shows to be put out to tender to independent production companies. I was on holiday in America when a few television producer friends contacted me. They'd seen the BBC tender document and couldn't believe my name was not on it. Apparently the BBC wanted to refresh the show with more diversity and appeal to a younger audience. I was gobsmacked. How did they think we weren't going to hear about this? We did not fit this brief. Thankfully many of the other companies that bid for the tender named Matt, Phil and me as their chosen three.

The BBC then stated that they didn't want to change the line-up – contrary to what I understood their tender document had said ... Who were we to believe? After Gareth went to make his final pitch, which he and producer Dave Gymer did brilliantly, they were given the job, but were asked to keep us on. We signed a one-year deal, but that wasn't unusual.

The next year I had a breakfast meeting to discuss the contract with BBC management and found out that they were offering the three of us one more year and me a further year, in which they would ask me to take on two new captains. I didn't need to think long about this. It was a 'no'. I said I'd leave with the boys. At that point I asked if, when they had decided on the 'refreshed' line-up, that we should get the three newcomers in to show them the ropes, welcome them on the show and introduce them on air as the new host and team captains. I was keen to have a friendly and supportive handover, just as David Coleman had done with me.

Nothing was decided over that next year so we all got another extension to our contract.

In the summer of 2020, rumours began circulating again about changing the line-up. Gareth warned me that talks were ongoing but absolutely nothing was mentioned to me, Matt or Phil. I understood that no job is for life and maybe our time was up. After all, I'd had 23 wonderful years – the equivalent of six Olympiads or a whole generation. I was preparing myself for the end but, again, all through the summer and well into our recording schedule, nothing further was mentioned. We began to believe we would get another extension. During our penultimate block of recording sessions, I asked Gareth about the situation. He said he hadn't heard anything yet. I told him that if they were going to get rid of us, we at least wanted to have a final farewell 'celebration' show. He agreed.

It was on the second night of our three-day recording block that Matt, Phil and I were winding down in Wagamama's as was our custom and my phone pinged. In quick succession we heard pings from the boys' phones too. We had all received messages inviting us to meetings after the last show the following day. We knew it was serious because they had split us up – I was to go in first for a talk with the management, followed by the boys. I knew what was coming and had done for a couple of years so it wasn't any great surprise. I realised that was it; I expected to be told my run in the host's chair was over, and I didn't have a problem with that. After all, I'd had a great run, but I was surprised that they had split the meetings. It made us believe that either me or the boys were staying, otherwise why not tell all three of us together?

I enjoyed every minute of my 24 years on *A Question of Sport* bar five minutes – that brief meeting in an anonymous back room in Salford. There was a bit of 'We love the show and you've been an amazing host', *but* … I was waiting for that 'but'. I accepted their decision and understood their reasoning, but I couldn't help feeling wretchedly sad that it was all over. Before my five minutes were up, I did manage to ask to have a farewell show. In the boys' meeting, Phil listened to the preamble of compliments and thought he was about to be offered a pay rise, not get the sack. Matt listened to what was said and was quick to tell them the story would break, and they should get a statement from everybody. The boys were devastated too. The show had played an anchoring role in all our lives; it was part of our identity – it's the first thing any member of the public who stops me for a chat wants to know about.

Matt says that despite being selected for three British and Irish Lions tours and being an England World Cup winner – the hero who fed the ball for Jonny Wilkinson to kick that drop goal in 2003 – his mother really only thought he'd made it when he joined *A Question of Sport*. We were all gutted.

We accepted that we had lost our jobs. We had no issue with that in itself, but we could foresee the public reaction. At the end of his meeting, when Matt emphasised that this news would make the papers he'd told them the BBC should own the story by getting their publicity department to help protect us and them through it. We heard nothing from BBC management for over a week. No email, no letter, no phone call. Silence. It got to the point when the filming of the last show was two weeks away so

I called Gareth and I said, 'We – that is me, Matt and Phil – are going to choose our guests for our final show.'

'Okay,' he said. 'And how are you, by the way?'

'Not very happy,' was my reply.

Half an hour later I had an email from BBC management to say they were sorry not to have been in touch – which made me feel worse, as it was clearly prompted by my call to Gareth.

That's when anger set in. Not just for me, but for the boys. Matt, very gallantly towards me, told them they should pause for five minutes and consider what they'd done to someone who had looked after the integrity of *A Question of Sport* since inheriting the chair from David Coleman in 1996. Naively, I expected more after 24 years. As did the boys for their longevity as captains. We'd all seen John Humphreys move on from *Mastermind* on his own terms, with a celebratory ushering-in of Clive Myrie a week later. I know it was amid the Covid pandemic and they couldn't give us a goodbye lunch or anything, but they could have involved us in their plans to evolve the show over that last year and let us play a part in the handover.

Three days later I got a call to say two of the red tops were going to go with the story on Sunday. I was told the BBC publicity department had sent me a statement that they wanted me to approve immediately. So they hadn't even bothered to get a quote from me. The statement said that the three of us had decided to step aside and leave the show. If this had been decided earlier, we could have worded it together so that all parties were happy. We hadn't decided to step aside at all. We point-blank refused to sign it and the drama continued.

That evening I started receiving calls. It was amazing how, suddenly now, the manner of our departure had become important. Why hadn't they reacted to our request earlier? Why had we been shown so little respect? Our disappointment made us less likely to help them. I was told we needed to nip this in the bud. I was then asked to say in my statement that I was leaving for the good of the show. I was astounded. Was that because I was too old or not good enough?

Either way, it was insulting. Did they actually expect me to sack myself and show myself no respect at all? I told them to own it themselves and to declare publicly that they wanted to finally do their refresh; then stand by it and believe in it. I wasn't going to lie to make it easier for them. They then offered me my job back, but as I couldn't help but feel they didn't want me any more, I declined. I was asked again the following day to say I was leaving 'for the good of the show'. What were they thinking?

It could have been so different if they had done as I suggested and allowed us to be a part of the changing-of-the-guard process. I knew my days were numbered when the BBC brought in a creative advisor. He had been present at all our recording dates in that final year and I told the boys that he was certain to have been brought in to think through a new line-up. That proved to be the case. He must have come up with the idea of having celebrities on the show. So at that point my fate was sealed.

This is something I have fought year after year. It amazes me that the BBC don't think sports stars are big enough names to carry a show. If you look at the highest viewing figures across the board in any given year, sport is way up there. Besides, this is *A Question of Sport*. The clue is in the title. It's fundamentally a sports quiz that is family entertainment. It's not light entertainment with a sports theme. It's a fun showcase for athletes who have achieved something special. To come on the show was a badge of honour. Viewers loved seeing their sporting heroes pitted against each other, revealing their 'off-pitch' personalities. I reluctantly accepted celebrities on the Christmas special as long as that was it.

But that was it for us. All good things come to an end and I'd had 24 magical years as the longest-serving host in the programme's history. It wasn't the ending of an era that stung, but the way it was handled. Matt, Phil and I are former sports professionals. We were brought up in the school of hard knocks. We would have accepted a situation if, for example, they'd planned ahead and said, 'This will be your last year, and we'd love you to help look for a suitable new host and new captains' – like the way David Coleman handed me his role. A good-humoured evolution would have been in the spirit of the show and easier for fans as well as for the new quizmaster and captains. There seemed little understanding of our chemistry and the way we worked together and little appreciation of all the years we'd put in to make sure each show was as good, if not better, than the last. The whole scenario was confusing and distressing. I had snappers stalking me when I was walking the dogs in my village. And then the auditions for a new quizmaster and captains went on for months …

What a time I had, though, working with some great captains. I'm still in touch with Ally, JP and Frankie, and I know

Daws, Tuffers and myself will continue to have many fun lunches and dinners in the future, laughing over the many hilarious moments we've experienced together. They've been a joy to work with and we will always be great friends.

Our farewell tour around the country was a tremendous tonic – and a wonderful way to end. The tour was supposed to be a 50th anniversary celebration, but because of Covid, it was 18 months late. With the blessing of the BBC, it became our swan-song. Over the autumn and winter of 2021, we took a live stage show with rotating guests to Manchester, Liverpool, Birmingham, Edinburgh, London, Brighton, Hull, Cardiff, Leeds, Glasgow, Nottingham, Plymouth, Southampton and Newcastle – and it was raucous and emotional to the very last sounding of the buzzer. We didn't expect that. After being sacked as has-beens, we were nervous about how much interest there'd be in people turning up to see us. We'd written the scripted bits in the bar the night before. The first night in Manchester was terrifying, Daws peeked at the audience from behind the curtain and whispered, 'It's packed. It's FULL.' There were the three of us croaking with emotion – and I've walked out and competed on Centre Court, Matt has won the World Cup on the biggest stage, and Tuffers played at Lords and the Oval. The whole crowd stood up as we walked out on stage to the iconic theme tune. The reception was electric; the warmth for us spine-tinglingly tangible. It really got to me. I had to borrow Tuffers's hankie.

CHAPTER 22

LET'S STITCH HER UP

People often remark on my near-zero public profile. You certainly won't have seen me welcoming readers of *Hello!* magazine into my charming Cotswold home or filling the weekend supplements with my idea of a perfect Sunday. With all the television I have presented for BBC Sport from 1993 and 24 years of being beamed into the nation's sitting rooms with *A Question of Sport*, I think people have seen enough of me.

Often during Wimbledon fortnight, the match being shown on BBC1 will overrun. When this would happen, I would have to say, 'Live coverage will continue over on BBC2.' I'd vanish from the screen on BBC1 when I moved across to BBC2, but would reappear immediately to viewers who hadn't changed channel, as next up on BBC1 was often *A Question of Sport*, pre-recorded of course. The Beeb would get letters, texts and tweets saying, 'How can Sue Barker be in two places at once?' I wish my dad had witnessed one of those summer moments – Sue Barker controlling the airwaves during Wimbledon! He'd have enjoyed that.

It was always a thrill to see my name and picture in the local newspapers when I first started playing tennis. I love flicking through Dad's scrapbooks now, seeing pictures of Mr Roberts's squad at the Bristol junior hard-court championships or a head-line proclaiming an IMPRESSIVE WIN BY 14-YEAR-OLD TORBAY STAR. There's one article that includes a photo of me perched on the arm of a chair in our living room as I clutch two trophies, above eight paragraphs explaining how I'd actually lost in the Great Britain final of the Nestle's schools' tennis tournament, but won a prize for coming top of the English schoolgirls. Below the article is a few lines of monthly bogey results from Churston Ladies golf, headed by Mrs B. Barker – Mum!

At the time, I appreciated the local press coverage as affir-mation of the progress I was making. Now, these records are just wonderful chronicles of the fun we were having along the way. Junior tennis at regional and national level was meticulously observed by a group of writers who were huge enthusiasts of tennis and all the players who had the potential to go far. The monthly write-ups in *Lawn Tennis* magazine chronicle every step of my junior career from our Marist Convent school exploits to the annual national Under-14, Under-16, Under-18 and Under-21 tournaments all over the country in forensic detail. Even stories I thought might be purely anecdotal are backed up in reports, such as Dan Maskell pointing out the 13-year-old me to Dewar Cup television viewers as 'one to watch'. The December 1969 issue of *Lawn Tennis* carried a panel of three photos from the

Dewar Cup final at the Palace Covered Courts, Torquay, with the caption: 'Four stars of today and one of tomorrow. L to R: Virginia Wade, Julie Heldman, ball-girl Susan Barker (remember the name), John Clifton and Mark Cox.'

Until I reopened Dad's scrapbooks, I had no idea my junior trajectory was so meteoric and that I never lost to anyone younger than me – I was just living it – but it's all documented in the lyrical style of the times. I am always described as 'the golden-haired Marist Convent schoolgirl' (graduating to the 'golden-haired princess from Paignton' when I had my milestone win over Glynis Coles). The correspondents were as engaged in the competition and rivalries as the players. Columnist Boris Harris nominated his two happiest moments of 1971 as 'Nichola Salter and Susan Barker winning the doubles at the National Junior Championships, and the Leningrad Philharmonic Orchestra's reading of Shostakovich's fifth symphony, as there was a great similarity between the two events. Both were executed with verve, tension and high emotionalism.' Crikey! In print, he very generously suggested I was, perhaps, 'another Chris Evert in the making' and offered me avuncular advice ahead of the most decisive and difficult years of my tennis career: 'Just listen to Arthur Roberts, and respect and take heed of every word he says.' Yes, sir!

Once I was on the tour, it was always nice to see the friendly faces of the British press corps at the majors and the tournaments in the United States when the organisers invited them over to help drum up much-needed publicity to satisfy the sponsors. Life could be very lonely on the circuit and there was great camaraderie among the press and players, as I most memorably recall from that night in Paris when the *Daily Mail*'s Laurie Pignon and his wife, Melvyn, the Dragon, took me out to Montmartre on the eve of the French Open final. With his bushy grey moustache, huge sunglasses and pipe, Laurie was a larger-than-life figure who liked to wear bright pink shirts under checked blazers with vibrant cravats. Lance Tingay, a distinguished tennis historian, was as measured in his manners as he was in his prose, and always wore a suit and tie or a sweater with a tie. His quiet demeanour was in total contrast to Laurie. John Parsons, who we knew as JP, started at the *Mail* and succeeded Lance at the *Daily Telegraph*. Then there was my old friend Gerry Williams and David Gray, another flamboyant personality who wrote fabulously about tennis. They were professional observers, passionate about tennis, who were scrupulously fair and honest in all they wrote, but also our loyal supporters – Laurie would stand up and cheer for us from the press seats. At the Italian Open, Virginia and I had an annual tradition of going out to dinner with them.

Everything said that night was 'off the record'. Even when they wrote the odd stinking article about my game, I never fell out with them. I used to visit Laurie and the Dragon for dinner in their cottage in Sunbury-on-Thames long after he retired. 'Let me show you my lower orchard!' he'd proclaim – and then lead me to one solitary apple tree in the corner of his garden. It was always fun to be around Laurie.

It was when tennis mushroomed into a global box-office attraction that we began to encounter a more intrusive style of journalism, focused on our off-court lives. The fairy-tale engagement in 1974 between Chris Evert and Jimmy Connors – both champions at Wimbledon that year – enshrined them as tennis's golden couple. The story of the 'lovebird double' came hot on the Fila-clad heels of Borg's hordes of hysterical teenybopper fans whose displays made front-page news of Wimbledon. Suddenly news reporters wanted to know who was dating who – and before you knew it tennis players were romantically linked to models, royalty, Hollywood stars, singers, television personalities, anything that made a headline above some paparazzi snaps.

I was happy to talk tennis on the circuit and enjoy the banter between the British players and the accompanying press pack. I was not so happy when reporters started pestering my family at home. My sister, who used to get so fed up being dragged to Eastbourne for our family summer holidays, would now come home from university or her teaching life in London and find herself parrying calls from reporters wanting snippets of information about my life. She used to pretend to be a cleaner.

I learned from my brief romantic friendship with Cliff that there were no boundaries, no respect. There was a story the press wanted – an ongoing relationship between Cliff and me – and one they persisted in perpetuating no matter what I said or what evidence there was to the contrary. Asking Cliff questions about me over the years, knowing we had long ago moved on, gave papers licence to print his response with yet another headline pairing our names together. I hated the feeling that the truth about my own life could be so wilfully misconstrued. By nature I'm private, and I didn't go into tennis – or television – in order to be famous. My professional careers just happen to be dependent

on an audience. The Cliff scenario took me into a different strato-
sphere of press attention. I wish I'd never gone there; I'll never get
away from it. Which is why I really shy away from doing anything
unless it's live radio or TV and I can't be misrepresented.

The experience that burned me came at the first Wimbledon
I hadn't played in since 1973 – an emotional milestone in itself –
and I was offered a lucrative, exclusive contract to write a series of
columns for a Sunday tabloid. I thought it sounded like a great
post-retirement gig, as I would have an involvement in the fortnight's action. Naively, I thought they wanted me to write about
tennis. Some of the newspaper's reporters came around to my
house for a chat about material for my first column, a preview
of the tournament. They asked if I had any personal photos and
I gave them an album or two to look at while I went to make
them cups of tea. What I didn't realise at the time was that they
removed some pictures from their mounting corners and took
them away with them.

On the first day of Wimbledon, I went off in search of my
friends in the players' facilities and received such a torrent of criticism that I retired to my flat. They were not happy in the dressing
room about my 'tournament preview'. When I read the words
printed under my name, I was horrified. I didn't recognise them
as my own. They stitched me up good and proper, putting words
into my mouth about players on tour. They had me talking about
Chrissie and John Lloyd, saying they'd never last as a couple,
which I would never have done because they're both really good
friends of mine. Over the course of this column I was sort of
slaughtering every player in the draw. It was truly awful. A friend

sought out Chrissie and John in the Players' Lounge and told them I'd never said any of these things, but they said they were angry. And they were right to be incensed.

Within months they understood, and could see how upset I was by it. But I think they wondered if I'd done it for the money – as I would have thought if someone did that to me.

So that was it. Never again. How naive had I been? What did the Sunday tabloid want for its money? Not me saying, 'Ooh, I thought so-and-so played a lovely match and so-and-so was unlucky.' The final straw was 'my' last column, which was all totally untrue stuff about Cliff, using my personal pictures to give credence to the whole fabrication. I was so angry I went to the newspaper's office and said I wanted my private photos back. They said I'd offered them. I asked IMG for advice and they said I didn't have a strong case to sue them because it was one word against another.

I knew where the editor lived – in Wimbledon village, up the hill from the All England Club – so I went and knocked on his door. I was so infuriated I needed to take action. I wanted to ask him why he'd do that to me. His wife answered the door. She didn't ask me in. She called out over her shoulder and a big bloke came to the door. 'Oh, yes,' he said, clearly recognising me. 'What do you want?' He was not friendly at all.

I said, 'I want to know why you would do this to me because I didn't say any of the things that were printed under my name. Why did you do that?'

He looked at me and said, 'Because you're yesterday's news.' Then he shut the door in my face.

And that hurt me even more, the fact that he couldn't care less. I wasn't with Cliff. I'd given up tennis. I wasn't going to feature in any stories, so it was like, 'Let's stitch her up.'

That incident was the final straw. I can't understand that mentality. Who gets anything out of that? I was missing my tennis life. I was feeling alienated from the world I'd grown up in and isolated with all my friends still being on the tour, and I walked into the players' facilities at Wimbledon so excited to be reunited with everyone – only to face a cold reception. It was a horrible era for news press coverage. And I was on the receiving end, too. The number of times I've phoned up someone and said, 'Why did you say that about me?' And they said, 'Do you think I said that?'

It's why I've shunned doing interviews. I have a public persona as a former athlete and a mainstream television presenter and I've always agreed to do associated publicity work as a player and a BBC face, but I don't enjoy being in the public eye for the sake of it. I don't go to awards dinners or red-carpet functions. I'm invited to a lot of glitzy events but I always send my regrets. Even on the many occasions when our *A Question of Sport* team was nominated for a BAFTA I didn't go. That's partly because my husband isn't comfortable in that showbiz environment, but also because, in terms of a work-life balance, my work is in the public eye and my life is time spent enjoying my privacy.

Lance did accompany me to two awards dinners. He was a police officer at the time and had to book a day of annual leave to travel with me up to London for the event. We arrived, dressed up in our finery, only to discover we were a day early. Obviously, he couldn't try again the next day. On the second occasion, we turned up as a couple and discovered there wasn't a seat for him at the dinner table. We joked about the perils of being a 'plus one', but that was enough for Lance. As he said, he wouldn't expect me to come along to any of his police functions.

· · ·

This Is Your Life, hosted first by Eamonn Andrews and then Michael Aspel, was a high-profile family entertainment show I'd followed all my life. It was always interesting to see who was being surprised with the big red book, just as today it's fun to see who's on *Strictly Come Dancing* or *Dancing on Ice*. I once said to Lance, 'I will divorce you if you get me on that show,' and I told my mum I'd never speak to her again if she had any involvement in signing me up for it. I did not want my life aired without me having any control over it (naively, I believed that people were genuinely ambushed on the day).

In my diary on 19 February 1996, I was down to do an early evening radio interview with John Dunn, who hosted the weekday drive-time show on Radio 2 in Broadcasting House – as I understood it, for something related to my role at the BBC. Lance casually suggested that we meet up for dinner with some friends we hadn't seen for ages while I was in London. We discussed booking a nice restaurant – he knew that I would stick on a pair of jeans, trainers and a baseball cap if I was just doing radio. I put on a reasonable shirt and trousers and off I went at the appointed time to do this interview. When I arrived, I realised John had just come off air. I thought maybe we were going to record a short item. I sat down and we chatted away for a few minutes. Then Michael Aspel appeared at the back of the studio with the big red book and I assumed it was for John. He was 20 years or so older than me. I was just 39. I mean, I thought I hadn't had a life yet. 'Oh, John, congratulations!' I screeched, clapping excitedly.

But Michael bypassed John and said, 'Sue Barker. This is your life.'

I thought, *This cannot be happening.* I must have had such a fixed smile on my face. I had a basic mobile phone in those days, which was whisked off me. I wasn't allowed to contact anyone. I was escorted to a room at BBC Television Centre and not allowed out. Food and drinks were provided. Recording would start in an hour. My first thought was, *Oh God, what am I going to wear?* I was told not to worry – Lance had brought me some outfits. Well, that was cause for worry. Needless to say, he brought me a choice of two suits, no matching shoes, no stockings and no top to wear under a jacket. I mean, absolutely no thought went into it whatsoever. We had to send out for stockings and matching shoes, but I wouldn't have chosen the shoes or the outfit. I felt ridiculous but out on to the stage I went in this cream skirt-suit and saw in front of me, assembled in the seats, a who's who of my life. Everyone thought it was hilarious. Michael said, 'Meet the person responsible for this … your husband, Lance!' When Lance came on to the stage, I moved towards him smiling, but if you can lip-read, it's clear I say to him, 'You're dead.'

Lance answered Michael's questions and he sounded like an alien. I don't know how he ever agreed to do it because he was so out of his comfort zone. And there was my mum, my brother and sister, cousins, extended family, my old school friends Giovanna and Melanie … friends from tennis such as John Barrett, Angela

Mortimer, John Parsons, Laurie Pignon and the Dragon, Gerry Williams, Roger Taylor, Mark Cox; people I've met through television, like Paul Dempsey, Robin Cousins, Duncan Goodhew, Harry Carpenter. Even Des Lynam was there. They had a link to Pam Shriver and Chris Evert in America. Other guests who walked on included our PE teachers, Mrs Chadwick and Mrs Embury – without either of those two selfless teachers I wouldn't have been standing there. Next came Sister Placidus, Sister Moira and Sister Evaristus. Crikey, two of them tried to expel me when I'd turned Sister Moira's plants upside down because she wouldn't let me go and play tennis, but they came on stage and it was such a surreal experience because they were so lovely in everything they said. Michael then announced there was one person who particularly remembered me at the Marist Convent who knew I was 'destined to be a superstar'. It was the sort of drum-roll entrance: 'You probably remember him, Sue, as Brother Alan, but he's now Reverend Alan. Please welcome the reverend …'

My mind went blank. I had no recollection of this brother. It was absolutely bizarre. He walked on and I still didn't recognise him. I glanced across at Giovanna and Melanie and they were looking at me quizzically. The reverend gave me a big hug and told these amazing stories about how talented I was and how he knew I was going to be this, that and the other. Thank you very much. Off he goes to take his seat.

Then my Australian friend Karen Scott came on. And when I saw her I had my head in my hands because Karen and I misbehave when we're together. I knew she would want to tell a naughty story about some silly antics we'd got up to and I was thinking, *Oh no, this is on national television!* Thankfully she largely managed to restrain herself, and after the final guests had said their bit, the party got under way. Des had popped in for the start of the show, but he was preparing for *Match of the Day* and said he'd pop back later.

The mystery of Reverend Alan continued. I sidled up to Giovanna and Melanie and asked if they knew him from the church, as they are both Catholic and had to go to Mass at the convent, unlike me. They couldn't place him. The party was in full swing and the reverend was hosing down the drinks, getting more and more p****d. Des came back and whispered, 'I don't think he's going to last long.' Within minutes, the reverend had collapsed and was out cold on the floor. The producers had him swiftly taken back to the hotel in a taxi. And we thought no more about it.

A week later the producer called to see how the programme had gone down with me. She revealed that the majority of people pretend they're surprised but in reality they have already discussed it with their family. I said I would have had a very different list if I'd had any say in this programme. I mean, where did that reverend come from? And what happened to him? Apparently, once he'd woken up from his drunken stupor, he cleared out the hotel minibar and scarpered. We still have no idea who he was, but he enjoyed a very nice trip up to London, got totally slaughtered and left with his suitcase clinking with miniatures. So well done him. Despite my misgivings, we had such a laugh at the party and it actually made it with the nuns coming on and the mysterious reverend. The holy barmy army was back.

● ● ●

Among the lovely fan letters I receive at the BBC, there are the occasional disturbing ones. My fan mail used to be opened by a kind girl in the office who would send back a reply with a stock picture I'd signed. I'd had a lot of 'I'm going to kill you' letters when I was playing tennis, which was something I learned to live with, but the young girls who opened the ones sent to the BBC told me they were traumatised by some of the cranky requests. I told them it wasn't their role to deal with them and to stick all the letters in a box and I'd go through them.

Some were difficult to know how to handle. Were they from a harmless weirdo or could it be a potential stalker? On one occasion I received a letter from an admirer who had taken a picture of himself naked in the bathroom and had the photo blown up. Over his manhood, he had scrawled, 'The speaking cock'. Typically I would have dismissed this, but it came with a weird letter as well. This was after my friend Jill Dando, a prominent face on the BBC, had been killed on her doorstep under circumstances that have never been solved. Lance took it to the police. The officer on reception took it into a back room and raucous laughter erupted. They didn't know what to make of it.

Des and I were recording a launch at Wimbledon for our summer coverage on 26 April 1999 when we heard the devastating news about Jill. I used to see her in the BBC canteen and at Cliff's birthdays and other events. As a newbie at the BBC, I confided in her about quite a few things and she was always generous in giving me her take. I respected her professionally because she was flying in her career and, on a personal level, she couldn't have been nicer.

Four or five years after her murder, I opened a letter, which turned out to be a five-page rant, that was very disturbing. The writer said he had watched me interviewing Serena Williams and he had then imagined weird things that Serena and I were doing together sexually. In his head, there was something going on between us, which he didn't like, and he threatened to kill me like Jill Dando. Then he started ranting about the BBC and other presenters, including Ray Stubbs, who was presenting *Football Focus* at the time. I dismissed it all as the crazy thoughts of a twisted fantasist, but there was one paragraph at the end that stopped me in my tracks. The letter writer stated: 'I'm going to kill the children in a Sunday school in Scotland while their parents are praying next door.'

As soon as I read this, I gave it to Lance. Should I be worried here? The letter had come from Thailand, but the writer had signed off with a British name. Lance said the fact that he'd signed it meant he didn't think he was going to go through with his threats. But we agreed we couldn't live with the bit about the children. What if we woke up to discover that kids had been killed in a Sunday school while their parents were next door and we hadn't reported this letter? Following Lance's advice, I handed the letter to a BBC security officer. He agreed that it probably wasn't anything untoward, but he said he'd give it to the Metropolitan Police in Hammersmith. And that, I thought, was the end of it.

Two days later, I woke up to hear my name on the third item on the news thanks to a headline in the *Sun* – SUE BARKER TO 'DIE LIKE DANDO' – and a front-page splash in the *Daily Mail*:

Sue Barker Death Threats. My phone was ringing constantly; the press were trying to get hold of me. I rang the BBC security and said, 'Oh my God, what's happening? How has this leaked?' The detective didn't know and said he'd find out. Later he called me back to say he'd discovered that the paperwork may have been put in the wrong in tray or processed the wrong way by the admin team at the police station and someone had read this and thought they could make a quick buck. I later received a letter from the police informing me an investigation had revealed that a police employee received £1,500 from the *Sun*. And so the story escalated out of all proportions. I had safeguarded my privacy for years but now there were press and photographers outside our house. Photographs of our previously undisclosed home address were published with the name of my village. No one cared about my security. The reports were about someone who wanted to kill me and they were pinpointing exactly where I lived. I told the papers I didn't want to take this further, I was letting the police deal with it.

The culprit was still in Thailand, but then he wrote a similar letter to the reporter who had written the *Daily Mail* articles about him, threatening to kill her. The *Daily Mail* went into overdrive on the grounds of protecting their writer. Well, thanks – let's show the world where I live, publish a picture of my house, photograph me on my daily routine, detail the events I'm going to be doing – but you're going all out to protect your reporter. The man was arrested. The *Mail* did take him to court for his behaviour towards their reporter and he went to jail. I never heard from him again.

CHAPTER 23

RULE BRITANNIA

Lillehammer, Victoria, Atlanta, Nagano, Kuala Lumpur, Sydney, Salt Lake City, Manchester, Athens, Turin, Melbourne, Beijing, Vancouver, New Delhi, London … Between 1993 and 2012, my diary auto-filled with the greatest sporting events on the planet. I've been lucky enough to have had a front-row seat as records have been broken and emotional personal milestones marked at summer and winter Olympic Games and the Commonwealth 'Friendly' Games. Add in the seasonal block-booking of tennis, racing and athletics in the summer, and I wonder: was I ever home? One summer, the lovely lady who booked my travel logistics and hotels also scheduled a hotel massage. 'You'll need it to get through this,' she laughed.

I had been heavily involved in our coverage of the Atlanta, Sydney and Athens Games, but in August 2005 Roger Mosey took over as Director of Sport and I realised I was never going to be his cup of tea. The former editor of *Today* had earned a strong reputation in his role as Head of BBC Television News. He moved across to Sport intent on changing the culture and redesigning the portfolio of sports programmes to reflect the loss of rights packages to ITV, Sky and Channel 4, and to maximise the benefits of digital services to traditional broadcasting. I had been presenting athletics for eight years when he told me he was looking for a new presenter. He made it clear I wasn't going to be the main presenter at the 2008 Beijing Olympics. But months later I ended up in my old role by default. It was almost like a last-minute thing – actually Sue, can you do it now? Which doesn't make you feel great. It was not an easy experience knowing that the day I finished, I was out, especially as the crew and studio guests knew it too. But I had a fantastic time in the studio in the Bird's Nest stadium: the opening and closing ceremonies were dazzling and it was a wonderful way to bow out.

My BBC contract was up at the end of 2008, and I was sure I would be leaving. So much so that, in late 2007, Lance and I moved from Surrey to a much smaller house in a lovely setting in one of the most beautiful villages in the Cotswolds. In my usual manner of trying to fly under the radar, I kept my head down and we moved in without fuss or rumour. On the first morning we woke up in our secluded idyll, I popped to the local shop to get some milk and tea. We had an estate car with one of those electronic handbrakes (which I hate). I came out of the shop to find my car had rolled out of the car park, crossed the road, crashed through someone's fence and was now buried nose-down in their back garden. That was my low-profile entry to village life …

At least it wasn't one of my supercars. I've owned three Ferraris over the years and probably most of the other super-cars out there. When we lived in Surrey, we were close to the track where *Top Gear* was filmed. I always wanted to appear in the Star in a Reasonably Priced Car segment, but was never invited. Racing around a track has always appealed to me. I loved taking part in the Goodwood Festival of Speed, driving a Ferrari up the hill. My all-time favourite car has to be the Lamborghini Urus. We flew out to Italy to have a tour of the Lamborghini factory and to test-drive the car. There is some-thing thrilling about the power and control of a Lambo and the sound of its trademark engine roar, but the downside is the attention they bring you. Some owners seem to make money on these cars; I've managed that a couple of times but generally found them a money pit. Following our move to the Cotswolds, I gradually became much more sensible and am now on my fifth Mini. Mind you, it is the fastest one they make. We also have a 20-year-old doggie car. It used to belong to my mum but when she was in her mid-nineties she started using it like a dodgems car, giving everyone a nudge as a gauge of how close she was to nearby vehicles.

• • •

Prior to the Beijing Games, London 2012 had obviously been under discussion. Roger had promised me I would be a major part of the home Games. He referred to his vision of a series of billboards lining the route from Heathrow Airport into

London with the BBC faces of the Games. I was to be one of them. Before Roger's switch to Sport, I'd been involved in the pitch to get London on the shortlist as host for the 2012 Games. Under Sebastian Coe's aegis, we created a short video indicating the planned locations for the venues. Seb asked me to wear something bright as I'd be standing in fields and wasteland. I dug out a turquoise jacket and navy trousers.

One segment had me standing outside Stratford station, repeating over and over again the line, 'The magic of Stratford is that you'll be able to get a train into the centre of London in less than ten minutes.'

Every time I said it, a commuter walked past and shouted, 'Are you kidding?' We got a lot of abuse.

I stood in Greenwich Park, pointing towards the site of the mooted Olympic Village on a de-industrialised brownfield site on the other side of the river, and filmed from Horse Guards Parade, the venue for beach volleyball. It seemed outrageous, but we had beautiful weather and London looked at its very best. And it worked. Months down the line, London was nominated to be on the shortlist alongside Paris, Madrid, Moscow and New York City.

Seb called again: 'Sue, have you still got that turquoise jacket?' We did another two days of filming for a video that I didn't know was to be screened during the actual bidding process. I was proud of our video and shared everyone's euphoria when the IOC awarded London the right to host the 2012 Games. It was a once-in-a-lifetime event for the whole nation. Following Steve Rider's departure from the BBC, I was the lead general sports presenter and had front-and-centre experience of summer and winter Games since 1994. I was excited beyond words about the prospect of helping present a home Olympics. It was a one and only shot to be part of the biggest event in recent British sports history, but the rug was pulled from underneath me when my 2008 contract negotiations became extremely strained.

I received a phone call from a person in the accounts department who informed me that there was to be a change in contracts and that each sport and programme I presented would have a monetary value. I was told, by the by, that I was being let go from athletics and racing. (I was quite happy about the racing, in fact I'd pushed to be relinquished of that for some time – but it was disconcerting to hear such news from the accounts department.) Then came the money offer. After totalling the fees, I discovered I was being offered a contract – like Steve Rider before me – that I could only refuse. It seemed obvious that Roger wanted rid of me. I have huge respect for Roger and his career but it was obvious that I didn't fit with his plans. The offer was considerably lower than the value of my previous contract. What's more, it was exclusive and the BBC could take me off any sport at any time. They confirmed that if the BBC took me off everything except, say, tennis, I would only receive payment for that sport and I could not work for anyone else. It was madness. I told the lady in accounts that no idiot would accept that offer and no idiot should offer it (I didn't mean her). I didn't have an agent, I didn't have David Coleman's advice any more, I had to deal with the highs and lows myself. I decided I would leave the BBC at the end of the year.

Many BBC people who I liked and respected met me to try and persuade me to stay but I was determined to leave. Roger Mosey, I felt, underestimated my ability. I told him I was leaving.

Further down the line, I was asked to discuss a joint statement about my departure. They said I should say I was leaving 'to explore other opportunities'. I told them I would compose my own statement, thank you very much.

Later that day, the director general Mark Thompson's secretary called and said he wanted to see me on Monday morning. He asked why I was leaving? I gave him my side of the story and described the way I had been treated. He seemed shocked. On the spot he offered me a deal, a contract organised personally by him. It was for five years.

Come the programming for London 2012, I suspected that Roger Mosey would not give me as prominent a role as in previous Games. I'd been the main face of the coverage of Beijing's opening and closing ceremonies but I was no longer fronting athletics. Roger rated Gary Lineker highly and Gary was duly named the host of the primetime evening coverage. I had the 4–7pm shift on BBC1, which moved to BBC2 for the last hour. Clare Balding didn't even have a studio show and was based at the swimming pool in the Aquatic Centre. Roger Mosey was a newsman and he thought an Olympics on home soil was a national event that needed the gravitas of prominent news anchors. I think his view was that I was not journalistically strong enough to be in the main presenter role, but I would argue that he underestimated what sports presenters, well versed in technically tricky outside broadcasts, bring to a multi-sports event in terms of an awareness of the depth and range of knowledge required, and the technical dexterity to jump from venue to venue. The telling of the story of a home Olympic Games is not just about the action that unfolds during those 17 days, not just about the 'breaking news'; often it's about the significance of a story for the athlete or country involved. The seeds of many of the stories are rooted in the years of the quadrennial cycle – the stuff that we sports presenters live and breathe and can react to instinctively, without scripts or autocue.

Huw Edwards was to be commentator for the opening ceremony. It wasn't clear who would be the presenters, but the rumour was that it would be a line-up from News. Roger's line was that the London Olympics were 'bigger than sport'. That was really disappointing: since 2000, I had co-presented the last three summer and winter Games formalities and the Commonwealth Games, and it was gutting to be denied a role in introducing the start of my home Olympics. However, the fiasco surrounding the Queen's Diamond Jubilee river-pageant broadcast prompted a re-think. In Roger's memoir, *Getting Out Alive: News, Sport and Politics at the BBC*, he described the coverage of that as 'very bad indeed':

> The weather was terrible, causing technical problems for the outside broadcast. The mood of the programme, which might have worked on a sunny day, felt wrong from the start. The casting of talent was not right. There were unforced errors in the presentation and commentary.

Late in the day when it comes to Olympic planning – ten days before the Games – Gary and I were told we would be co-presenting the opening and closing ceremonies after all. I just got on with it.

We knew why we were doing it and we were determined to do a top job and not let Sport down. After the years of being downgraded, I felt very fortunate to get the opportunity to present the curtain-raiser live from the Olympic Stadium in front of the Queen, the Duke of Edinburgh, the Prince of Wales, the then prime minister David Cameron and several of his predecessors, and numerous IOC dignitaries. That emotionally stirring night stands out as one of the most gratifying in my career. Gary and I came on air at 7pm and for two hours hosted the build-up to Danny Boyle's 'Isles of Wonder' sound-and-vision spectacular. The Red Arrows flew past at 8.15pm. From the depiction of 'A Green and Pleasant Land' and the Industrial Revolution through to the Queen's cameo appearance with James Bond, it was a love letter to Britain with quirky touches – featuring 23,000 costumes, 12,956 props, 10,000 volunteers, 40 sheep, 12 horses, 10 chickens, 10 ducks, 9 geese, 3 cows, 3 sheepdogs and 2 goats. A UK audience of 26.9 million people tuned in that night – one of the 20 most-watched programmes in UK TV history – and I felt fiercely proud to be British.

BBC politics aside, London 2012 was memorable in so many ways – starting with a pre-Games lunch with the Queen. A wonderful embossed envelope arrived at home from the Palace with an invitation to lunch at Buckingham Palace with Her Majesty the Queen and the Duke of Edinburgh. It was to be a small, intimate lunch with six guests. I couldn't reply quickly enough. What an honour! On the day, I drove myself down the M40 to London from our home in the Cotswolds in my Mini. The invitation had said parking was available and I thought I would be in a little car park around the corner somewhere. Incredibly, I was beckoned in through the famous gates with a 'Hello, Ms Barker, we are expecting you.' To my amazement, they directed me through the famous arch into the quadrangle. It seemed so ridiculous, and slightly embarrassing, to steer my little car into the famous central court of the Palace, which was empty except for my humble Mini. The other guests had been dropped off in chauffeur-driven cars. I was shown into a beautiful reception room for pre-lunch drinks before the Queen and the Duke arrived accompanied by the corgis.

It's protocol not to report private conversations with royalty but it was a fascinating and enjoyable couple of hours that rank among my favourite memories. Lunch was delicious and we had a lot of laughs along the way. It was a very relaxed atmosphere. I was seated next to the Duke and opposite the Queen. The hilarious chap to my right who I won't name (David, you know who you are) decided at the end of the lunch that we should, on this very special occasion, have some sort of memento to treasure. I was to sneak two lovely menus into my handbag and he was going to slip our two place cards into his jacket; we would swap outside. We were giggling like children. As we descended the stairs we were met by a Palace official who wanted to formally send us off with some gifts ... which included a beautifully embossed menu. As he handed them over, he said, 'You see, you didn't need to take them after all. Don't worry,' he added as we dissolved into laughter, 'you're not the first and you won't be the last.'

During the Games themselves, how can I forget the windy day over at the All England Club, redressed in London 2012 livery, when Andy Murray won the gold medal – just weeks after his tearful on-court interview following his loss to Roger Federer? I also had an amusing chat with Prince William and Prince Harry, when they visited the studio in the Olympic Park. After we came off air, William asked if I received questions through my earpiece, because he noticed I hadn't looked at my notes.

'Give her some credit,' chipped in Harry. 'She's done her research!'

William revealed he was going to the velodrome later with Catherine. 'Ooh,' I said. 'You might get on the old kiss cam.'

He looked alarmed. 'You don't think they would do that to me?'

In unison, Harry and I said, 'Oh yes, they would.' And needless to say, they did – and they had to kiss!

For the closing ceremony, my long-time friend and producer Carl Hicks was overseeing the creation of a three-minute montage of the highlights, shaped around the sentiments of Seb Coe's inspiring speech at the start of the Games.

'There is a truth to sport, a purity, a drama, an intensity, a spirit that makes it irresistible to take part in and irresistible to watch,' Seb had said. 'In every Olympic sport there is all that matters in life. Humans stretched to the limit of their abilities, inspired by what they can achieve, driven by their talent to work harder than they can believe possible, living for the moment but making an indelible mark upon history.'

Carl called me over for an advance peep at the tape that he wanted to reflect those emotions. To the soundtrack of Emeli Sandé singing 'Imagine', it captured glimpses of athletes from starting gun to podium in gestures of jubilation and despair, in the agony of effort and the disbelief of victory, looking up to the skies in hope or thanks or celebration. As well as athletes from around the world, there were our gold medallists Mo Farah, Andy Murray, Nicola Adams, Victoria Pendleton, Jess Ennis, the rowers, the riders … It was so moving, I burst into tears. So did Carl, and so did Gabby Cook, the creative director. Thank God he'd shown me then and I didn't see it for the first time live on air. I'd have been incapable of speech.

Roger Mosey's billboards never became reality, but in the run-up to the Games, I'd been involved in an advert for Go Compare, the financial-services comparison website. My role was an undercover sniper who shot (not fatally) Gio Compario, the irritating opera singer with the twiddly moustache played by Wynne Evans. Everywhere I went in the Olympic Park, children would look at me in awe and excitedly point me out to their parents, 'Look, that's the lady who shot the Go Compare man!' Fame at last!

I've always been careful about the brands I represent, turning down advertisements for betting companies, for example, but that Go Compare ad caused some controversy, sparking a debate on a radio phone-in about whether it encouraged terrorism.

Thankfully, someone with an army background called in to point out that he'd seen terrorists use all sorts of weapons but never a giant banana-yellow bazooka. It did teach me how delicate some people's sensitivities can be and how a sense of humour can't be taken for granted. By contrast, my longest-running commercial association by a country mile is with Holiday Property Bond (HPB), a company that offers holiday investment opportunities in the most fabulous properties across Britain and Europe. I am so proud to represent HPB. I'm a bond holder myself and have enjoyed amazing holidays – with my dogs. I love meeting fellow bond holders and hearing how happy they are. I know all the bosses, who are now friends of mine. My reputation couldn't be in safer hands and that means a lot to me.

The saga leading up to 2012 made me want to draw back from my commitments at the BBC. Roger Mosey left the corporation after the Games, but the damage was done. From then on, I decided to stick to *A Question of Sport* and the tennis. I told them that after 2012, I no longer wanted to present the London Marathon, the Great North Run, the summer and winter Olympic Games, the Commonwealth Games or *Sports Personality of the Year*. Carl Doran, the executive producer of *SPOTY*, spent an entire year trying to persuade me to carry on with the year-end show – his argument was that it would be good to complete 20 years in the presenter's role, rather than 19! For me, to step back after the glorious year of our home Olympics seemed like perfect timing. Carl even called Lance to get him onside. I gave in to their request to continue presenting the ice skating, culminating in Sochi 2014, as they wanted to take their time to find the right replacement. I thought I owed them that.

I have great memories of the camaraderie forged during the big Games. I've had lots of laughs in the name of work and made many friendships that endured long after the events. After the Sydney Olympics, I received an invitation from the office of the former prime minister Sir Edward Heath to Sunday lunch at his home in Salisbury. My husband, who never wants to go to functions with me, was intrigued and persuaded me it could be fascinating to meet Ted, as he was always known, and actually a good hoot. The letter indicated that the lunch was in honour of Steve Redgrave, who had won his incredible fifth gold medal in Sydney. We drove down on the designated day to Ted's magnificent home, Arundells, in the Cathedral Close.

Armed guards let us through to park. We arrived at the front door at the same time as former athlete Sir Chris Chataway and his wife Carola. Ted himself answered the door. I had brought a pot plant for him as a present – I know, ridiculous – and he clearly thought so too. In that famous voice he boomed, 'Oh. What's *that*?' My plant was shoved into the hands of a housekeeper, and we were let in. Ted told me and Lady Chataway that we were to go to the last doorway on the left. He then told Lance and Chris to go to the second door on the right. *Weird*, I thought. *Why are we splitting up now?* I know that at some parties the ladies leave the room after dinner, but I'd never heard of it on arrival. My husband gave me a sideways look but went along with Ted's request. Carola and I were led by Ted into the reception room in which about twelve guests were chatting and drinking champagne. I now know that my husband and Chris had been directed to the downstairs toilet. Much to their amusement. Ted had obviously thought the men would need a piddle after their journeys. Chris took advantage while Lance stood guard outside. They then made their way to join us.

As my husband entered the room, Ted started to tap his champagne glass with a spoon. The room fell silent. He handed my husband a glass of champagne and with his hand on Lance's shoulder boomed, 'Ladies and gentleman, this man deserves a glass of champagne. What an outstanding achievement. Five gold medals over five Olympic Games ...' I will never forget my husband's face. I raced to his rescue: tall and blond he may be, but Steve Redgrave he was not. I explained to Ted that this was my husband and not Steve the great Olympian. He looked at Lance and said, 'What? What do you do then?' No reply was needed as our host wandered off and sat alone in the window seat.

Just at that moment – with the best comedic timing – Sir Steve and his wife Lady Ann entered the room to silence. Ted didn't even look in their direction. Steve noticed a weird atmosphere and looked for an explanation. Lance said, 'All that training, all that hard work and I've just taken all the credit for your five gold medals,' and we were laughing like schoolchildren. At the lunch, the four of us were put at the far end of the table and Ted didn't speak to Steve all day. We still mention it in our Christmas cards to each other, 22 years on.

CHAPTER 24

THIRTY YEARS OF MAGIC

2022 marked my lightest workload since signing for the Beeb in 1993. Without *A Question of Sport*, I was back where I started – at Wimbledon. This year, the centenary of Centre Court also marked my 30th Championships – a couple of nice round numbers to retire on, but the nature of an annual sports event is that there are always anniversaries to note. I've always said I will never be ready to go.

For me, Wimbledon is a case of friends reunited, literally stretching back 53 years. When I walk through the gate, I know I might bump into the family who used to live in the same street in Paignton or someone I played against in a regional Under-14 tournament, as well as my mates from the tour and the people I've met through television. When Des Lynam left in 1999, one of the concerns about promoting me to anchor the programme was that I wouldn't be able to fill the rain delays as Des did with his effortless gift of the gab. That's when I invited all my friends on to have a chat – Billie Jean, Chrissie, Martina, Mac, Tracy, Andrew Castle, Pam Shriver, Virginia and Co. As the younger stars retired, they too wanted to join in – Boris, Pat Cash, Tim Henman, Andy Roddick, to name a few – and we created a genuine insiders' bubble of conversation for viewers to feel part of. The installation of the Centre and No.1 Court roofs mean we no longer have those desperate, waterlogged days when Des would have Daisy, his West Highland terrier, in the studio for Bring Your Dog to Work Day or get me to do a tongue-in-cheek weather forecast – anything to break up the back-to-back reruns of great matches. The days are long but, with such a long-standing, close-knit crew in the studio, I love every minute.

Well … apart from the on-court interviews at the end of the finals. I don't enjoy them. It's not nerves; it's almost dread. When they were introduced in 2000 I walked on to Centre Court to talk to Pete Sampras, the winner, and Pat Rafter, the runner-up, with Martin Hopkins's voice in my ear: 'Sue Barker, at Wimbledon, just the 500 million people watching you right now. Good luck!' Thanks very much. The difficulty is that I'm speaking on a PA mike as well as to television cameras and I've still got talkback in my ear. I have to wait to hear my television cue while I'm hearing myself on the stadium speaker. With Pete and Pat, or Roger and Rafa, Andy and Novak, I'm talking to athletes with good English, but some players don't have English as their first language and I have to make sure they can understand the questions and then respond to them with humour and empathy.

I know how much it hurts to lose such a big match – a semi-final hurt me enough – and I hate thrusting a microphone under someone dazed in defeat. The last thing a player wants to do is answer questions or listen to some crowd-pleasing jokes. I try to keep it positive and say how well they've done to get there. Poor Karolína Plíšková in 2021 just burst into tears. But then with Murray in 2012, his tears were the making of him. I could have easily just taken the microphone from him and said, 'You don't have to speak, it's all right.' But I could see how emotional he was and I knew that the public hadn't warmed to him. I thought this was his chance to show the public what this loss meant to him. I was hoping he would win over a few more fans and he ended up being taken to heart by the nation. So you never know how much to ask and how much not to ask – I have to trust my instinct. There's the added pressure of the traditional format and the Royal Box – and people thinking, what *is* she wearing? I save my best two outfits for the last days of the Championships regardless of the weather.

As a team, we've been working together so long, we have our own customs and lingo. There's what Sally Richardson, the producer, calls the 'Sue Barker dash'. I might be down by No.1 Court, on air, introducing a match while the players warm up, only to hear on talkback that I need to leg it back to the studio because the match on Centre is coming to an end and I'm needed to manage the break before the next match comes on. We've got 90 seconds – that's me, my floor manager, camera and sound. I'll whip off my heels, slip into some flats and sprint back to the Broadcast Centre. We're all blonde so we're easy to spot as we charge back together: it's a sight that those in the studio looking out for us call 'the Sue-nami'.

There's only been one year when I felt out of sorts – when, in fact, I quit. It was at the end of a hot and cloudy Thursday in the first week of Wimbledon 2017. We were four days into the Championship. Two big seeds had fallen in the women's singles draw – the Czechs, Petra Kvitová and Karolína Plíšková. In the men's, the Big Four of Andy Murray, Roger Federer, Novak Djokovic and Rafa Nadal had eased through to the third round. Players left, right and centre were complaining about the slipperiness of the grass, criticism that intensified when poor Bethanie Mattek-Sands, the entertaining American doubles specialist, suffered a horrific knee injury and was stretchered off Court 17 in full view of our studio window.

The threat of thunderstorms lingered in the night air when I left Television Centre with my night's homework spilling out of my rucksack – printouts of the next day's order of play, competitor biographies, head-to-head match statistics, a list of records that could potentially be broken. My mind was mulling the next day's likely stories, wondering what questions I'd direct at which of our studio guests. It was business as usual ... but I walked back to the flat I rent close by feeling strangely on edge.

Minutes later, on the phone to my husband, I just burst into tears. It was so unlike me, *so* unlike me. No matter how gruelling a schedule at an Olympics or a Commonwealth Games or a World Championship, or a back-to-back run of major events, I had never even got close to this feeling before.

'I want to quit,' I blurted. 'I've had enough.'

Lance listened calmly as I let out my emotions. 'Let's talk about it on Sunday,' he said. 'Don't do anything rash!'

Throughout the spring of 2017 I'd travelled the world to talk to my favourite champions for a documentary called *Our Wimbledon*. Officially, it was to mark the 90th anniversary of the BBC's coverage, but it was also the most personal film I'd been involved in. I travelled to New York to track down my childhood hero and life mentor Billie Jean King. I walked in Central Park with Virginia Wade, joking – as I am fated to do – about the different paths the Wimbledon semi-finals of 1977 sent us on. I went to Florida to sit down with Chris Evert at her tennis academy in Boca Raton and cried with laughter when she muddled Keith Richards for Cliff Richard, recalling my brief romance with the pop star in 1981. Now that would have been a story …

I was fascinated to hear how the greats of tennis felt their lives had been changed by the Championships. Or vice versa. In California, Rod Laver recalled his prize for winning the trophy was 'a voucher for 20 pounds and a firm handshake and that was it'. I flew out wanting to thank Rod for all he has done for the game. His decision to turn professional in 1963 in order to support his family meant that he couldn't compete at the Grand Slams, which at the time only allowed amateur players. But Laver's star quality was immediately missed, prompting the then chairman of the All England Club, Herman David, to organise a one-off televised professional event the week after the 1967 Championship. This was so successful the club announced that in future the annual fortnight would be open to all players. It was Rod who made Wimbledon as we know it possible. At the end of the interview for this documentary, I couldn't resist delving into my bag to show him a photo I've treasured all my life.

It's the picture of the pair of us jumping the net – his trade-mark celebration – at a junior invitational tennis clinic that he and Ken Rosewall hosted back in the early 1970s when he picked me out as a star of the future.

Flying to and from these interviews was time-consuming – and expensive. Carl Doran, the producer, called me with the usual 'We have no budget… Where did you say you were going on holiday?' We had a laugh, and I thought here we go again. It was decided that my holiday in Carmel, California, was a great way of ticking off the interviews with Rod and Pete Sampras, who both lived along the west coast. The budget wouldn't have stretched to me flying there especially. But I must point out how big California is. I ended up flying up and down the coast, renting cars and staying in a hotel at my own expense to get the job done. When I hear of BBC big budgets and wastage, I think back to those days and wish they'd wasted a bit more on me.

But I'm very proud of the film. It was far more than a professional assignment. As I said at the end, 'From kissing the champions to sitting with my idols, I have laughed and cried with people I've played against and those I've admired from the stands.' The visit to Pete was particularly emotional. Focused more on results than style, Pete went about his record-breaking dominance without fanfare. After Borg's five Wimbledon titles, and Mac and Boris with three apiece, Pete's seven titles between 1993 and 2000 represent an incredible era of dominance. We showed footage of his final triumph in 2000 – the year he climbed up through the spectators to hug his rarely seen parents, Sammy and Georgia. As Pete relived the moment he got to celebrate with them, he welled up, swallowing hard to prevent tears from flowing. As a parent now, he said his regret was that he hadn't encouraged his parents to be a part of those special moments often enough. 'I carry a little bit of that today,' he admitted ruefully.

In Sweden, I reunited with Björn Borg and travelled back in time with him to relive his run of five titles and the rock-star allure he brought to the sport. Björn opened up about the personal cost of that time of competitive intensity and over-whelming fan adoration. After losing on Centre Court to John McEnroe in 1981, at the age of 25, he revealed he could no longer live 'that kind of life', and practically vanished the following year.

Mac, we managed to nail down in London. It's hard to think of any other player who has gone from being so universally booed for his brattish behaviour to being so adored by the Wimbledon faithful. Would he have been a better player had he curbed his temper? He thinks so. Or maybe not … Here was another player still mulling over 'what could have been' despite his success.

When it came to Wimbledon 2017, many of the champions who had featured so candidly in the documentary came into the studio as guests. And all of them were saying, 'Oh, we're going up to the Royal Box now,' or 'I'm just going off to meet so-and-so.' They breezed in for their slot and went off to have fun. And I was stuck in my studio chair thinking, *I'd like to go and catch up with Billie Jean and Rosie [Casals] too. I'd like to have lunch with my old tennis mates. I'd actually like to see a live ball hit!* Having had so much fun with them putting together *Our Wimbledon*, I was a little bit envious of 'their Wimbledon' – to the extent that I began to question whether I wanted to continue my TV role.

When Lance arrived at the weekend I said, 'I still feel the same. I've had enough.'

Lance always came up for the weekend when Wimbledon still kept Middle Sunday as the traditional day of rest. (The 2022 Championships saw the introduction of a Middle Sunday of scheduled play so that the men's and women's singles fourth-round matches could be played over two days, instead of all being fitted in on what became known as 'Manic Monday'.) We'd go out for dinner on Saturday and then have Sunday lunch. That time, we just talked about whether I wanted to carry on. Maybe it was the weariness of doing that documentary, all the travel, flying to California, to Florida, to New York, and then straight into the busy build-up to Wimbledon with Queen's? Or was I just frazzled by the demands of hosting the live coverage of Wimbledon for eight and a half hours a day, often across both BBC1 and BBC2, with the continuous updates required to keep pace with social media? Whatever, I had decided that was it, but I wouldn't say anything to anyone at the Beeb until the end of the tournament.

Federer won that year, becoming the first man to win the title a record eight times. After his straight-sets victory over Marin Čilić, he came up to the studio to close the show with me. I am a great admirer of his and I really appreciated his presence as a final hurrah. As I heard the countdown in my ear, I said, 'Thanks ever so much, Roger, for doing that. What a wonderful Wimbledon it's been. From all of us here, it's Roger and out.' Everyone came in and said, 'Oh Sue, that was lovely.' And Philip Bernie, then Deputy Head of Sport, came in as he always does after the credits roll, generous with his praise.

'Okay, thanks for that,' I said. 'I'm going to tell you this now. That's it. I'm done. I didn't want to say it before because, trust me, the one thing I don't want is one of those naff videotapes of my best moments. That's so not me. But I've just had enough.'

That was five years ago. As I've said, at heart I'll always be a player first and a broadcaster second – and I toppled off the tightrope between my two careers in the course of making that documentary. The emotional trip down memory lane catapulted me back to my childhood dreams and my playing days. Talking to the figureheads of my generation, I embraced that feeling of kinship and the rapport we have through our shared experiences – and I craved more of that camaraderie.

Over the next few months, the conversation with the BBC turned from my retirement to one about reducing my hours. Barbara Slater, head of BBC Sport, said that if they were plan-ning Wimbledon coverage from scratch now, they would never expect one person to front eight and a half hours continu-ously, much of it across two channels. The way the BBC covers Wimbledon has evolved from the days when the show started at 2pm, hosted with inimitable coolness by Des Lynam, and ran until the *Six O'Clock News*, followed by a late-night highlights show presented by Harry Carpenter. Today, live coverage starts at 11am and can continue until 11pm with the roof on both Centre and No.1 Court closed and the lighting that was installed to meet the demands of high-definition television. Barbara said that if I did leave, they would use two people to front the cover-age, so why couldn't one of them be me? I said I'd think about it and discuss it with my producer and editor. After much thought,

I decided I'd try it for one year. And that's how it went for the next five years; I'd found a better balance. When I signed out at 6pm, Tim Henman and I had a glass of champagne, and I would take my place in the members' seat. He even sneaked me into the Royal Box. It was the ideal way of maintaining my presenter role, which I loved, and getting to meet up with old friends and see some tennis.

It was about time I saw a live ball hit. One year, when we were only on one channel – the football Euros were on – Liz, my floor-manager friend, said, 'Look, we've just handed to a match of Andy's, shall we nip into these spare seats under the scoreboard for a few games?' We both kept our earpieces in, in case we were needed back urgently. What we didn't realise is that the scoreboard we were sitting under is the one the BBC cameras focus on – and very soon we had our producer Martin Hopkins in our ear. 'Sue Barker, I'm looking at you! Get back to the studio!'

One experience I haven't had at Wimbledon is coming to the All England Club as a spectator, with the freedom to plan my day. What would I do? Well, as soon as the honorary stewards lifted the barrier, I'd run to get a seat on the outside courts. For me, Wimbledon is about trying to earn your airfare home. Okay, there's more money in the game than when Arthur was sending me off to the South of France without the wherewithal to get back unless I progressed far enough to win prize money. But those lower-ranked players, the wild cards and qualifiers, are competing for their survival. They'll be dreaming of pulling off a big upset, of making a headline-grabbing run. I appreciate that fighting spirit. And I love watching juniors. I like to observe how they react when they get into a tight spot; you can predict the future stars from the way they deal with knockbacks. And it's amusing to see whose mannerisms they are mimicking – the Roger fist clench, the Rafa shrug, the Djokovic ball bounce, the Kyrgios head tilt ... Sometimes, something will remind me of a moment in my career, and it's quite salutary to tap back into what it felt like when I was 14 with my life ahead of me.

Thanks to Arthur Roberts, my passion for tennis, guided and channelled by him, has given me two careers I hardly dreamed possible. I've had an absolutely magical time in both. I didn't come into television to be a pioneer, and smash glass ceilings, but if I've made it easier for Clare and Hazel, Gabby, Jill or Alex Scott, I'm thrilled. I've just gone with the flow, following Arthur's advice to 'never turn anything down' and do the very best I can. He always encouraged me to take things on, 'and if it doesn't work out, laugh at yourself'. I never look back and think 'what if ...'

People ask if having children was incompatible with making my way in television. I can honestly say that if it had been that important to Lance and me, I would have given up what I was doing, but we were both always so busy that in the end we decided it wasn't for us. My career kept me so occupied and so excited that I didn't feel I needed anything extra in my life. We've just been incredibly happy as we are.

I find myself in 2022 aged 66 and looking back on a tennis career cut a little short by injury followed by a TV career that has extended beyond my wildest dreams. I remember very clearly signing on for the BBC and thinking that if I could get five years out of this I would be a very lucky girl. Thirty years later and I'm still here, albeit in a much-reduced fashion.

Some reduction in my roles has been my own choice, such as stepping back from *Sports Personality of the Year*, the Olympics and the London Marathon; some events, like the horse racing, were taken away from me. For many years I presented the Derby, the Grand National and the Prix de l'Arc de Triomphe, and for many years I wanted to stop presenting those events. The enjoyment had gone. I wasn't a natural in the world of racing and the research required became all-consuming. It will forever look as though I was dropped because at one particular contract renewal, racing simply wasn't listed any more, but I had been asking Dave Gordon to get me out of the job for several years! His argument had always been that standard coverage of racing presented by Clare Balding drew about one million viewers. The Grand National drew about nine million viewers. 'That's about eight million viewers who are not regular racing fans and they want to see someone they know,' he said. It seems incredible now given Clare's rise in stature that this was once a consideration.

The ending of my athletics role falls very much within the sacked category. As, of course, does the way *A Question of Sport* ended after 24 years. I learned nothing from the athletics sacking other than that some people have their own ideas of who they want in certain positions and that, in the world of television presenting, the arrival of a new boss often signals upheaval. I look back on my many years as the top BBC athletics presenter through three Olympic Games, Commonwealth Games and World Athletics Championships with nothing but pride.

When I reflect on my career and where I am today, I have to say the sacking from *A Question of Sport* has left me slightly damaged. I have to stress that I have no problem with being replaced as the host. Producers must always have the right to refresh a programme and take it in a new direction. No new talent will ever get the chance to flourish if people can't be moved on. Everyone has their day. It was the way it was handled. It taught me there is actually no way of leaving a role in a nice, pleasant and helpful manner with your head held high. I tried. How I tried to make it that way. How many people, knowing the end is coming, offer to 'bring on' the newly chosen and make sure the show doesn't suffer in any way? That's still the producers' choice, though. The lack of planning to prevent the news becoming public before a press release led to me being ambushed by photographers at my home. My worst nightmare.

The overwhelming feeling I was left with was a determination that this sort of treatment, this lack of care and consideration, was never ever going to happen to me again.

I'm going to 'own' my retirement from the BBC. I'm going to decide how and when I go. I'm not going to wait to be told that it's all over or to be chased out of the door. This inevitably means I will be leaving earlier than I would have normally chosen. At the time of writing, I only have the Queen's tennis tournament and Wimbledon left on my contract. I decided after *A Question of Sport* that I wouldn't wait for a hint that the end was coming before owning the decision to step back. There was a time when the BBC was chasing me with a new contract well in advance of it running out. Those days have gone ... and after this year's Wimbledon so will I.

When my contract ran out in 2019 it was the end of a five-year deal, as they had all previously been. It surprised and rather shocked me that the BBC was unaware that my contract had expired and was talking to me about various upcoming events for 2020. I had to tell them I would be out of contract. I was then offered not a five-year deal but three years going forward. I just accepted this, but it was a big hint to me that my time was nearing the end.

My contract was due to expire the moment Wimbledon 2022 came to a close. In fairness to the BBC, I had a late offer of a new three-year deal to present Queen's and Wimbledon. It was late because it came only eight weeks before my existing one expired and only by my prompting. These things happen but they never used to happen to me. It gave me too much time to evaluate my position and think about my future. My bosses spent days on end trying to persuade me to stay but, once I started to question my role, it was a door that wouldn't close.

The Championships of 2022 were to be my 30th Wimbledon for the BBC, which seemed to be a perfect punctuation point. It just felt right. I decided to announce my departure to the press just before Queen's via the *Daily Mail*'s tennis writer Mike Dickson because I wanted to stress that this was my decision, and my choice, and I wanted all of the fuss out of the way before Wimbledon got under way.

That didn't work too well.

Little did I know what an emotional rollercoaster Wimbledon would be. From the very first day, the light-hearted digs from John

McEnroe as he tried to cajole me to reconsider my decision became a regular talking point – and that was fun. However nothing prepared me for what happened elsewhere. On the final evening following the men's final, I stood on a platform in the sunshine with No.1 Court as backdrop alongside Billie Jean, Tim, Mac, Pat Cash and Clare Balding. For the first time in his life, Tim interrupted me on air to introduce a BBC video of my time at Wimbledon, both as a player and broadcaster. It was surprising … it was embarrassing … but strangely wonderful. I would like to thank Clare for her kind words and her friendship and support. Her tears set me off again and I was blown away by the words from my fellow players, both past and present. It's a video I will treasure forever: Billie Jean calling me the GOAT (greatest of all time) of sports broadcasting and Mac calling me the Roger Federer of presenting. It just doesn't get better than that. I couldn't be more proud!

That said, the memory that will linger the longest is the ovation I received on Centre Court during the Parade of Champions on the Middle Sunday. Mac and I had introduced an incredible procession of Wimbledon singles champions onto the grass as part of the centenary celebrations, starting with Angela Mortimer and including Rod Laver, Billie Jean, Björn Borg, Chrissie … so many great players … and ending with today's stars and the incomparable Roger Federer, who surprised the crowd with his appearance even though he hadn't been fit enough to compete this year. To my mind the ceremony was closing when Mac took over the microphone and turned to address me. He said he was speaking on behalf of the players. 'We will be lost without you ...' I started to laugh, but he pressed on. 'After 30 years covering this tournament magnificently ...' The crowd just erupted and I could see row after row of people getting up out of their seats. I no longer heard any more of what Mac was saying. That tribute brought me to tears. It was so unexpected. I fought so hard not to cry. There was still a closing to do and this Parade of Champions wasn't about me. I think I more or less managed it. To have that response from tennis fans meant everything. Their reaction was overwhelming, it was the most special and the proudest moment of my entire career. And I will never forget it.

I always knew that however and whenever I called time on my broadcasting career, it was going to be a difficult day and the final walk out of the BBC compound would be emotional. When the moment came, I had to leave a room full of cheering friends and colleagues wearing ridiculous Sue Barker masks. What a glorious send-off they gave me. I have no regrets though. I know it was the right thing to do.

What a wonderful run I've had, working with the most amazing people. I am BBC through and through. I have huge pride in the quality of the programmes I've worked on and that will never change. I have worked with Harry Carpenter, David Coleman, Brendan Foster, Des Lynam, Steve Rider, Barry Davies, Clare Balding and Gary Lineker. I have been directed and produced by true legends of sports broadcasting such as Dave Gordon, Martin Hopkins, Ali McIntyre, Sally Richardson, Carl Doran, Paul Davies, Sharon Lence, Carl Hicks, Michael Cole, Barbara Slater, Philip Bernie and Ron Chakraborty. There are so many more I could name. My Wimbledon couldn't work without the likes of Suzi Ross Brown, Penny Wood, Phil Jones, Liz Thorburn, Angie Jullings, Sophie Brown, Jo Salisbury, Helen Harrall, Carl Wilson, Tim Moses and Grant O'Neill ... the list is endless. I've also worked alongside tennis royalty, so a huge thank you to Mac, Billie Jean, Chrissie, Martina, Tim, Andrew, Lloydy, Pat, Tracy, Pam, Annabel and Sam. You made my role in front of the camera so much fun.

It's the hardest thing in the world – to stop doing a job you still love while you are somewhere near the top. I will miss it terribly when it's not an annual part of my life. The BBC coverage of Wimbledon has changed dramatically over the past decade. When I started, the days were much shorter and far fewer courts were televised. Today much more information is demanded and more frequently. My job was live sport – no script, no autocue, it's fly-by-the-seat-of-your-pants stuff for eight hours or more, and on BBC1 and BBC2 at the same time. It's very rare within television to have one person presenting live action simultaneously on two channels. As you get older, you don't get quicker or smarter and you don't have more energy. So I said to myself: leave at the top. Don't drop down the rankings. Don't start making mistakes and, above all, leave with your head held high. Better to walk away too early than too late.

I have loved working for the BBC and I've loved the events I've worked on. I've met some incredible people and made some great friends. I've worked with the best of the best. Thank you BBC but, most of all, thank you to my parents for their support and sacrifices through the early years, and for their faith in my passion for tennis and where it might take me. Without their blessing I would never have met the two men who changed and shaped my life.

David Hill, who was brave enough to give me a chance on television, I can never thank him enough.

And Mr Roberts, who gave me the tools to lead a life I could never have dreamed of.

God bless you, Arthur.

ACKNOWLEDGEMENTS

Two careers ... 66 years behind me ... too many people to thank. If I named them all here we'd have another book, but I must mention some.

Firstly, my parents Bob and Betty, who are no longer with me, but thankfully I was able many times to tell them how grateful I was for all they had done for me and to tell them how much I loved them.

To all those who helped contribute to this book, telling their stories, thank you to:

Billie Jean King, Chrissie Evert and Martina Navratilova. Three great champions I'm proud to call friends. I have to thank John McEnroe for his insight, knowledge and wicked sense of humour. I could sit and listen to him all day. Actually I did.

The wonderful Tim Henman, who I've known since he was a kid. Now 'young man', remember my seat in the Royal Box ... please.

My incredible US mum, Carole Hoffman. Always there for me.

Karen Happer. We've enjoyed 40 years of fun together. Here's to many more.

My besties from school and still today, Giovanna Ficorilli and Melanie Walker. Thank you for remembering so many embarrassing stories I'd conveniently forgotten.

My friends and rivals from our junior days, Nuala Dwyer, Glynis Coles and Linda Mottram.

Daws, Tuffers and Coisty … three of the funniest guys you could ever meet. Thank you for all the laughs. I look forward to our next catch-up. I'm paying. Again.

Gareth Edwards and Dave Gwymer, thank you for making us look good on QOS.

To all my wonderful BBC colleagues. I've mentioned many in my final chapter, but there are so many more. Thank you for your professionalism and all the fun we had behind the scenes.

David Luxton. From the very first steps through to completion of this book you were always so supportive. Thank you for all your help and advice.

Richard Thompson, Chairman M&C Saatchi UK, thank you for your wise words as always. Emily Rees Jones, M&C Saatchi UK, thank you too for all your help and support.

Sarah Edworthy. Little did you know the immense challenge you were taking on!! Thank you for your patience, your understanding and your outstanding detective work, particularly in the early years. Thank you for making the whole process so enjoyable.

Ebury. Thanks for being so easy to work with and for the care in making sure everything is perfect.

I know I've made it clear earlier, but thank you, Arthur

Roberts, for all the lessons on tennis and life, and thank you, David Hill, my TV hero.

Finally to Lance. He didn't want me to do this book and he didn't want to be in it ... OOPS!!

• • •

In addition, Sarah Edworthy would like to thank the following people for generously giving their time to share memories and observations of Sue's early life, tennis years and television career, often laced with the funniest (unprintable stories! In particular, Giovanna Ficorilli, Melanie Walker, Nuala Dwyer, Linda Mottram, Glynis Cole, Jane Greatbatch, Sue Mappin, Billie Jean King, Martina Navratilova, Carole Hoffman, Karen Happer, Tim Henman, Steve Rider, Clare Balding, Dave Gordon, Ron Chakraborty, Gareth Edwards, Liz Thorburn, Sally Richardson, Carl Hicks, Matt Dawson and Phil Tufnell.

Thanks are also due to Robert McNicol, librarian at the All England Tennis Club, who, during lockdown, photocopied and posted reams of junior tennis reports from the early 1970s to keep research moving and, once restrictions were lifted, allowed me to visit the library to access its unique resources.

I'd like to thank Frederick Waterman, author and former international sports writer, for the 'Does this work for you?' exchange; Liz and Patrick Edworthy for providing a haven when writing required a boot camp timetable; Rory Ross, for his writerly support and for doing more than his fair share of domestic chores and late-night dog walks; to Isabella, Alexander and Emily Ross for their understanding. And big thanks, as ever, to my agent David Luxton for so sensitively air-traffic-controlling the project from proposal to final proof, and to his colleague Rebecca Winfield. Finally, I am hugely grateful to Lorna Russell and Claire Collins at Ebury for their expertise, patience and unflagging enthusiasm.

IMAGE CREDITS

All images from the author's private collection or copyright of the following rightsholders:

PA Studios / The British Petroleum Co Ltd (Image 9)

Tommy Hindley (Image 14)

PA Studios (Image 15)

Getty Images / Hulton Archive (Image 18)

Herald Express Torquay (Image 20)

Evening Standard Pictures / A. McDougall (Image 32)

The BBC (Images 35, 37, 38, 44, 52, 53)

Zoke / Sunday People (Image 40)

Matt Dawson (Image 50)

INDEX